The Epic in Film

D1559058

The Epic in Film

From Myth to Blockbuster

Constantine Santas

ROWMAN & LITTLEFIELD PUBLISHERS, INC.
Lanham • Boulder • New York • Toronto • Plymouth, UK

ROWMAN & LITTLEFIELD PUBLISHERS, INC.

Published in the United States of America
by Rowman & Littlefield Publishers, Inc.
A wholly owned subsidary of The Rowman & Littlefield Publishing Group, Inc.
4501 Forbes Boulevard, Suite 200, Lanham, Maryland 20706
www.rowmanlittlefield.com

Estover Road, Plymouth PL6 7PY, United Kingdom

Copyright © 2008 by Rowman & Littlefield Publishers, Inc.

All rights reserved. No part of this publication may be reproduced, stored in a
retrieval system, or transmitted in any form or by any means, electronic, mechanical,
photocopying, recording, or otherwise, without the prior permission of the publisher.

British Library Cataloguing in Publication Information Available

Library of Congress Cataloging-in-Publication Data

Santas, Constantine.
  The epic in film : from myth to blockbuster / Constantine Santas.
    p. cm.
Includes bibliographical references and index.
  ISBN-13: 978-0-7425-5528-0 (cloth : alk. paper)
  ISBN-10: 0-7425-5528-3 (cloth : alk. paper)
  ISBN-13: 978-0-7425-5529-7 (pbk. : alk. paper)
  ISBN-10: 0-7425-5529-1 (pbk. : alk. paper)
  1. Epic films—History and criticism. I. Title.
  PN1995.9.E79S26 2008
  791.43'658—dc22

                                                    2007012387

Printed in the United States of America

∞™ The paper used in this publication meets the minimum requirements of
American National Standard for Information Sciences—Permanence of Paper
for Printed Library Materials, ANSI/NISO Z39.48-1992.

Contents

Preface   vii

Introduction   1

Chapter 1   The Classic Epic Form   23

Chapter 2   The Mythological Epic   53

Chapter 3   The Religious Epic   73

Chapter 4   The Historical Epic   87

Chapter 5   The Women-Centered Epic   111

Chapter 6   The Comic Epic   127

Chapter 7   The Anti-Epic   157

Chapter 8   The Information Age Epic   179

Chapter 9   The International and Art House Epics   205

            Appendix: Significant DVD Editions   217

            Selected Bibliography   221

            Index   225

            About the Author   235

Preface

This book intends to bring proper critical attention to and encourage the study of the epic film. Despite the fact that the epic film has been the most popular, most honored (in terms of Academy and other awards), and the most durable genre in film in the more than one hundred years of its existence, no major critical work has yet appeared to define the genre, or to discuss it in detail as a separate and distinct format. College textbooks make passing references to the epic, and sporadic discussions of individual epics do exist, but no textbook has so far been dedicated to the epic form exclusively. The reasons for this neglect may have to do with the reputation of the epic film as a crassly commercial venture, a vehicle for entertainment void of content. In this book we propose to demonstrate that the epic film has often risen to the artistic level aspired to by other film genres, thus deserving more serious attention than it has received so far.

In addition, this book purports to place the study of the epic film in its broader context, exploring its roots in the long literary tradition of the West and numerous other cultures, a tradition that the epic film has adopted and expanded upon in format and content. The great literary epics of the West have repeatedly become film epics or have inspired stories of epic breadth, exploring in depth the mythic dimensions of the cultures represented. The film epic avails itself of this tradition both on aesthetic grounds, where the epic form offers spectacle, length, and multiplicity of plot and characters, as well as in the treatment of serious subject matter, as epics of note such as *Judgment at Nuremberg*, *Schindler's List*, or *Gandhi* have shown. The epic, a

distinctive form of literature since antiquity, has undergone significant transformations from a long narrative poem, to epic drama, to the novel, and, finally, to film—where it thrives. When the epic became film, it split into numerous genres and subgenres (and continues to do so) at an accelerated pace,
dynamically reinventing and transforming itself, often representing the highest ideals and aspirations of the cultures where it thrives, and gaining momentum in popular and often critical appeal.

This book intends to offer as comprehensive a treatment of the epic form
and its various subgenres as space allows. To that end, it presents an extensive introduction, which contains definitions of the epic in general terms, its
mythological origins and literary background, an assessment of its commercial character, and definitions of the epic hero/heroine. The introduction
also outlines the present status of the epic form, its tendency to expand and
intermingle with other genres, availing itself of changing technologies affecting movies in general. Finally, the introduction outlines the method followed in examining the epic film form. The nine chapters that follow illus-
trate the various formats that modern epic film has taken to express itself in
screen terms and are intended to show how the epic film has become a distinct form in itself as well as an intrusive medium that has branched off into
various subgenres and categories. Discussions of epic film are given in fully
developed essays but also in capsulated form in order to encourage study of
many more than those discussed. References to works consulted, or other related films of subjects are given in notes at the end of each chapter, and a selected bibliography is provided both for reference and as an aid to those who
would like to pursue the subject further.

Many have helped me in this endeavor, both in terms of moral support
and in reading and offering suggestions in the format, subject matter, style,
and in actual research. First I wish to thank numerous colleagues who have
read parts of the manuscript and offered suggestions, among them Professor
Gerasimos Santas, Professor Antonio T. de Nicolas of Stony Brook, and his
wife Dr. Maria Colavito, all of whom read and commented on the introduction and the general design and ideas in the book. I would like to thank Professor Carl Horner of Flagler College for inviting me to read chapters of the
book in his Colloquium of Literary Studies; Professors Todd Lidh, Vince
Puma, and Darien Andrew for their continuing support of the project; and
director of Library Services at Flagler College Michael A. Gallen and his as-
sistants, Margaret B. Dyess and Jenny Eason, for helping me with tracking
down numerous sources through interlibrary loans or microfilm materials
that became an essential part of my research. I would like to extend gratitude
to my sons, Xenophon Santas of Atlanta and Professor Aristotelis Santas of

Valdosta State University, who read parts of the manuscript, commented and argued (often vehemently) with me on the merits (or lack thereof) of the lengthy movies that I like to watch when they visit; and my daughter Christiana, for her generous wallet contributions to the purchase of expensive multidisc DVDs that certainly contributed to the task. Finally, I would like to thank my wife Mary for her unstinting support and enormous patience in viewing scores of lengthy films with me—an epic task of its own.

Introduction

What is an epic? The word is associated with fictional tales that offer size, length, spectacle, and, above all, unusual human feats—possibly of heroic proportions. A story that possesses these characteristics is usually called an epic, the Greek *epos* (επος) meaning "word," "tale," "story," "prophecy," "oracle," and, in literary terms, "a poem written in heroic verse,"[1] or "heroic measure,"[2] as the poems of Homer are. Used only for the epic form, the heroic measure implied "largeness" and dignity in both subject matter and style. Today, an epic is characterized as "an extended narrative poem in elevated or dignified language, celebrating the feats of a legendary or traditional hero."[3] But an epic can also be a real-life event, an achievement that entails great effort, a struggle to attain something significant, or an inspired action that brings about admirable results. Any venture of large proportions, a war, a trek, an exploration, a social struggle, a trial, a lengthy football game that went into overtime, an election campaign of unusual length—all of these endeavors associated with size, length, complexity, and heroic action could be categorized as epics. In the fictional sense, the word goes back to numerous literary works in the West[4] and throughout the world—tales of fights against monsters, of hard-fought victories, lengthy adventures, and heroic achievements of many kinds. Western and world literature are filled with epics: Babylonian, Greek, Roman, Hindu, Anglo-Saxon, African, and other literary masterpieces can be cited.[5] History also cites descriptions of epic struggles—mostly wars, but also of expeditions to unknown parts (like the travels of Marco Polo) or space travel (like the

1

moon landing or the Rover expedition to Mars). Real life has provided numerous episodes that in the collective memory have been retained and recorded as epics.[6] Epics, in the real or fictional sense, are associated with collective and national events and are projections of tribal wishes and instincts, and, according to Sigmund Freud, epics are based on myths that represent collective wish fulfillments.[7] Thus the epic, in any form, real or fictional, can become the means of survival, a way to facilitate and glorify collective feats. In its most exalted instances, an epic serves as the apotheosis of human action, an escape from pedestrianism to an ideal fashioned by tribal struggles. Above all, the epic is a product of the human imagination as it strives to conceptualize the victories of humanity's heroes in the millennia-old and never-ceasing battle between good and evil.

The Mythic Dimensions of Epic Film

Introduced in literary forms since antiquity, epics can be seen as the embodiments of collective myths and symbols that enable a society to establish its own identity and to face its severest tests. A society's consciousness is shaped by events within its most immediate historical past or present, and the different eras express their wishes collectively in the art forms available to them. Just as in the literary forms that preceded it, the epic film can be seen as an embodiment of aspirations, hopes, fears, and other collective emotions and feelings, and therefore is and must be primarily valued for its mythic dimensions above and beyond its formal properties[8] or its all too obvious commercial character.[9] Notable film epics are testament to that: religious feelings are expressed in such epic productions as *Ben-Hur* and *The Ten Commandments* at a time of spiritual and social crisis—the Cold War of the 1950s and the Joseph McCarthy era investigations—conflicts that threatened to endanger world peace and disrupt social values. Fear of defeat, craving for victory, or subconscious tribal wishes for a return to heroic times were given expression in numerous war movies, such as *Sink the Bismarck, Tora! Tora! Tora!, Pearl Harbor,* and *Saving Private Ryan.* Horror at the Holocaust may have been responsible for epic productions such as *Judgment at Nuremberg* and *Schindler's List,* while space exploration inspired popular epics such as *2001: A Space Odyssey, Star Wars,* and *Apollo 13*; social conflicts resulted in *Giant, Gandhi,* and *Dances with Wolves*; and real and imagined human disasters fueled the creation of *The Towering Inferno, Titanic, Armageddon,* and *Independence Day.*

Myths, we are told, "are, by nature, collective and communal; they bind a tribe or a nation together in that people's common psychological and spiritual activities."[10] And film is one of the most visible expressions of the re-newal and perpetuation of myths and thus can be seen as the embodiment of humanity's most cherished dreams and desires. In some form or another, whether in film or another medium (in Mozart's and Wagner's operas, or in Mahler's symphonies, for instance), the epic has related to communal myths more than any other art form, and it will continue to thrive and pros-per as long as audiences find a deeper need for it. When film itself arrived early in the twentieth century, epics became a means of reflecting social changes that had become the feeding ground for modern cultural myths: the numerous scientific discoveries of the previous century; prophecies of moon landings, as in the novels of Jules Verne; momentous social events, such as the massive immigration to the New World and the movement to the American West; folklore and the supernatural, as the legends of Franken-stein and Dracula; and great conflicts, such as war. Even a brief list of early epics is a testament to that: A Trip to the Moon (1902), The Great Train Rob-bery (1903), The Count of Monte Cristo (1910), Cabiria (1913), The Birth of a Nation (1915), Intolerance (1916), The Fall of Babylon (1917), Nosferatu (1922), Napoleon (1927, 2003), Ben-Hur (1907, 1926, 1959), Gone with the Wind (1939), Jesse James (1939), and many more are a testament to the mythmaking power of the epic film. Later in the century, epic film achieved its greatest popularity during the 1950s and the 1960s, spurred, in part, by the rivalry of television and the arrival of the wide screen that allowed heroic action to be magnified and glamorized by the new technology. Though the epic waned in the following decades, it did not by any means disappear, and epic productions resurfaced in the 1970s with the gangster yarns The Godfather (1972), The Godfather: Part II (1974), The Godfather: Part III (1990), and Apocalypse Now (1979) and in the 1980s with Gandhi (1982) and A Passage to India, (1985), though some critics have expressed doubts as to the epic's survival.[11] Yet, a look at the epics produced in the last dozen years or so (1993–2007) alone will convince skeptics that the epic form has made a thunderous comeback with Schindler's List, (1993), The Age of Innocence (1993), Amistad (1997), Titanic, (1997), The Patriot (2000), Gladiator (2000), Pearl Harbor (2001), Black Hawk Down (2001), Gangs of New York (2002), Master and Commander (2003), The Last Samurai (2003), Cold Mountain (2003), The Lord of the Rings: The Return of the King (2003), The Passion of the Christ (2004), Troy (2004), The Aviator (2005), Flags of Our Fathers (2006), and Letters from Iwo Jima (2006), to mention some of the most prominent examples. The resurgence of the epic film is partly owed to advances in technology—digital photography, for instance—which materialized in the tendency to popularize the sci-fi thriller and fantasy

epic, and partly to the mythic yearning for preserving and resurrecting yes-
teryear's heroes, as the latest Superman epic attests, or to revisit national
crises, such as 9/11 (*World Trade Center*, 2006, and *United 93*, 2006) or Hurricane Katrina (*All the King's Men*, 2006).

But the enduring popularity of the epic film can be explained largely by its
ability to preserve and re-create mythical patterns and thus remain in touch
with the deeper wishes of national identity. Its apparent omnipresence and
continuing appeal can be partly explained by its larger-than-life personae and
partly by its stress on action and spectacle, but mainly because it is capable
of embracing popular trends and ideals that define or represent an era. In the
mere span of a hundred years, epic film has re-created, reshaped, and expanded the heroic images and archetypes of the past, connecting them to the
present: from Gilgamesh to Hercules, from Icarus to Luke Skywalker, from
Orestes to Hamlet, from Odysseus to James Bond and Harry Potter, from
Moses to Superman, and from Buddha to Gandhi—epic film has revisited
and retooled these heroic images as no other narrative medium has, perpet-
ually using them for its own ends while forging new ones. From the outset,
epic film has feasted on the collective myths of East and West, dipping into
the inexhaustible resources of stories from the Bible; from Greek, Egyptian,
Babylonian, Roman and medieval cultures; and from Oriental and Eastern
myths (*Crouching Tiger, Hidden Dragon* is a recent example).

Developing technologies have allowed the epic film to bring into our consciousness heroes who can fly (Superman), and who can reach the moon in
reality and in fantasy (as in *Apollo 13* and *Star Wars*). The epic hero's archetypal qualities are undeniable: According to anthropologists and myth critics, an archetype is a universal symbol, a phenomenon common to all cultures, even those isolated from each other by geographical ties.[12] In a Jungian
sense, archetypes find expression "in tribal lore, mythology, fairy tales, religious systems, and primitive art."[13] They reside in the collective unconscious,
which is "a part of the psyche which was the first to evolve and now provides
the necessary links with humanity's ancestral past."[14] As an archetypal character, the hero undergoes trials and ordeals in cyclical patterns that involve
submersion, mystical death, and regeneration. All Western (and world)
mythical heroes were subjected to these cycles and thus undertook quests,
progressing from initiation to maturity, and finally making triumphant returns to their peoples. According to psychologist Otto Rank, such heroes—
including Moses, Hercules, Oedipus, Siegfried, and Jesus[15]—lived lives that
exhibited the basic components of the heroic saga: a high or divinely marked
birth of the hero preceded by barrenness or prohibition, a prophecy warning

of the perils such birth (Oedipus), a loss or wandering of the infant in a far-off land (Moses, Jesus), a recovery or suckling of an infant by an animal (Romulus, Remus), a discovery of distinguished parents (Oedipus), a revenge if appropriate to the hero's mission (Hamlet), and the achievement of rank or honors.[16] The hero, often conceived as both tribal and religious leader (Jesus, Moses), may be exiled or die in the end (Oedipus, Hamlet), but his action has cleansed his land of a pestilence (Oedipus), or brought about the end of a corrupt system (Hamlet).

All mythical heroes underwent similar cycles, progressing through various trials, achieving glorious feats, until they returned victorious to the tribe. While conceding that epic heroes are representative of their community's hopes, aspirations, and fears, one must also admit that a certain strand of the epic is capable of embodying heroes that leave their imprint on the collective psyche in a manner that elevates them to the status of universal heroes. It is their "drawing" power as archetypes that make them such attractive screen personas, capable of inspiring crowds of viewers, who then are reminded, in their collective consciousness, of desires that have remained unfulfilled and can be satisfied by their projected visual counterparts on the screen. Such are warriors of extraordinary merit; are so-called prophets—even in the most secular of societies—who can be seen as mythological heroes; and so are saviors of humanity, who, even in the most technologically advanced cultures, can be seen as mythical heroes. Such are lovers who arouse sexual passions in both sexes, and men or women of nature, who bring man back in touch with lost paradises. In film, epic heroes are often depicted as leaders of society in numerous forms and categories, whether derived from real life or fiction. Warriors responsible for ridding humanity of tyrants, such as General Douglas McArthur, General Dwight Eisenhower, and General George Patton have all been depicted in epic films fighting America's enemies during World War II. Civil rights leaders, such as Mahatma Gandhi and Martin Luther King, Jr. have both been the subject of films, while scientists like John Forbes Nash and Marie Curie have also been featured in epic screen presentations, and in most cases have been invested with mythical qualities. On the other hand, mythical film heroes of the technological era of the last fifty years are found in James Bond, Luke Skywalker, Frodo Baggins, Batman, and Superman. A mythical hero then, whether derived from life or of pure fiction, becomes the embodiment not just of a specific tribe or nation, but of all humanity. These heroes are invested with qualities admired, held dear or sacred, or found spiritually wholesome by most cultures. Though terrifying or destructive figures are also present in myth, it is the wholesome ones who hold an audience's attention and lift the average viewer to the imaginative heights projected in the illusory worlds of the epic (and other) cinema.

The Literary Origins of the Epic: Myth and Tradition

The epic is an ancient form of literature that has thrived on the exultation of the epic hero and the mythic qualities associated with bravery in battle, divine guidance, and great spiritual, moral, or intellectual leadership. Epics were literary works, either written or orally delivered as early as 3000 BC.[17] Among of the best known were *The Epic of Gilgamesh*, the Sumerian epic whose hero embarks on a search for immortality; *Enuma Elish*, the Babylonian epic of creation, written between 1500 and 1200 BC; and the Greek epics, *The Iliad* and *The Odyssey*, attributed to Homer in the eighth century BC. All of these, and many others, projected indelible heroic archetypes of bravery, high moral status, nobility, and cunning, human traits that have helped fashion heroic images down to our own day, while their authors exerted more influence than any other on Western literary thought. Homer, in particular, spawned numerous imitators during antiquity, among whom were the "cyclical" poets of the Ionic school who completed the tales of *The Iliad* and *The Odyssey*, devising an introduction up to the beginning of *The Iliad*, and finishing the story of the war by adding the death of Achilles, the sack of Troy, and the return of the heroes to their homelands.[18] Of these poets, Laches of Mytilene authored *The Little Iliad*, which details the destruction of the city in four books and which is criticized by Aristotle in *The Poetics* for its lack of structure.[19] Generally, these poems were inferior in literary merit to those of Homer and only fragments of them survive. Some poets followed the models left by Hesiod in his *Works and Days*, written in the eighth century BC, recommending practical pursuits, expounding upon the fruits of honest labor, and exploring the world of art and industry. Hesiod's *Theogony* became the source of myths about the genesis of the gods and heroes, providing a larger view of the progression from the divine to the human order and becoming a feeding ground for later poets, painters, sculptors, and mythmakers. Generally, however, Hesiod's poems were preoccupied with didactic subjects and influenced later antiquity, the Alexandrians; Callimachus, around 250 BC; Phranius; and Apollonius of Rhodes, famous for his *Argonautica*. On the whole, the Hellenistic period, culturally fragmented and imitative, adhered to the tradition of Hesiod, producing some worthwhile didactic epics on subjects as varied as astronomy (Aratus of Sicyon), medicine, and geography, and on some subjects as trivial as angling and hunting.[20] Even at its relatively early stages, the epic showed a tendency to expand and pro-liferate, becoming larger in scope and subject matter though producing no other works equivalent to Homer's in literary merit. Roman authors, often imitating Greek models, were mostly preoccupied with patriotic themes re-lated to their own history. Virgil's *The Aeneid*, composed on the request of Emperor Augustus to glorify the founding of the Roman Empire, spawned nu-merous imitators during the Middle Ages, and Virgil became the spiritual guide of Dante in *The Divine Comedy*, where the subject matter changed from heroic feats to human salvation. The Middle Ages generally ignored both Aristotle's guidelines of the epic and Homer's epics, which were written in Greek and not available in translations until the fourteenth century.[21] Me-dieval epics were for the most part fraught with Christian themes, differing both in form and content from the Greek and Roman prototypes of the clas-sical periods. Some of these, *Beowulf*, *Chanson de Roland*, and *Sir Gawain and the Green Knight*, were epics whose spirit of heroism was permeated by chival-ric and Christian virtues, showing knights combating monsters, conquering sin, fighting non-Christian invaders of the Holy Lands, or embarking on a quest for salvation. Even Chaucer's *The Canterbury Tales* and Boccaccio's *The Decameron*, though not strictly epics in the traditional form (they are called "frame epics," requiring a narrator for each tale[22]), expressed ideas conform-ing to the beliefs of Christian morality espoused by medieval society. Dante's *The Divine Comedy* was the culmination of these epics and projected ideas and paradigms not only for the condemnation of sin but also pointing to the road of ascending to heaven.

Since antiquity and even at the dawn of the modern era, epics were gen-erally divided by scholars into primary and secondary formats.[23] The primary were written (or composed orally) by societies close to the conditions de-scribed in the narrative, while the secondary were written by more advanced cultures and had a distinct social or national purpose. Homer's poems (and those of his imitators) and Dante's *The Divine Comedy* (along with most me-dieval epics) were in the primary category, while Apollonius' *The Argonau-tica*, Virgil's *The Aeneid*, and Milton's *Paradise Lost* consciously imitated events[24] that occurred in the far past. But their themes followed a natural his-torical evolution, reflecting, in one way or another, the times in which they were composed, as film epics do today. Milton's *Paradise Lost*, for instance, was undertaken as a metaphysical and religious quest—to "justify the ways of God to men,"[25] as its opening line states—a theme fitted to the seventeenth-century Puritan ethos. After Milton, the epic survived in reduced scale dur-ing age of romanticism, and poems like "The Rime of the Ancient Mariner," by Samuel Taylor Coleridge; "Sohrad and Rustrum," by Matthew Arnold;

and "Enoch Arden," by Alfred Tennyson, all shorter works, were written with the express purpose of following the Homeric tradition in such areas of human experience as visits to exotic lands, warring among tribes, and ship-wrecked mariners.[26] Numerous poets in the twentieth century, T. S. Eliot, W. H. Auden, and Robert Greeley,[27] among others, showed no taste for long verse narratives and wrote poems that revisited the epic hero in his contemporary transformations, a seer or visionary meandering through the chaos of modern life, as Eliot's Tereisias in *The Waste Land*. Some long verse narratives on the grand scale were attempted in the twentieth century, showing a resurgence of the epic form in the lengthy poem *The Odyssey, a Modern Sequel* (1936) by Nikos Kazantzakis and in *Omeros* (1990), by Derek Walcott, a story set in the Caribbean, with many parallels to the Homeric poems.[28]

Though maintained in such sporadic works, the epic form had in the meantime relinquished its domain to the novel, which acquired epic dimensions in the eighteenth century in the works of Daniel Defoe, Jonathan Swift, Samuel Richardson, and Henry Fielding, whose prose narratives combined the primary epic's elements, such as the description of the wandering hero, explorer, and discoverer of lands, with the didactic elements of the secondary epic. The novel acquired new epic dimensions in the nineteenth century in the massive works of Balzac, Dickens, Dostoyevsky, and Tolstoy, whose explorations of psychological and social conflicts invested the medium with fresh outlooks and social relevance. In the twentieth century, the novel flourished in the pioneering works of James Joyce, Marcel Proust, D. H. Lawrence, Thomas Mann, Nikos Kazantzakis, William Faulkner, Franz Kafka, Albert Camus, George Orwell, Vladimir Nabokov, and Umberto Eco, among many others; their works introduced such techniques as the narrator's voice as the primary means of narration (stream of consciousness), the establishment of the multiple point of view, and the break from the syntagmatic, or chronological order of narrative. The novel was in part a transformation of the epic form, though its prose format deprived it of the grandiosity of the Homeric hexameter or the elegant beat of the iambic pentameter of English poetry. But the novel in many ways functioned like the ancient epic: it carried on the narrative tradition with its multiple plots and descriptions of grand spectacular scenes and, though in written rather than oral form, it addressed large audiences, often elaborating on social or national issues or projecting heroes with archetypal and mythic qualities. Its most significant characteristic was the development of a viable prose narrative style that made the epic novel available to the masses. The verse form, on the other hand, though not totally extinct, ceased to connect with mainstream audiences, and, like drama in the nineteenth century, assumed the closet from—it was written not to be recited or performed but to be read, and that of course changed its dynamics, making it the prerogative of the learned and the elite, thus diminishing its popularity and narrowing its political and heroic spectrum. The novel, on the other hand, gained momentum, expanded its geographical boundaries and social horizons and achieved unmatched popularity during the times of its greatest triumphs—the latter part of the nineteenth century and the early part of the twentieth century. The novel, using its scope and power, dominated audiences as "emphatically" as the ancient epic form had, and for a while became the dominant form of literary expression. That is, until film came along, to borrow from it as one borrows from a parent, antagonizing it at times,[29] and competing for attention. Film, derivative and autonomous at the same time, has assimilated the main characteristics of the epic form, and at least from an aesthetic point of view, it bears a striking similarity to both the novel and to the ancient epic.[30] More so than the novel, however, film has assimilated the mythic qualities of the ancient epic, depicting heroes meant to project tribal and collective wishes and to have the power to inspire. Before we get into this subject further,[31] a few words must be said about the evolution of the epic hero.

The Evolution of the Epic Hero

From antiquity on, the epic hero must be seen in the context of his social milieu, in which his function is to represent, embody, or defend tribal and communal interests. Without such a collective spirit, the hero is an isolated individual who is more likely to express an author's personal views than those of the social group.[32] Some epics present archetypal heroes whose valor, intelligence, craft, and other highly individualist qualities enable them to surpass difficulties and achieve feats impossible to common mortals. Ancient heroes embarked on long quests to reach superhuman goals, often under divine guidance (Gilgamesh, Moses), fought monsters (Hercules), avenged the death of friends (Achilles), or visited the underworld to gain knowledge of mysteries prohibited to others (Odysseus, Aeneas). When provoking the gods, they suffered retributions and had to undergo additional trials before ending their quests. Ancient heroes who combined brawn and brains resurfaced in medieval and Renaissance literature, as Orlando, in *Orlando Furioso* (1532) by Ludivico Ariosto; Roland, in *Chanson de Roland* (twelfth century) by Turoldis; and Hamlet in *Hamlet* (1603) by Shakespeare.

On the other hand, the advent of Christianity in the medieval period demanded a hero whose moral qualities superseded valor and craft. The Celtic legends of King Arthur and his knights, Gawain, Lancelot, and Tristram, were expressive of both romantic ideals and of Christian piety.[33] Though the Celtic hero Cuchulainn was also distinguished for his physical strength and war skills,[34] Christian knights in general were known for their lengthy and adventurous quests for truth, love, and the expunging of sin. A quest for the Holy Grail became part and parcel of a medieval hero's search for the salvation,[35] while Renaissance critics expressed their preference for Virgil's Aeneas, who was especially popular in the Middle Ages and whose primary virtue was *pietas*.[36]

In the seventeenth and eighteenth centuries, the epic hero often took the form of the picaro, a wandering vagabond in search of fortune or romance, or of an idealistic fool (Don Quixote), an ironic caricature of the medieval knight errant who set out to help widows and orphans. Such heroes were found in the works of Cervantes, Gil Blass, Henry Fielding, Tobias Smollett, William Makepeace Thackeray, and Mark Twain. The picaro did not always represent tribal or communal interests, often being perceived as an amoral adventurer in search of position or fortune—Thackeray's Barry Lyndon, or Becky Sharp, his female counterpart, being good examples. Amoral or antisocial heroes surfaced during the romantic era in the works of Byron (especially *Don Juan*), Shelley, and Victor Hugo. The influence of the romantic tradition brought on the concept of the antihero, a man (or woman) decidedly antisocial, a person functioning underground, harboring hostility and antagonism against the social environment, and often exploding into antisocial behavior. This duality split the hero's persona into a protagonist and an antagonist, a format that had its roots in antiquity, in such dual figures as Gilgamesh/Enkidu, Moses/Ramses, Achilles/Patroklos or Achilles/Hector, Dante/Virgil, Satan as the fallen angel in Milton, Hamlet/Horatio, Faust/Mephistopheles, Alyosha/Ivan Karamazov, and in Nietzsche's figure of the anti-Christ. In Jungian terms, the dual nature of the hero can be seen in the "anima," the part of the projected image of the hero that becomes the "shadow," or the darker side of the unconscious self, and, as Jung puts it, "the invisible saurian tail that man drags behind him."[37] Every villain is a representation of Jung's shadow, the flip side of the heroic coin, the heroic counterpart that inevitably provides the spark in the action of the epic in its most intense moments of confrontation. The villain thus becomes the counterpoint of the heroic archetype and survives in most literary forms or any other mythic narratives accessible to the community.

From the end of the nineteenth century to the first, middle, and latter parts of the twentieth, the concept of the hero has been enlarged and diversified to even a greater degree, becoming any number of figures—soldier, cop, spy (for a good or bad cause), space flyer, western hero, underground fighter,

fighter for social causes, even a terrorist intent on destroying social order while using heroic methods; and of course these multiple personas have been incorporated into film, having been re-created in the numerous archetypal forms that populate the medium, in most cases the epic form. Here continuity exists with the preceding media, the verse epic and the novel, especially the latter, which has provided film with numerous storylines since its inception at the beginning of the twentieth century. Thus, several media—most prominently the film and the novel—run nearly parallel lives. But the typical characteristics of the epic hero still lie in his ability to strike a chord, whether of sympathy or hatred, adoration or revulsion, in the heart of the community itself.

The film epic hero is the natural descendant of the heroic figure previously known in history and fiction but surpasses all the earlier types in popularity. Hollywood stars, whose personalities were glamorized on the screen, exerted enormous influence on audiences everywhere, often greater than that of athletes, musicians, war heroes, scientists, writers, sculptors and painters, and theater actors and poets, personas that they routinely represented. Stars were worshiped worldwide, commanding mass appeal unparalleled in recent human history. Screen idols enjoyed instant recognition, the following of millions of devoted fans, and had the power to shape public opinion and set social trends or establish mores to a greater degree than fashion designers and media moguls. During Hollywood's early decades, the so-called golden era (from the mid-1920s to about 1960), the powerful studios took pains to groom and mold their stars' images, stressing their physical attractiveness (their sex appeal), sympathetic personalities, honesty, religiosity, and social awareness, even as some of them portrayed despicable, dishonest, malicious, and treacherous villains. Many of the biggest Hollywood stars were perfectly suited to epic roles: Claudette Colbert and Fredric March in *The Sign of the Cross* (1933), Ramon Navarro and Charlton Heston in two versions of *Ben-Hur* (1925, 1958), Clark Gable and Vivian Leigh in *Gone with the Wind* (1939), Victor Mature and Hedy Lamarr in *Samson and Delilah* (1949), and Kirk Douglas and Jean Simmons in *Spartacus* (1960). Big Hollywood stars continue to shine in the modern era: Tom Hanks as a war hero in *Saving Private Ryan* (1998), Russell Crowe as an arena warrior in *Gladiator* (2000), and Mel Gibson as a charismatic fighter and martyr as Scottish rebel William Wallace in *Braveheart* (1996). Moviemakers are quite aware of star power and have adjusted the heroic images to suit the public's fantasies, choosing the right actor to play a popular role. Thus, the hero supersedes the star: at a time of space exploration, *Star Wars* projected an interplanetary hero (Skywalker), while *Superman* (and its sequels) featured a savior as a visitor from another planet. A grand epic such as *The Ten Commandments*, with its source material from the Bible, was perceived not only as a vehicle for entertainment but as a contributing factor to a culture's spiritual outlook, and its hero Moses assumes the mythic role of a redeemer, though, in some cases, an epic's broader themes have eclipsed the more narrow appeal of a star's attraction (*Judgment at Nuremberg* and *Schindler's List* may be such examples). Still, it is the appeal of a star's personality on the collective psyche that mostly accounts for the epic film's popularity—in early times and today.

Film epic heroes can be broadly seen as adventure or romantic heroes, though these two personas often intertwine. Usually, romantic lovers are known by their similarities—good looks, appealing personalities, strong emotional natures—while action heroes fall into numerous groups: detectives, government agents (spies), western heroes, warriors, space explorers, men and women of science, and even desperadoes, gangsters, and terrorists (villains or antiheroes)—each having characteristics of his or her own. Hollywood thrived on romantic heroes, and even in the epic genre the romantic hero dominated the screen for decades in the early cinema, and still does, though his persona has evolved, from the almost pure lover of post-Victorian times to the man or woman of action who loves incidentally and as occasion arises. The greatest of screen lovers was Rudolph Valentino (1895–1926), the embodiment of the Latin lover, inspiring passionate reactions, sometimes amounting to hysteria, among female audiences. Subsequent romantic lovers often merged with the adventurer, and that combination worked well with the epic. In the 1930s, every major studio production featured male stars that combined both qualities: Gary Cooper in the film version of Hemingway's *A Farewell to Arms* (1930) paved the way for such polished performers as John Barrymore, Ronald Coleman, and Cary Grant, while other stars combined male sex appeal with the rough and tumble of the adventurer—Douglas Fairbanks Sr. (of the silent era), James Cagney (also known for his early gangster roles), Paul Muni, Errol Flynn, Clark Gable, Humphrey Bogart, and, in later decades, Kirk Douglas, Rock Hudson, Burt Lancaster, Charlton Heston, Sean Connery, Steve McQueen, Harrison Ford, Michael Douglas, Tom Hanks, Tom Cruise, and a host of others. The female persona—usually forgoing adventure, which is mostly left to men—still had its share with such luminaries as Greta Garbo, Ingrid Bergman, Bette Davis, Rita Hayworth, Elizabeth Taylor, Barbara Stanwyck, Grace Kelly, Jean Simmons, and, in more recent decades, Meryl Streep, Glenn Close, Michelle Pfeiffer, Annette Bening, Cate Blanchett, Geena Davis, Angelina Jolie, Keira Knightley, and many others. Women actors are more or less distinguished for their romantic or dramatic roles, while men can readily slip in and out of their romantic and epic persona/images. Few women (Elizabeth Taylor in *Cleopatra*, and Meryl Steep in *Out of Africa*) are featured in purely epic roles, but when they are they are as strong willed and capable of leadership as their counterparts in literature.[38] The role of woman in the epic film is inextricably linked with the persona of the actress that plays that role. This was truer in the era of the Hollywood studio system—the 1930s, 1940s, 1950s, and 1960s—for in those days the images of actresses were carefully honed and maintained throughout their careers. Greta Garbo, for instance, was equally adept when playing a seductress (*Inspiration*, 1931), a queen (*Queen Christina*, 1932), an ill-fated prostitute (*Camille*, 1938), or an intriguing bureaucrat (*Ninotchka*, 1941). Marilyn Monroe's projected image of a sex symbol catapulted her to fame in the 1950s, while Bette Davis became known as a southern belle (*Jezebel*, 1936), a woman capable of evil (*The Little Foxes*, 1938), a queen (*The Private Lives of Elizabeth and Essex*, 1939), and a romantic heroine (*All This, and Heaven Too*, 1940). Katharine Hepburn (playing a queen, in *Mary of Scotland*, 1936) had both comedic and dramatic talents, and Ingrid Bergman combined an alluring romantic image with a heroic persona (in *For Whom the Bell Tolls*, 1943 and in *Joan of Arc*, 1948).

The Epic Film as Commercial Art

The steady rise of epic film on box office charts during its one century of existence can be broadly attributed to its mythic power and its ability to express and uplift (and also occasionally depress) the communal spirit. But in the public mind the word "epic" is usually associated with advertising slogans intended to promote a product rather than define a cinematic/literary term. To the average viewer an "epic" has become a catchword for size, action adventure, "casts of thousands" (as in the previous eras), and special (read "digital") effects. Thus, the term "epic" has become interchangeable with "blockbuster," an expression familiar to distribution, marketing, and advertising agencies, whose aim is to attract large audiences rather than to define a genre or to elaborate on plot and characterization. Like the word "symbol," the term "myth" is never used in advertising and it is often perceived as an antonym to "fact." And, as if taking a cue from advertising, many film critics, sometimes justifiably, generally dismiss the epic as shallow spectacle—as a blockbuster—devoid of artistic merit, a vehicle for Hollywood to cash in on the screen presence of its stars and its technological wizardry. Indeed, advances in technology—color, wide screens, elaborate stunt work, digital effects—have been regarded by many as means for rampant consumerism that have helped the epic at the box office as much as they have harmed it critically.[39]

It would be inadvisable, however, to exclude epic film from serious critical discussion simply because it has enjoyed enormous success at the box office. As a genre in general, the epic has amassed, and profited by, a tradition of significant literary works that have paved the way for its continuity and built the basis for the various formats or subgenres the epic is capable of taking today. Historically, epics, in verse form or other narrative medium, have been both popular genres and major artistic achievements though not always at the same time. Some of the epics of antiquity and of later times have been masterpieces, while others are quite forgettable works. The novel, which many regard as a continuation of the epic form, has been praised as "the most magnificent of forms" by Henry James, but also branded as one of the shallowest of mediums.[40] Like the novel, film was created to entertain, and, as such, it sometimes cannot avoid being called crass commercial spectacle; but, like the novel, or any other entertainment vehicle, it has the option of providing thought-provoking screen yarns (*Intolerance*, *Battleship Potemkin*, *Gandhi*, *Schindler's List*) when it chooses, to say nothing of its ability to reflect society's values. If, as usual, it produces low-grade commercial fare that makes no claim to artistic merit, criticism gains nothing by denigrating epic film in its entirety. By its nature, epic film is a large economic venture firmly tied up to the commercial interests of its producers and will probably remain so for the foreseeable future.

The epic's popularity and commercial character have actually contributed both to its success and its longevity—a fact understood by Hollywood, the first to discover the epic's profit-making capacity. The epic's potential for diversity and its wide popular appeal did not escape the notice of astute American filmmakers who discovered early that, of all film genres, the epic is the most commercially viable. Of the early producer/directors, it was D. W. Griffith who saw the epic film as a vehicle for both commercial success and artistic work and used both history and myth (*The Birth of a Nation*, 1915; *Intolerance*, 1916; *Orphans of the Storm*, 1921) to explore the new genre. Griffith discovered the potential of the epic for grand spectacle that would please the masses, but he was also conscious of the epic's artistic value and strove to produce epics—some would say unrealistically—that would combine both ends. By contrast, it was Cecil B. DeMille who shrewdly discovered and steadily explored the moneymaking potential of the large spectacle, practically inventing the western format and the biblical epic.[41] DeMille, a producer, director, and at different times head of such major studios as Paramount and MGM, branched off into the creation of the various formats the epic genre offered him, especially those with religious topics that mixed pious storylines, spectacular adventure sequences, sex, and violence, all in the same package.

Some of the movies that made him notorious as an epic maker include *The Virginian* (1914), *The Ten Commandments* (1923, 1956), *The King of Kings* (1926), *The Sign of the Cross* (1934), *Cleopatra* (1934), *The Crusades* (1935), *Union Pacific* (1939), and *The Greatest Show on Earth* (1952). During the 1930s, 1940s, and 1950s, most major studios—Paramount, RKO, Warner Brothers, Universal, Twentieth Century Fox, and MGM—produced adventures, musicals, war stories, and westerns, types of films that either were epics or contained epic elements. In more recent times, franchises, that is, films with sequels (or a film "series"), such as the James Bond movies, *Star Wars*, *Jurassic Park*, *The Raiders of the Lost Ark*, and many others, have been among the most lucrative industrial ventures of the late twentieth century. Though at times risking financial failure, epic films practically guarantee, or promise, big returns at the box office.[42]

Studios attempt to gain an advantage by exploiting the term "epic" in the commercial promotion of their films and count on the exaggerations implicit in the term to attract audiences. Thus, the commercial character of the epic has given it its distinct characteristics: it is not strictly speaking a literary product, though some of its plotlines have been borrowed or adapted from literary epics (*Vanity Fair*, *Barry Lyndon*, *War and Peace*); nor is it an art film, made for and by a distinct film group or school (French new wave directors, for instance) aimed at limited, discriminating audiences. Literary epics do exist—Sergei Eisenstein's *Alexander Nevsky*, Kurosawa's *Seven Samurai*, and a few other exceptions[43]—but the overwhelming majority of epics are movies made to appeal to large audiences and hence are mainstream, commercial ventures mindful of box office receipts. As we have seen, the problem in defining epic film arises partly by the use of the term "epic" by the media, partly by the commercial character of the epic venture: Almost without exception, epic terms such as "big" or "long" translate into a wide-screen spectacle with obligatory (and often nerve-racking) special effects. The success of *Titanic* reinforced that point as recently as 1997; the sinking of the world's largest ship, cinematically compelling because of the huge catastrophe shown on the screen, lured audiences as no other epic of that era had. In addition, *Titanic* won eleven Oscars, matching the record of *Ben-Hur* of several decades earlier (1959), a film remembered mainly for its celebrated chariot race. Thus, the use of the term epic by the advertising agencies often causes confusion if one attempts to assess a film's stature by literary standards rather than by its commercial potential. While it is obvious that such things as size, spectacle, or large casts are meant to attract large audiences, it is not clear, or admissible, that an epic film possesses, or that it should possess, distinct literary qualities.

The Status of the Epic Today: Why the Epic Film Continues

Today, the word "epic" is tossed about regardless of a film's particular form, popping up into the vocabulary of critics and filmmakers to mean anything that is long, adventurous, action packed, suspenseful, with plenty of special effects, and always relying on a heroic persona to carry on a mission. Thus, it is harder to define the epic because of this proliferation of its subgenres that dilutes the original concept of the term, as we shall see in chapter 1. It can be said that at this point (in 2007), however, that while the "classic" type of epic that was made in the 1950s has run into a buzz saw, the epic in its general forms is not threatened with extinction. In the last decade or so—roughly since 1995—classic epics like the 1950s *Ben-Hur* or *Spartacus*, with big casts and lavish sets, or spectacular action sequences have either faced failure or quick oblivion. An exception, however, is *Titanic* (1997). While it went over budget and nearly "sank" the fortunes of its producers, it was a hit at the box office, and won numerous Oscars, including Best Picture and Best Director. But more recent classic epics like *Troy* (2003) and *Alexander the Great* (2004), made with well-known directors, flopped both with audiences and critics, though the cause of these failures ought not to be attributed solely to their format. *Pearl Harbor* (2001) offers more than three hours of superbly filmed action sequences, but its plot is diluted with a triangle romance that the alert viewer of today has seen repeated dozens, if not hundreds, of times.

Still, the epic enjoys a considerable resurgence in its recent transformations, mostly aided by digital technology, which gives it an ability to adjust to modern sensibilities and to quiet fears generated by new concerns, like the war on terrorism, for instance. Thus the epic has retained its power to communicate and has become, once more, a convenient medium to channel these anxieties. Even in the pre-9/11 world, thrillers and action epics were injecting new blood into the genre. Films like *Executive Decision* (1996), *The Peacemaker* (1997), *The Siege* (1998), *Air Force One* (1997), and *Black Hawk Down* (2001), all films of epic sweep, brought hints of impending national crises. Post-9/11 movies, *United 93* (2006) and *World Trade Center* (2006), imprint indelible images of the horror of the attacks on the national consciousness. Meanwhile, the fantasy genre has breathed new life into the epic. The fantasy epic got its real start with the sci-fi, George Lucas epic *Star Wars* (1977) and its sequels in the early 1980s and its prequels in the late 1990s and early 2000s. Trilogies, in fact, seem to be the new format of the fantasy/digital epic of the information age,[44] as such popular fantasy films like *The Matrix* and *Lord of the Rings* testify. These genres coincide with digital photography and the expanding areas of satellite transmission and the Internet, which also help them thrive. A new cosmos is being invented, but the epic, retaining some of its original traits—length and emphasis on action and spectacle—has embraced these new forms, or perhaps has been forced to adjust to their technical transformations. In addition, the epic has taken upon itself to accommodate outdoor dramas (*Cold Mountain*, 2003; *Brokeback Mountain*, 2005), the martial arts (*Crouching Tiger, Hidden Dragon*, 2000; *Hero*, 2003), thrillers (*Collateral*, 2003; *The Constant Gardener*, 2005), tales of heroic women (*North Country*, 2005), and even urban dramas (*Crash*, 2005), which have traces of epic elements to them (the hero's search for identity, for instance). One gets the impression that the epic form has weathered the assault of a monstrous technology, one with long and pliable tentacles that threatens to embrace, if not suffocate, the epic's traditional forms. The result is a constant fragmentation of the epic form into newly generated subgenres—those mentioned above and many others.

A complete categorization of the kinds of epic films being made today is not likely to produce definitive results. The epic form, as said already, is the most protean of forms, and, though the basic traits (length, action, and spectacle) of the epic are retained, the form has proliferated into genres and subgenres to such a degree that any attempt to pigeonhole them with accuracy is bound to have limitations. One can only suggest the most common divisions and subdivisions as they seem to be almost haphazardly formed, and constantly being formed, for a great number of reasons—some pointed out already. The causes for change are not formal—that is, epic filmmakers do not consciously wish to imitate Homer or Virgil (or Aristotle's rules). The changes are mostly due to financial considerations, for the epic film is the most expensive; therefore, epic structure has to be adjusted to market values, distribution, weekly charts, and general popular and critical acceptance. If the epic did not happen to also be the most popular form—speaking of films as single units, rather than, let's say romantic comedy as a whole—it probably would have vanished from the film horizon by now. In its heyday, the 1950s and 1960s, the epic's popularity was unquestionable. In the last three decades, epics have become sporadic, due mainly to the demise of the great studios and the reluctance of independent producers to venture into big budgets. But the grand epics are still around (*Titanic, Gladiator, The Lord of the Rings*), despite the fact that some critics have announced their demise,[45] and the epic subgenres continue to proliferate, readjust, and reappear into myriad other forms: action and spy thrillers, war movies, mysteries, the supernatural, and so forth. For convenience, and for the sake of orderly discussion, in this volume we have divided the epic genres into nine chapters. The epic form is basically intrusive: it will insert itself into whatever format it finds convenient, and the epic elements—as will be shown in chapter 1—resurface and take over anytime or anywhere that is convenient for them. Length and spectacle, for instance, two essential elements of the epic, are staples in most adventure stories, and that includes war, spy thriller, and fantasy. Even musicals achieve epic dimensions (*Amadeus, Moulin Rouge*), not to mention docudramas and biographies (*Patton, Gandhi, Nixon, JFK*), which may be characterized as epics. The epic form is dominant: it requires bulk, substance (more often than not), and mass appeal. Moviemakers are certainly not bound to give up the boon that the epic form has brought to cinema or abandon film formats that have given solid proof of box office success. After all, epic film is part of the entertainment industry—and profit motivates as nothing else does.

The Method of This Text

The method of this text is consistent with its aims: to show that the epic has maintained its mythic qualities, connecting its heroes and their actions with the collective psyche of the community and its common goals. In addition, this book shows the multiplicity of forms the film epic has attained, having pervaded almost every film genre—films of war and history, drama, adventure, social comment, and even comedy; these are basically the principles used to divide this volume into nine chapters, each chapter showing the main aspects of each of these subjects. The plethora of material dictates a certain kind of sequence, and also allows some room for overlapping. Epics cross over to mainstream dramas, action movies, war movies, fantasies and thrillers, and generally to every form that has come to be known as genre, and these suggest a progression from the lengthier and more spectacular form to the lesser or shorter epics, where the aim may be characterization or focus on subject matter. In fact, the epic form in film has become increasingly fragmented and has crept into other forms or genres, shaping and reshaping, and even hiding behind nonepic genres. Epic elements can be found nearly everywhere in film, even in musicals (*Cabaret, The Magic Flute, Amadeus, Chicago*), comedies (or mock epics), in movies about heists (*Topkapi, The Score, Ocean's Eleven, The Italian Job*), animations, fantasies, sci-fi, thrillers, western adventures, and in war stories, as long as these formats offer action-packed sequences, spectacular elements, and a hero/heroine or villain that embodies tribal interests, ending up in tragedy or fulfillment. Love stories can appear within the epic framework, for lovers' stories frequently intertwine with larger themes—war, for instance (*Gone with the Wind* is an example). The chapters of this book are designed to follow this concept of multiple transformations, bearing in mind that these categorizations do not attempt to cover the entire spectrum of the epic form, but are given as highlights (avoiding the inconvenient term subgenres) that will provide some guidance and indicate that future studies are needed in this subject to fill in the gaps or examine each category in greater detail. Chapter 1 offers a definition of the classic literary form as inherited from antiquity and adapted in epic film, thus providing the basic aesthetic parameters that characterize the epic form; it also offers discussion of several epics to which such definitions apply. Chapter 2 examines the mythological hero, more or less along the lines presented in the introduction. Chapter 3 offers definitions of the religious Roman/Christian epic that prevailed in the "golden era" of Hollywood, especially in the 1950s, when the religious epic reached its apex with such spectacular movies as *The Ten Commandments* and *Ben-Hur*. Chapter 4 examines one of the most popular epic forms, the historical epic, especially the war adventures that reached epic proportions following World War II. Chapters 5, 6, and 7 examine areas of the epic form hitherto unexplored: the women-centered epic, which attempts to point out that epics are not the exclusive domain of men; the comic epic, specifically the "mock epic" and the "comic strip epic"; and the anti-epic, which elaborates on the origins and explorations of the antihero persona in film. Chapter 8 illustrates the changes brought on the epic form by digital (or "information-age") technology. And chapter 9 offers a brief account of international and art house epics of note. Hopefully, these discussions will provide the student of the history of film—especially of American film—a broad scope of the origin and evolution of the epic form and will encourage further study and analysis of the subject. To attempt to describe all the epic transformations alluded to in this volume is an impossible task, given space limitations. Another, more general and overall aim of this volume is to place the epic film within the parameters of its social milieu and to show how it relates to the general aims of cinematic art—how it shapes social consciousness and defines the epic hero. Discussions of form are essential but cannot be dissociated from the other aspects of film epic, for the form and subject matter are interrelated. Bibliographical references to film aesthetics and references to others works are offered for a broader discussion for students of this particular area of film studies.[46] It is all too obvious that the epic, at its best, provides audiences with spectacle and entertainment, but also a reminder that its appeal penetrates deep into the national psyche by stirring up the nobler instincts of survival during times of global crisis.

Notes

1. Henry George Liddell and Robert Scott, *Greek-English Lexicon* (London: Oxford University Press, 1964), 309.

2. The "hexameter," consisting of seventeen-syllable dactylic lines, a dactyl being a three-syllable foot, of which the first was accented.

3. *The American Heritage Dictionary* (Boston: Houghton Mifflin, 1985), 459.

4. See "The Literary Origins of the Epic: Myth and Tradition" section below.

5. *The Aeneid, The Bagahvad Ghita, Beowolf,* and many others are included.

6. Pearl Harbor and September 11 qualify as such collective memories.

7. Sigmund Freud, "Creative Writers and Day-Dreaming," in *Criticism: Major Statements,* 3rd ed., eds. Charles Kaplan and William Davis Anderson (New York: St. Martin's, 1991), 427.

8. This is discussed in chapter 1, "The Classic Epic Form."

9. This is discussed below in the section "The Epic Film as Commercial Art."

10. Wilfred Guerin, Earle G. Labor, Lee Morgan, and John R. Willingham, *A Handbook of Critical Approaches to Literature* (New York: Harper & Row, 1979), 156.

11. See Richard Corliss, "Maybe Nobody Told Martin Scorsese the American Film Epic Was a Dead Form," *Time,* December 2002, 66.

12. Philip Wheelwright, *Metaphor and Reality* (Bloomington: Indiana University Press, 1962), 197.

13. James F. Iaccino, *Jungian Reflections within the Cinema: A Psychological Analysis of Sci-Fi and Fantasy Archetypes* (London: Praeger, 1998), 1.

14. Iaccino, *Jungian Reflections,* 1.

15. Guerin et al., *A Handbook of Critical Approaches,* 162–63.

16. Otto Rank, ed., *The Myth of the Birth of the Hero* (New York: Random House, 1959), 65.

17. Derek Elley, *The Epic Film: Myth and History* (London: Routledge & Kegan Paul, 1984), 9. See also Margaret Drabble, ed., *The Oxford Companion to English Literature* (Oxford: Oxford University Press, 1985).

18. Oskar Seyffert, *Dictionary of Classical Antiquities, Mythology, Religion, Literature and Art,* eds. Henry Nettleship and J. E. Sandys (London: S. Sonnenschein, 1898), 219.

19. Aristotle, *The Poetics,* quoted in Kaplan and Anderson, *Criticism: Major Statements,* 47.

20. Seyffert, *Dictionary of Classical Antiquities,* 220.

21. Katherine Callen King, ed., *Homer* (New York: Garland, 1994), 2.

22. A frame epic, or frame story, establishes a working framework of a group of people assembled for some social function, each person telling a story with a common theme. *Ship of Fools* (1965) is a film that uses this format.

23. Seyffert, *Dictionary of Classic Antiquities,* 219.

24. Anne Ferry, *Milton's Epic Voice: The Narrator in Paradise Lost* (Chicago: University of Chicago Press, 1983), 1, 88.

25. *Paradise Lost*, Book I, l. 26, quoted in Mary Ann Caws and Christopher Prendergast, *World Reader: Antiquity to the Early Modern World* (New York: HarperCollins, 1994), 1220.

26. George A. Waltrous, *Three Narrative Poems* (New York: Allyn and Bacon, 1924), 116.

27. John Alexander Allen, "The Hero," in *Hero's Way: Contemporary Poems in the Mythic Tradition* (Englewood Cliffs, N.J.: Prentice-Hall, 1971), 127.

28. King, *Homer*, 12. King also cites the poems of Constantine Cavafy, Rainier Maria Rilke, and George Seferis as belonging to the epic genre in her introduction, pages xx–xxv.

29. Joy Gould Boyum, *Double Exposure: Fiction into Film* (New York: New American Library, 1985), 23.

30. For more on the historical background of the epic literary form, see the selected bibliography at the end of this book.

31. See chapter 1, "The Classic Epic Form."

32. For an extensive discussion of this point, see Joseph Campbell's "The Hero's Adventure," in *The Power of Myth* (New York: Anchor Books, 1991), 151–206.

33. William Vaughn Moody and Robert Morss Lovett, *A History of English Literature*, 8th ed. Fred B. Millet (New York: Scribner's, 1964), 28.

34. Jean Chevalier and Alain Gheerbrant, *A Dictionary of Symbols* (London: Penguin, 1996), 502.

35. For general information, see Jesse Weston, *From Ritual to Romance* (Cambridge: Cambridge University Press, 1920), in particular, chapter 2, "The Task of the Hero"; chapter 5, "Medieval and Modern Forms of Nature Ritual"; and chapter 11, "The Secret of the Grail."

36. Philip Sidney, "An Apology for Poetry," in Kaplan and Anderson, *Criticism: Major Statements*, 129.

37. Carl G. Jung, *Psychological Reflections* (New York: Harper & Row, 1961), 217.

38. Worth mentioning here are Dido as Queen of Carthage in Virgil's *The Aeneid* and Clytemnestra in Aeschylus' *The Oresteia*. For more on women as epic heroes, see chapter 5, "The Women-Centered Epic."

39. See Corliss, "Maybe Nobody Told Martin Scorsese the American Film Epic Was a Dead Form," 66.

40. The reputation of *The English Patient* has been marred by its categorization as an "epic romance," according to Bronwen Thomas, "Piecing Together a Mirage: Adapting *The English Patient* for the Screen," in *The Classic Novel, from Page to Screen*, ed. Robert Giddings and Erica Sheen (Manchester: Manchester University Press, 2000), 145.

41. Steven C. Earley, "The Epic/Spectacular," in *An Introduction to American Movies* (New York: New American Library, 1978), 146.

42. *Batman, Star Trek, Back to the Future, Lethal Weapon*, and *Superman* count among the most successful epic films. See also Martin Wolk, "James Bond as the Moneyraker," MSNBC website, www.msnbc.com/news835307.asp?vts=11210020440.

43. One might mention here Fellini's allegorical epics, *La Dolce Vita*, *Eight and a Half*, and *Satyricon*, or Jean-Luc-Godard's allusions to Homer's *The Odyssey* in *Contempt* (*Le Mepris*).

44. See chapter 8, "The Information Age Epic."

45. See Corliss, "Maybe Nobody Told Martin Scorsese the American Film Epic Was a Dead Form," 66.

46. Constantine Santas, *Responding to Film: A Text Guide for Students of Cinema Art* (Lanham, MD: Rowman & Littlefield, 2002), 54–95. See also Christian Metz, "Some Points in the Semiotics of Cinema," and Alfred Guzzetti, "Christian Metz and the Semiology of Cinema," in *Film Theory and Criticism*, 2nd ed., ed. Gerald Mast and Marshall Cohen (New York: Oxford University Press, 1985), 164–93.

CHAPTER ONE

The Classic Epic Form

An Epic Poem, the Critics agree, is the greatest Work Human Nature is capable of.

—Alexander Pope[1]

When epic film made its first appearance at the beginning of the twentieth century, it already had at its disposal many recognizable formal epic traits that had been associated with the epic narrative for centuries, even millennia. Perhaps more than any other factor, the temperament of the historical era during which an epic was made is what determined the form of the film. Early epics were influenced by the preference of audiences for spectacle that had been denied them by earlier art forms—the opera and the stage theater, for instance, both means of entertainment reserved for the middle or upper classes. For the first time in history, a popular medium of potentially artistic merit was affordable, with epic movies offering spectacle unimaginable within the range of previous media. Action, length, and spectacle, the most essential ingredients of the epic, became accessible to large audiences projected on a screen, unlike earlier narrative forms that required either a lengthy oral delivery or an equally lengthy reading. Thus, like all forms of art, the epic film is directly linked to the historical conditions dominant during the particular era in which it was made. Such a view is especially favored by Marxist critics,[2] who maintain that the historical era during which an artwork is produced determines its content and form. Content and form thus become indistinguishable because one relies on the other. "Form itself," claims Frederic Jameson, a Marxist critic, in his "Marxism and Form," "is but the working out of content in the realm of the superstructure."[3] Marxists in general entertain the notion that superstructure, the material, economic, and political conditions that determine social consciousness, is also the deter-mining factor in the form that art takes.

Periods of turmoil are sharply reflected in artistic expression, and film is no exception. A crisis, such as the Second World War, the Cold War, or the terrorist threats of today, calls for the presence of heroic figures to lead a na-tion to victory, and such figures, though they may be based on real life, are usually cast in mythic archetypal forms through an art form available to the community at the time. Epic film is an art form particularly suitable to play-ing such a role, and has been a tool used to incite the popular imagination to real or imaginary triumphs. Early in the twentieth century, epic film re-flected the uneasy feelings about disasters—the sinking of the RMS *Titanic*, and the outbreak of the First World War—events which affected public mood. War, for instance, determined the form film took—lengthy narratives with battles—creating an aggressive or defensive (or patriotic) mood among the public; and many epics spawned by the outbreak of two world wars rep-resented in grand spectacle the struggles of nations to dominate over or to defend against enemies. War movies proliferated in the 1940s and 1950s, af-ter America was attacked by Japan at Pearl Harbor and had opened a sec-ond front to help defeat the Nazis in Europe. Later, during the height of the Vietnam War and its aftermath, in the 1960s, 1970s, and even into the 1980s, when antiwar sentiment grew, war epics became antiwar movies (*Apocalypse Now*, 1979; *Platoon*, 1984), while the 1990s and early 2000s prowar sentiment allowed for the development of epic movies that extolled patriotism (*Saving Private Ryan*, 1998; *Pearl Harbor*, 2001). Today, epics like *The Lord of the Rings* or *Troy* may be expressions of undercurrent wishes that good defeats perceived evil forces. In a sense, the content of the epic goes along with the prevailing social trends, changing as eras change and with them social aspirations and conditions.

The genesis of new forms may be consistent with social conditions pre-vailing at the time, as the novel, for instance, was the outgrowth of social changes in the eighteenth century caused by urbanization and the oncoming Industrial Revolution as well as political changes with philosophers such as Rousseau preaching dogmas of liberation of suppressed peoples or social classes. It is also possible to argue that while form is determined by social conditions, certain formal elements are ahistorical, and thus universal, and common to the epics of all peoples, ancient or modern, regardless of histori-cal circumstances. Such formal elements provide society with a sense of "aesthetic truth," which is different from the discovery of scientific facts, according to Kenneth Burke, who sees the truth of art as "an exercise of human propriety, the formulation of symbols which rigidify our sense of poise and rhythm."[4] Formal elements in any work of art, including the epic, must be reviewed and accounted for, for it is the structure of the epic film that will help us understand its mythic underpinnings and its social dimensions as it made its appearance one hundred years ago, evolving from its early crude structures to the polished spectacle of today. If the epic helped raise the level of our social consciousness, it is because its formal qualities enabled it to do so.

Though definitions of the epic have varied over the centuries, perhaps a convenient way of discovering formal qualities that have endured would be to go back to the first articulated views on the subject, *The Poetics* of Aristotle (335–322 BC), which provides not only definitions of the epic but also comparisons with the genres of tragedy and comedy, as well as an aesthetic overview of the epic in general. Though Aristotle's definitions of these genres have often been misinterpreted as "rules," an idea that has been in decline since the Renaissance, most writers of drama and later of the novel (and now filmmakers) have been consciously or unconsciously emulating these "forms" (kinds, genres) that Aristotle collected from his observations of Greek poetry and thence are the beneficiaries of a critical inheritance that has been in existence for nearly three millennia. Aristotle did not give a history of the genesis of the epic but only provided an outline for the theoretical basis for its form. All poetry consists of forms of imitation of action, he said, and those forms "differ in three respects—the medium, the objects, or the manner of imitation."[5] Since the epic is an expression of spoken or written literature, the objects are higher types of men, and the manner is a narrative, as contrasted to the tragedy or comedy, both of which are staged productions.[6] The poets of epics and tragedies preferred serious or elevated subjects, while comedians turned to lampooning. Both epics and tragedies often had plots ending in a catastrophe, evoking pity and fear, subsequently producing a catharsis of such emotions. Aristotle discussed the epic sporadically throughout *The Poetics*, allotting the bulk of his attention to tragedy. The two genres are closely related, he insisted, being the two most important kinds of poetry, since the tragedians picked their topics from the epic writers—especially Homer—who preceded them.[7] Both epic and tragic poets described "higher" types of men: heroes or heads of great families; thus tragedy and epic share this particular characteristic. Their main difference is length: the action of a tragedy must be confined to "one revolution of the sun,"[8] while in the epic, action has no time limits. The plot of the epic, however, like that of the tragic action, must be unified; it must be a complete, organic whole, and not a series of episodes in chronological sequence. The least artistic epics are those that attempt to depict either the entire life of a hero (a biography) or an entire historical period; such epics lack plot unity, for their subject matter may be diluted and lacking structure. The best epics are those that attempt to describe a single action, rather than an entire period. Thus, *The Iliad* by Homer detaches one single portion of the Trojan War, rather than attempting to embrace the entire ten-year war—a subject too large for one epic, although some authors have attempted to do that, unsuccessfully, Aristotle insisted.

The epic action shares many of the important characteristics of tragic action: as with tragedy, the epic plot can be simple or complex, pathetic, or ethical, and must contain reversals of fortune or recognitions—states of mind during which one must pass from ignorance to knowledge. Therefore, the epic hero, like the tragic hero, must also be a great person, or a person of stature who falls due to a frailty (αμαρτια), rather than from a vice or depravity; he must suffer reversals and experience recognitions, as the tragic hero does. An epic action must have a beginning, middle, and end, and it must have a complication (δεσις) and a denouement (λυσις), as happens in a tragedy. Catharsis of pity and fear must also occur in the epic, as in tragedy. Events must follow each other in causal links, out of probability or necessity, rather than haphazardly. Thus, *The Odyssey*, an epic due to its length and narrative form, contains recognition scenes, its plot has a double reversal, and its action in general conforms to the principle of cause and effect.[9]

While the similarities between the tragic and the epic form are treated as being rather self-evident, the differences are stressed. Length (or size), the main characteristic of the epic, entails a scale of action larger than that of tragedy. Because of its enlarged dimensions, the epic writer is able to carry out, not one, but "several lines of action"[10] simultaneously. The advantage that the epic gains by the multiplicity of its plot—or subplots—is that it lends mass and dignity to its subject, a "grandeur of effect"; moreover, epic plot allows for the "element of the wonderful," that is, the ability of the author to "tell lies skillfully."[11] That is, in narration (as indeed, in film), an exaggeration may be overlooked, or appear more convincing if well told, whereas on the stage an improbability cannot pass the test of a viewer's close scrutiny.

Whether these distinct qualities of the ancient epic can have a direct relevance in distinguishing modern film genres is a question that should remain open in film studies. The main stumbling block to carrying on Aristotle's definition may be the fact that modern film is more akin to stage production than to an epic oral narrative, as modern film derived from essentially photographed stage action. But what strikes the modern reader of Aristotle's theory is the fact that while Aristotle stressed the basic affinities between the narrative and staged forms of action, he also stressed the differences. In his time, the term epic could not apply to stage action. The term, however, has changed meaning from indicating both oral narrative and length or size, to length or size alone—whether this particular quality is applied to a written lengthy narrative (the novel, for instance), or to a lengthy film, but not to a lengthy stage play of today; for a modern stage play still complies with Aristotelian economy. Stage demands that its performances are short (shorter than an epic film anyway). Lengthy plays, such as those of Shakespeare or Ibsen, are truncated in most actual stage productions. Length alone, however, does not seem to be an artistic limitation in the production of film—rather it is an economic, as well as an aesthetic factor. Filmmakers—Griffith, Lean, Kubrick, and many others in subsequent and modern times—found that film, as an art form, offered itself, in a way that a stage play never quite could, to the presentation of massive historical events, or lengthy adventures, where both multiple plots and large casts of characters could be used.

If a distinction between different film genres is attempted based on the differences between tragedy and epic, one could apply the Aristotelian distinctions made above, concluding that, although the differences of length or size do exist, the similarities are also evident—such things as the unity of plot, complications and denouements, as well as reversals and recognitions. Just as these are the basic ingredients in both tragedy and epic, so they are in the normally sized drama of two hours and in the epic film of three to four hours. If the modern epic film then possesses these qualities of plot, which were found in the ancient epic, then it also must share its similarities with ancient tragedy. The modern epic does indeed possess the characteristics of a tragic plot as well as the qualities of the ancient epic—which are compatible with changes in what Aristotle had called "the medium of imitation"—that is, the change of ancient narrative epic form, delivered in hexameter, to modern narrative film. The legitimacy of that change is a question that could be examined separately. Here, suffice it to say that a basic structure in narrative form, whether one is talking about an oral or written form of narrative, or filmic narrative, is that the plot must be a single action as far as possible, though the multiple line of action is more characteristic of the lengthy film. But even with a multiple plot, the whole length of a film must be perceptible in one view, and the action as a whole must be unified. A hero, or heroes, must suffer reversals of fortune and must undergo recognitions. The entire plotline must follow the principle of cause and effect, hammered throughout *The Poetics*, thus avoiding episodic sequences as far as possible. A happy ending is possible in the epic, though not in tragedy, but there could be opposite outcomes for the villain and the heroes, as Homer's *The Odyssey* demonstrates.

In shifting such principles as outlined above from theory to practice, one must keep in mind that it is no longer possible to apply such generalizations verbatim. In modern film, for instance, we often talk of "awareness," "consciousness," "epiphany," using terms which are more applicable to modern critical readership. Film critics rarely talk of tragedy in cinema, and when they do, they draw their examples from Renaissance and post-Renaissance dramatists, Shakespeare (*Macbeth*), Schiller (*Wallenstein*), or Ibsen (*Ghosts*), whose characters suffer self-inflicted wounds, without the intervention of fate, or, to use Siegfried Kracauer's substitute phrase, "the fortuitous."[12] However, the basic idea of tragedy, in film or literature, is perspicuous: to have a modern epic hero who is also tragic, it is necessary that such a hero undergo some kind of self-awareness, or "αναγνωρισις"[13] which is the recognition of the cause of one's mistake. That could be termed as a state "where one goes from ignorance to knowledge,"[14] and Aristotle did indeed sort out in great detail several kinds of possible anagnorises,[15] including recognition by signs, tokens, scars, processes of reasoning, or, what he called best, "by natural means."[16] Anagnorisis is knowledge, which includes self-knowledge. Oedipus indeed obtains knowledge of who he is—in terms of his family connections—and yet his most important knowledge is the knowledge of the self, of a mistake committed in a certain course of action that has contributed to a fall. That is why the most important tragic element is self-knowledge which coincides with a reversal of fortune—and which is indispensable to tragic action.[17] Without anagnorisis coinciding with a reversal, there is no tragedy. As already demonstrated, it is impossible to have an epic action that leads to tragedy (instead of to a happy end) without these particular ingredients—anagnorisis and reversal (peripeteia), for the same reasons already advanced. In this particular sense, then, the epic and the tragedy work their plots along the same lines of action—both bringing their heroes to calamitous ends. In modern film, however, spectacle, the "least artistic" of artistic elements, according to Aristotle, since "the production of spectacular effects depends more on the art of the stage machinist than that of the poet,"[18] has defined the epic, and when the word is applied, it is understood mostly in its commercial sense, as "epic" attempts to attract an audience to a movie theater. Though the epic film has laid legitimate claims to the aesthetic form derived mostly from antiquity, in reality it is an accommodation that reduces it to the general financial denomination that the film industry will dictate. That does not mean formal aesthetic criteria should not be applied to epic film criticism.

The Formal Qualities of the Epic Film

The basic epic qualities could be summed up in several generic qualities that a modern epic film shares with the classical epic, as follows.

1. Length
    The length of the modern epic film must be greater than that of the average film. There is no need to confuse chronological length with actual running time. The action in a film of normal running time may use longer chronological time, but the epic film will have both a longer running time than the average film and an often-greater chronological dimension. The length of the epic film evolved out of the necessity to tell longer stories without entirely compromising the time limits that audiences are forced to adhere to, since viewing a film has restrictions quite unusual in other media. A novel can be read at one's leisure (more or less); a painting or sculpture can be viewed regardless of time limits, and the other arts, with the exception of music, which has time limitations similar to film's, are not time constrained. This is very important for film, which faces limitations of time forced upon it by production and distribution costs.[19] But the long films, filmmakers and producers often decided, were worth that additional time and expense, for a longer-than-average story has its special needs and audience expectations. Length was the signifying mark with the original literary epics, all of which exceeded the length of stage narratives by several times the number of lines. An average film runs two hours or less; an epic runs from three to four hours. Still, a three-hour film is enormously long, and, if not gripping, it tires out an audience—a factor that many filmmakers did take into consideration. But the factor of length remains a hazardous enterprise in film, and thus the pressures for its box office success are far greater than, let us say, for average, low-budget B-grade movies. Those pressures have, generally, been significant factors for the relatively higher quality of most epic movies, although standards have changed over the decades. Today, for instance, four-hour-long epics like *Ben-Hur*, *Lawrence of Arabia*, and *Cleopatra*, made in the 1950s and 1960s and containing fifteen-minute intermissions, are an impossibility. For entirely practical reasons, the multiplex theater demands a shorter time span, two-and-a-half to three hours, and modern epics (*Gladiator*, *Master and Commander*, *Gangs of New York*, *Alexander the Great*, *Flags of Our Fathers*) have generally conformed to these economic factors. Length limitations work to the disadvantage of

today's epic making, and producers seem reluctant to loosen their money belts and bet on uncertain prospects or a fickle public spoiled by numerous means of entertainment and faced with multiple options for a four-hour span of time. Thus, the uncertainty of popularity, the big expense, and the doubt of prospective Oscars to be won also become rather negative factors in making a long movie. An expensive long epic MUST gain at least a measure of popularity. But while some popular epics have won Oscars (and other awards), their popularity may have detracted from the amount of critical nods that a respectable film with artistic pretensions must receive. Most critically acclaimed films are not the longest ones, and critics often do not consider the long epic respectable enough, ironically for the same reasons that Aristotle gave twenty-four centuries ago: their message is diluted because of length, and they rely on spectacle, the least artistic of tragic qualities.

2. Unified Action
   Unified action means that the scriptwriter and director must select and focus on one single portion of a long story and not attempt to treat an entire historical period that lasts several decades, something that in most cases has become an unattainable goal. As pointed out already, Homer was commended by Aristotle (and Horace) for not attempting to represent the entire Trojan War but for selecting a single portion— only about nine weeks—to tell his story in *The Iliad*. In modern times, film epics often need to allow their action to develop over many years, aging or replacing their stars for that purpose. Such large chronological gaps require an episodic plot, frowned upon by Aristotle and his followers, but something that the modern novel knew much about and was forced to adopt. Still, some epics managed unified action (*The Bridge on the River Kwai, The Great Escape, Titanic*), and they were the better for it. Unified action can of course be achieved by other means: unity of theme (*Schindler's List*), plot coherence (*Ben-Hur*), or unity of character (Kenneth Branagh's *Hamlet* and David Lean's *Lawrence of Arabia*). Some epics lacked unity on any of these grounds, and appeared fragmented. One example is *Cleopatra* (1963), where the story is broken into two parts—Cleopatra's affair with Caesar seems to have little link to the subsequent events, the intrigue with Antony and the battle of Actium. Indeed, these two parts seem to belong to two different movies. Despite its several great stars, *Cleopatra* was a relative failure at the box office.[20] Some modern epics, like *Pearl Harbor*, practi-

cally benefit by managing to reduce potential sprawl by focusing on a single war episode (though they may fail for other reasons).

3. Multiple Plots

   Multiple plots may be parallel evolving plots, as in D. W. Griffith's *Intolerance*, which has four plots; *The Godfather: Part II*, where two parts of a plot become unified through expert dovetailing of two strands of the same story; or as in *The Bridge on the River Kwai*, where reversals (ironies) and recognitions become vital tools in merging elements of an epic plot. The multiple plot is a characteristic of *The Odyssey*, which set an example of telling two stories, one of Telemachus embarking on a search for his father and the other, the main line of action, involving the adventures of the returning Odysseus. The two strands are united at the end. The point here is that the size of the epic allows for the development of more than one strand, something that movies of two-hour length may attempt, but not as successfully. Modern epics can use any of these models, retooling them to adapt to their specific needs: *Schindler's List* has a double thread, using two points of view: one representing Goeth and the Nazis and the other representing Schindler and the Jewish prisoners; *Pearl Harbor* has unity of action and unity of time (with episodic elements), basically carrying two plots, that of the war and that of a trio of lovers; *Gangs of New York* shows unity of time and place; and *The Passion of the Christ*, focusing on the last twelve hours of Christ, has unity of both time and place. Unity of plot seems to be more of a problem in the epic than in shorter dramas, but the great film epics seem to be able to overcome this by using cinematic means at their disposal—as Steven Spielberg's use of rapid pacing in the sprawling *Schindler's List*, which is tight despite its great length. Multilayered plots, or interlinking episodes, can also be included in this category, with their seeming fragmentation, such as Atom Egoyan's *Ararat*, connecting a number of stories to a common theme.

4. Hero

   In general outlines, an epic hero may resemble the tragic hero or heroine. The epic hero, however, as has already been pointed out,[21] possesses qualities that go beyond those of the tragic hero: the tragic hero suffers a reversal and falls, usually because of a flaw of his own, though he can also suffer in order to redeem some sin of the tribe, as Oedipus, whose downfall and catharsis brings about a liberation from a curse. In the modern sense, the tragic hero can also be an epic hero, for the two ideas are not incompatible. *The Godfather: Part II* provides an example of a tragic hero in a complicated epic, but he too is an archetype in the Jungian sense, a "shadow" that maintains the reptilian tail and must be defeated, morally if not otherwise. The archetypal hero who uplifts his race remains the most popular type, in male or female form, of the hero/heroine who represents wishes of the tribe. Examples abound and will be explored in this and subsequent chapters.

5. Pity and Fear
The tragic effects of pity and fear, as defined by Aristotle, are not necessary ingredients of the modern epic, for such (or other) emotions have been enlarged and modified (or nullified) by psychology and modern sensibilities. To these feelings, horror and shock may be added, for the modern epic is able to represent, more realistically than any previous medium, catastrophic events that may shatter the audience's sensibilities (or scare them to death). Examples are seen in *Towering Inferno*, *Jaws*, *Earthquake*, *Armageddon*, *Schindler's List*, *Titanic*, *Pearl Harbor*, many war movies, and in the so-called disaster movies.

6. Happy Resolutions
Epic resolutions are as a rule happy rather than unhappy, contrary to tragedy, which has an unhappy ending. Since the evocation of pity and fear is the purpose of tragedy, such unhappy endings should be appropriate if the epic has a tragic theme, though the mainstream epic has generally preferred happy endings.

7. Spectacle
Spectacle is a term that translates into "special effects," almost obligatory in the modern epic, despite Aristotle's warnings, as already noted above, that it is the "least artistic" of the tragic elements. Spectacle—meaning special effects, costume design, art direction, and sets—however, has become a staple in the modern epic film. Spectacle today is mostly the result of digital technology, thus cheaper and more accessible to filmmakers, but it does not mean it should be less organically connected to plot and theme. As always, it does mean that the epic form requires its presence.

Modern epic film has retained a great many of the above classic formal traits, but at the same time, as film has in general, the epic has developed aesthetic forms of its own. Film language—montage, the visual reading of imagery, and so forth—has become the equivalent of what in Aristotle's time was called the "heroic verse," or "hexameter," of the classical epic. Today, battle scenes, for instance, which are staples in the epic spectacle, are carefully edited montage sequences (the Odessa steps scenes in *Battleship Potemkin*, for instance, or the clashes between rival gangs in *Gangs of New York*) that render a sense of grandeur of complex action required in the modern epic. Examples of modern epics are *Titanic* (1997), in which humans falling from the deck of the sinking ship are represented digitally, and *Gladiator* (2000), in which the Coliseum in Rome (among other things) is partly reconstructed with digital imagery. In the sci-fi or fantasy epic, computer-generated imagery dominates and shapes the desired effect—choreographed movement, for instance, in *The Matrix*; *The Truman Show*; *Crouching Tiger, Hidden Dragon*; *Minority Report*; *The Lord of the Rings*, and in other modern feature films—epic or not. Thus, computerized imagery becomes practically the essence of the story, modifying the aesthetic responses of audiences in the most fundamental ways, for we now live in a computer-controlled "virtual reality," an environmental state of illusion totally fabricated by machines.[22] Today, the classic epic film is part fantasy, having replaced the casts of thousands that fed its physical dimensions in the 1950s and 1960s in such films as *The Land of the Pharaohs* (1955), in which director Howard Hawks employed literally thousands of extras (something financially infeasible today); *Ben-Hur* (1959), its famous chariot race a real race in practically every sense because stunt work was minimal; and *Cleopatra* (1963), in which Elizabeth Taylor sits atop a huge glittering sphinx (which, of course, was a set, but was closer to a real structure than a computerized version of might be) as she triumphantly enters Rome. Still, modern epic films have retained many of the elements of the classic literary epic—length and massive action scenes, for instance—while at the same time they have become significant new epic forms in their own right. Evolution does not mean rejection of previous forms, for new forms are both continuations and modified versions of classic forms. Generally speaking, epic film as a whole is only a hundred-year-old creation that has shifted its emphasis from the purely narrative form (oral or written) to one which is represented on film, and film, at least in its initial forms, was nothing but a replacement of the stage, projecting and extending its already elaborate sets.[23] Initially, cameras were centrally positioned and static, photographing action strictly in the space before them. With the invention of dollies, crane shots, and camera movement in general, the action was captured as never before, and the camera could focus on an actor's face or on the entire Monument Valley—where many western epics were filmed. The modern epic film took advantage of technical innovations—trick shots, mobile cameras, tracking, helicopter shots, digital photography, costuming, makeup, elaborate studio sets, montage, filming on location, underwater photography, and many other techniques that modern technology enabled it to develop. Forms unimaginable in the ancient forms of the epic, except perhaps in the mind of the writer, or in the novel, where descriptions of grand scenes could only be given to the reader one sentence at a time, were developed in film with its massive varieties of projected images that modern film technology has furnished. The epic film chose to place a great deal of emphasis on spectacle, or special effects, reserving an Oscar category for it. But elements of the oral epic—length, multiplicity of plot, unity of action, depicting heroes, including mythical, historical, or modern types, who undergo initiations, reversals, and recognitions, evoking of the emotions of pity and fear—have been retained and incorporated in the modern epic film and have even been enhanced and reinvented by modern technology.

The Formal Elements in Noted Epics

Seven Samurai (1954); Director: Akira Kurosawa

Akira Kurosawa's eleventh film, Seven Samurai (Shichinin no samurai) displays the main epic characteristics known to narrators in the West since antiquity: length, battle scenes, tribal conflicts, and heroic action. Kurosawa learned epic film techniques partly from his Japanese mentor, Kajiro Yamamoto, a director of both comedies and epics in Japan in the 1940s, and partly from his American model and master for western epics, John Ford, whose film methods he adopted and imitated. As a director of note, who rose to fame in the West with his Rashomon in 1951, a film that won both a Foreign Film Oscar and the Grand Prix at the Venice Film Festival, Kurosawa embraced Western ideas and took "his cinematic inspiration from the full store of world film, literature, and music."[24] His mastery of the epic form is shown not only in Seven Samurai, but also in such later monumental works in the genre as The Hidden Fortress (1958), Kagemusha (1985), and Ran (1985), the latter being an adaptation of Shakespeare's King Lear.

With all its assimilated Western techniques and themes, Seven Samurai is an original work, showing the conflicts of a war-torn Japanese society of the sixteenth century, when warlords ruled the country among themselves, leaving anarchy behind when their rules ended. Then marauders raided villages, took the farmers' crops, raped the women, and left devastation and chaos behind. The villagers had a last resort: they could hire unemployed, and often starving, samurai to protect them. Thus, the legend of the samurai that emerged from these particular circumstances was not that of a swordsman at the service of a warlord, but of the defender of the weak. The "ronin," as he calls himself, is a roaming independent man of arms who, out of compassion, or the mere need of a meal, makes it his business to protect the tribe, leading it to victory and then once more dissociating himself from it. He has no master, no social connections, and the tribe has adopted him only momentarily. With the end of his task, he is again alone to roam the countryside, wiser perhaps and independent, but shiftless and homeless. His only satisfaction seems to come from accomplishing the task. He knows that the defeat of the villains is only a momentary triumph and that evil is cyclic and bound to return—and fought and defeated again to ensure survival. By skillfully blending philosophical and technical elements, Kurosawa achieves a perfect aesthetic whole, offering unity of action, characterization of both the individual and the group, and a concept of a hero who achieves mythical/archetypal dimensions as the defender of the tribe.

Despite its great length (over three hours), *Seven Samurai* is distinguished for its economy and relative leanness of action, which is achieved through quick editing, expert montage of battle scenes, and details confined to the absolutely essential points in describing character. There are few establishing shots here, so frequent in the gratuitous spectacle offered by the grandiose Hollywood epics of the time. Unity of action is achieved by focusing on only one episode—the saving of a village from bandits, in what must have been a prolonged civic strife that devastated Japan in the sixteenth century. As usual in great narrative epics of the past, such as *The Iliad*, war is given in capsulated form, and the viewer is informed indirectly, through dialogue and action, of the social unrest caused by the shifting of power from the aristocracy to the peasant, and the resulting dispossession of the professional warrior—the samurai. *Seven Samurai* achieves its unity of plot through the singleness of purpose that a group of peasants exhibit when they decide to enlist the help of these unemployed ragtag warriors to help them save their village from bandits.

This initial action precipitates a sequence of episodes organically connected and conforming to this general idea of protecting the village from outside dangers. After a brief shot of bandits, who stop short of raiding the village but whose presence is known, the desperate peasants call a meeting, consult an old wizard who tells them they must hire unemployed samurai to protect them from the bandits, and take off to the nearest town (or central village) where samurai are known to flock, presumably in search of employment. Here, the samurai are individually introduced and a distinct characterization of the principals is achieved. Kambei (Shimura) is the first samurai to come to the viewer's attention when he rescues a young baby that was abducted by a thief and held hostage in a hut. Kambei has his head shaven, dons a priest's robe, and, in a lightning move, kills the thief, who is seen staggering out of the hut and drops dead in front of an amazed crowd. Watching him is Katsushiro, a young man who aspires to become a fighter of equal valor with Kambei, asking the latter to take him on as a disciple. Kambei declines modestly but soon agrees to take him under his wing, suspecting that Kikuchyio (Mifune), a vagabond competing for attention, might lead him to unworthy habits. Kambei has considered the peasants' request to hire samurai to protect them, but thinks the plan is unrealistic if only two or three samurai were to fight a band of forty bandits. Soon, however, he revises this decision when Corobei, one of the numerous unemployed (and hungry) samurai who roam the villages, joins the group. He says he wants to join not for the job, which pays no wages and will bring no fame, but because, as he tells Kambei, "your character fascinates me." Three other samurai soon join the group: Heichachi, who cuts wood for a living; Shikiroji, an old friend and fellow fighter (the "right hand") of Kambei; and Kyuzo, a swordsman of dazzling skills. The six men start for the village, followed at a distance by Kikuchyio, a laughable character carrying a fake document to prove his claim to be a samurai. After many jokes at his expense, they good-heartedly accept him as their own, and Kikuchyio becomes the seventh member, though never officially titled as a samurai. Kambei, who possesses a strategic mind, plans the defense, making a camp of the village, devising a map with signs for the fortifications, which will include a flooded field as a ditch. Each samurai is assigned a post and is responsible for his position. Villagers are recruited and trained in the handling of weapons—bamboo spears. They have not shed their fear of the samurai, and Manzo, always suspicious of their motivations, cuts Shino's, his daughter's, hair and makes her dress as a boy. His measure does not prove too effective, for Shino and Katsushiro meet accidentally on a field of blossoms—a staple in Kurosawa films—and fall in love. This marks the young warrior's rite of passage, for now he will fight "as a complete man," as his colleagues will tease him later.

The numbers of the samurai are reduced by one when Heihachi is killed during a raid trying to protect Richichi, whose wife had been abducted by the bandits. Kyuzo, meanwhile, has killed two bandits who came to scout, and Kikuchyio kills one and captures a gun. The assault soon begins in earnest, and the village is in commotion. Methodically, Kambei eliminates the bandits one by one, letting them pass through an opening in the fortifications and be killed by his troops, as the villagers gradually become expert warriors. But in the final and decisive battle, which is fought (and masterfully shot) during a downpour, the chief bandit forces his way to the women's quarters, and from there he shoots and kills both Kyuzo and Kikuchyio. Before he dies, in an act of extreme heroism, Kikuchyio, though fatally wounded, spears the chief bandit to death. Corobei has also died in the battle. The four samurai are buried in a burial mound outside the village, their swords wedged into each individual grave. "Again we have survived," Kambei says to Shikiroji, as they are about to depart from the village. The two and Katsushiro linger briefly before the mounds, to look at villagers now working on the rice pads, singing their tribal song of victory and harvest. Katsushiro looks wistfully at Shino, who passes by him to join her group. "Again we have been defeated," Kambei mutters. "These villagers are the winners."

The film is an epic/heroic struggle of defeat and victory; a battle of good versus evil; a story of the humanity (and inhumanity) of man; and it is a cinematic masterpiece expressing its ideas through the medium of film language and film techniques. Kurosawa's vision rests on the concept of the struggle of good versus evil and of the necessity of defeating evil by any means possible to ensure survival. Man (and woman) as an individual and as a group is thrust into an amoral, inexplicable world, where chance reigns and evil—in the form of conquest, rapine, force, and violence—threatens existence at any moment. Chaos (the title *Ran* of the 1985 movie means chaos) is a condition of human existence. Escape from chaos is social order—an order which is threatened constantly by disruptive and evil forces often beyond that social order's control. Man's harmonious relation with nature is also disrupted by these forces. Heroism and human understanding can offset these disruptive forces and save humanity, but even heroes—rare phenomena in the spectrum of human existence to begin with—can be defeated and annihilated by social disruptions. However, heroes and humanism (fragile as these may be) are the best means humankind can offer in its efforts to avert disaster and conquer evil.

To Kurosawa, at least in this film, the ideal of hero is found in the samurai, trained warriors of the sixteenth century often selling their services to the warlords of Japan, in the same way that medieval knights made their livelihood by attaching themselves to feudal lords. Their roles were similar, but Kurosawa, unlike his European literary counterparts (Sir Walter Scott, for instance), does not always idealize the samurai. The average samurai is an amoral warrior roaming the countryside in search of employment, often at the service of a warlord, on occasion being as villainous as the bandits he will on occasion run down. Only the ronin seems to escape that categorization. The ronin is an unattached samurai, with no allegiance to any authority, preferring to fight for causes of his own choosing, though he will occasionally collaborate with a lord.

Kurosawa's concept of the ronin in this film is the vital part of his vision. Here the ronin is presented in the person of Kambei, who proudly declares he is one when the young aspiring warrior Katsushiro begs him to take him as a disciple. When Kambei humbly declines, he is thus implying that he does not consider himself worthy enough to have followers, but also declaring his independent nature. Kambei, however, is not aloof, and soon allows Katsushiro to come along with him, seeking to protect him from the unmannerly Kikuchyio. Kambei is proud, but also hungry. The request of the villagers, which promises "neither reward nor fame," attracts him, for in it he sees a challenge that will allow him to put to use his wily warrior's nature, but he also seems to be moved by the villagers' desperate plea. Though a skilled warrior, he is also a planner who can calculate the odds and the impossible situation of the villagers—a handful of untrained farmers against a band of forty trained warriors—seems to him a great challenge, no doubt as great as or greater than those he has faced before. His previous life, never revealed in any detail, seems to have been a series of hardships and defeats. He is a hardbitten realist, used to losing, but not disheartened, not a pessimist, and not cynical—as many of his Western counterparts in western American movies are (one example is *The Wild Bunch*). His inner strength is untouched by the everyday rampant evil he has seen and faced. He is stoic, self-assured, approaching every adverse development with determination and firmness. During a moment of panic in the village, when somebody has sounded an alarm signal, he remains firmly in command, beginning with asking rational questions. His sharp mind matches his inner courage; he is tough, courageous, compassionate, and unpretentious. Even tempered and calm in a storm, he is endowed with a strategic mind, characteristically scratching his shaven head in a dilemma, keeping to himself rather than voicing his troubles. He is good-natured, devoid of the usual arrogance and hubris of warriors, never making condescending remarks, assuming leadership but also treating all his fellow fighters with respect, as equals. He is unlike Western literary heroes, who have been traditionally presented as courageous or sharp minded, but also as flawed human beings. Achilles (*The Iliad*) is valorous but subject to catastrophic rages; Odysseus (*The Odyssey*), farsighted, prudent, and calculating, brags after a victory and is punished by a god who resents him; and Hamlet (in *Hamlet*) suffers inner collapse when faced with momentous decisions.

Epic film has followed suit with such flawed heroes as Lawrence in *Lawrence of Arabia*, who is both victorious and vainglorious, and Jake LaMotta, in Martin Scorsese's *Raging Bull*, whose unfathomed bitterness destroys everything in his life he is trying to build.[25] Kambei knows he is an outsider and that the peasants, who do not even thank him for his pains, will forget all about him and turn to their own daily tasks as soon as the danger is over. Kambei is resigned to his lot—that of a wandering, rootless hero, hungry and in tatters, but proud, confident, displaying his inner strength when needed, doing good but seeking no reward or fame. The other samurai in *Seven Samurai* exhibit similar traits: they are brave and even tempered, accepting their leader's superiority and working flawlessly as a group, each offering to serve when called upon by necessity or his leader's command.

The farmers, on the other hand, are as a whole downtrodden, disloyal (to anything but their own cause), treacherous, inhospitable, fatalistic, distrustful of authority, and amoral. "Foxy beasts," Kikuchyio calls them, while adding that it was the samurai who are responsible for their plight. It was the samurai who plundered their land, stole their crops, and violated their women. Having learned their hard lessons, the farmers are mistrustful, only striving for survival and nothing else. Outside their immediate tribal concerns, they have no interest in anything else. And yet, Kurosawa does not present them as hateful or despicable. They are the end result of the chaotic times they live in and the indifference of the outside world. Authority has betrayed them and religion does not succor. "God has abandoned us," the group complains at the beginning of the action, as soon as the bandits have left. The magistrate, if appealed to, will arrive only after the destruction is done. Only the old man sees the solution ("Hire hungry samurai," he admonishes), and the frightened villagers find in him the only reliable counsel.

Perhaps no other film conforms to the ideal of the epic to a greater extent than Kurosawa's *Seven Samurai*, for Kurosawa combines classic lines of action with modern themes—something reflected in the works of American directors whom he has inspired.[26] In the classic sense, *Seven Samurai* follows a single plotline (the "simple" plot and "ethical" plot of Aristotle), the defense of a village from marauders by a group of hired warriors (the samurai). The plot has a classical dimension, since it is noted for its economy. Though the struggle of the villagers against marauders encompasses a large time frame, for it is repeated yearly, this particular battle covers only a certain segment of this time period, the victory of the united forces of villagers/samurai against the attackers. Despite the three-and-a-half-hour duration of the movie, this plot is noted for its unity of action, and the episodes are tied together to tell essentially one story. The plot also follows the cause-and-effect sequence that

Aristotle deemed as characteristic of the epic (as well as the tragic) plot. Events are linked together: The initial appearance of the bandits compels the villagers to seek help, which results in the hiring of a group of hungry samurai. All the rest of the episodes follow the necessity of this logic: The samurai arrive at the village and begin preparations for the battle. Some of the villagers suspect them and try to hide provisions and their womenfolk, but when the danger becomes imminent they all unite and defeat the marauders. Some of the samurai are killed, buried with honors, while the rest depart with some philosophical observations. In the modern sense, *Seven Samurai* offers the viewers what they crave most, a suspenseful story, albeit with only minimal spectacle, not the "big show" that one finds in Hollywood epics. Kurosawa's style is noted for its economy, and that applies to the famous final battle scene, which goes on for nearly twenty minutes. Film relies on its own means of expression for its effectiveness—the language of film, which includes montage, panning, crosscutting, deep focus photography, and brilliant camera work. *Seven Samurai* is a film that redefines the epic; it is action filled to appeal to a broader public, but also thoughtful enough to be a draw to discriminating audiences who seek levels of meaning embedded in film techniques and language.[27] Above all, it is a redefinition of the modern action hero, whose violence-prone nature often deprives him of the means to seek self-knowledge and self-exploration. Here the hero of thought combines with the hero of action whose service to tribal interests has considerably expanded to include those of entire humanity.

The Bridge on the River Kwai (1957); Director: David Lean

The Bridge on the River Kwai (*TBRK*) can been considered a classic epic in the context of the above aesthetic parameters in two ways: first and foremost, in the context of this discussion, it has the contours of a classical plot that fits the formal elements of the ancient epic, reversals, and recognitions, and a two-strand plot comparable to that in Homer's *The Odyssey*. Second, though perhaps no less important, it marks a departure from the typical Hollywood religious spectacle that reached its peak in the mid-1950s with *The Ten Commandments* by bringing back the classic elements of the literary epic, long neglected by Hollywood. Film historian Steven C. Earley states that David Lean "recognized the potential of the epic and treated it with artistic respect,"[28] thus raising the level of the epic from mere popular entertainment to classic literary status, a trend that continued with *Spartacus* in 1960, *Lawrence of Arabia* in 1964, *The Great Escape* in 1963, and a host of others that appeared with regularity from that point on.[29] But what marks this departure from the usual epic spectacle more that anything else is the plot design with its discernable classic lines, character that becomes complex and ambiguous, while ironic utterances throughout the action become the film's most potent thematic tool.

The main epic plot elements are unity of action and unity of time. The film features only a single portion of the Second World War, the conflict in the Pacific (though the action takes place in Indochina), and focuses on an even smaller portion of that conflict, a Japanese prison camp, where a group of British prisoners of war are assigned to build a bridge in a crucial railway connection between Indochina and Burma in the early months of 1943. Colonel Saito, the commander of the Japanese camp (Camp #16), seems to have encountered some difficulties in completing the bridge, due mainly to lack of men and equipment. Therefore, he is in a hurry to get his project underway, and he counts heavily on a new group of British prisoners, who arrive after marching through the jungle, singing an uplifting martial tune and led by their indomitable commander, Colonel Nicholson. The main conflict in the plot is the clashing personalities of Saito and Nicholson. Saito, hard driving and anxious to finish his project, orders all the prisoners to work, including their officers. Nicholson, a stickler for military etiquette even in the middle of a jungle, resists having his officers doing manual labor, and refuses to obey, citing the regulations of the Geneva Convention regarding prisoners of war. As a consequence, he and his officers are shut in the camp's punishment huts. Nicholson obdurately refuses to succumb to Saito's threats and, later, rejects the latter's attempts to cajole him by offering him a dinner, and the building of the bridge comes to a veritable standstill. After about a month of such delays, Saito desperately gives in and frees Nicholson and his officers from manual duty. Under Nicholson, the British begin the task of building the bridge, proud to have won the "battle" with the Japanese.

Meanwhile, a British commando group, led by Major Warden (Jack Hawkins) and an American, Commander Shears (William Holden), who had escaped from that camp earlier, and a young Canadian officer, Lieutenant Joyce (Geoffrey Horne), arrive exactly at the time when the bridge is finished intending to blow it up. Thus, the plot of *TBRK*, though rather economical as epics go, carries a double line of action, beginning in *medias res*, as Nicholson clashes with Saito, while a second plot line simultaneously develops with the escape of Shears, whose story is briefly documented without dialogue, as the Saito-Nicholson feud goes on. Eventually, Shears is rescued by a British rescue seaplane, and, while recuperating at a Ceylon Hospital, he reluctantly volunteers to join the group of commandos assigned to blow up the Kwai bridge. The crosscutting is a device employed by film to replace the old narrative method of doubling plotlines—something that stage productions normally do not achieve. The double plot is, artistically speaking, a perilous experiment, since the viewer may be alienated if new characters are added in the middle of the action. But in TBRK the viewer is not thrown off center, since the bridge building is never out of sight for long through crosscutting, and of course, enough interest in that activity has already been generated. Tension is built, as the two separate activities begin to merge. As the bridge is finished by Nicholson and his men, Shears and his group arrive with intent to blow it up; thus the two strands of the plot unite. The commandos place the explosives under the bridge, which is to be blown up next morning when a train carrying a Japanese official passes over it, but Nicholson suspects something when the waters of the river subside overnight and he notices the wire connecting to the plunger a few hundred feet downstream. He alerts Saito, the two walk toward the plunger, and Nicholson attempts to cut the wire. Joyce attacks and kills Saito, and Nicholson shouts for help. He is soon wounded by a mortar shell fired by Warden and falls on the plunger, which blows up the bridge. Shears is killed while trying to reach Nicholson—who in utter amazement recognizes him, just before he dies.

As we have noted, reversals and recognitions are typical of tragic stories but are rarely found in the epic structure. Modern epic films usually ignore or bypass these classic traits, not deeming it necessary to present the epic hero as a tragic figure, especially when it comes to investing him with the element of recognition. In a classic epic, such as The Iliad, Achilles, bowing to Priam's plea and returning his slain enemy's body to him, gathers a glimpse of his own cruelty and barbarism, though he has known the wrath of revenge. In TBRK, the confrontation with the commandos gives depth to the character of Nicholson, who recognizes his mistake ("What have I done?") and falls on the detonator to blow up the train. Such self-knowledge is crucial to the understanding of this film, and it is basic to the understanding of film in its epic form. Nicholson's ignorance has been foreshadowed and fulfilled by chorus-like reverberations throughout the film's action. English efficiency, which is part and parcel of Nicholson's mentality, is highlighted by such phrases running repeatedly through the action, as "there's always the unexpected," or Colonel Greene's "in our job, there's always one more thing to do," and the decidedly ironic phrase of Saito's, "Be happy in your work."

Throughout the course of the action, Nicholson, however, displays an enormous capacity for self-deception, at the expense of sanity and common sense. Soon after he is freed by Saito, he embarks on the ambitious project of building a "proper bridge" (though a less perfect one, he was told by his medical officer, would do), despite severe limitations of resources and personnel. He can do no wrong, so they enthusiastically back his efforts, also gloating at the prospect of building a bridge that will "last six hundred years." Flush from his victory and vainglorious, Nicholson rises to heights of conceit and self-deception by seeing this as an opportunity to build on his victory—he surmises—by demonstrating how inefficient the Japanese are. The stiff-necked colonel, symbol of the conquering British Empire, though waning in prestige at this point in time, conceals his true motives from his officers and troops, letting them believe that his reasons for this huge undertaking, bound to exhaust them physically, is done for their welfare. All but one or two fully share his self-deception. This is a mass brainwashing, equaled by few such metaphoric statements in literature, film, or history. The enormity of the potential for catastrophe here is staggering. Only God could see its dimensions, and of course only God does, so to speak, in the image of the flying vulture. The film director's concept of detachment here is similar to the objectivity of Homer, the calm viewer of the massacres perpetrated in the battles of Greeks and Trojans. The camera may be detached, but the viewer knows what is going on. A slightly changed atonal music note or two is heard every time Nicholson goes into one of his trancelike fits of self-deception.

The epic hero, as the tragic hero, must reach self-awareness, anagnorisis, which is his qualifying characteristic. By this criterion, four other persons, in addition to Nicholson, may share tragic characteristics in *TBRK*: Saito, Shears, Warden, and Clipton, the British battalion's medical officer. Of these, Warden does not achieve full self-knowledge, though he comes close when he is forced to kill a young Japanese soldier in the jungle in order to maintain the secrecy of his mission. Warden is a Cambridge scholar learned in Oriental languages, now an expert in demolition and explosives, and the leader of a commando group called Force #316 with orders to blow up the Kwai bridge that Nicholson is building. Culturally and socially, he is the typical "officer and a gentleman" (something the amoral Shears is not), a specimen that the British Empire proudly produced and exhibited to the world, as a model to be adopted and copied. He comes across as a loyal, modest, courteous—even when he is being deceptive—self-sacrificing officer, a model for the military code of obedience and a stickler for the rules. He is totally dedicated to his mission and despises Shears for making such a fuss about going back to perform what to him seems a patriotic duty. Casually, Shears (and the viewer) hears from Warden's superior officer, Colonel Green, that Warden had been the hero in many sabotage missions, that he had already been captured by the Japanese (and presumably escaped), and that he is ready for another mission. Warden never has scruples about the murderous nature of his mission, but tosses his mortar away in disgust, saying, "I had to do it" to the uncomprehending Siamese women, after its shells killed one of his own men.

Clipton is Delphic, possessing common sense that his leader lacks, but not displaying any dimension of real depth; he is merely an announcer, and a very distressed one, impotent to influence events as an innocent by-stander. His knowledge is not self-knowledge, but knowledge of what duty means, but on medical or humanistic, not military levels. (Ironically, Nicholson tells him that he is a good doctor, "but that [he has] a lot to learn about the army.") His own duty is to save men from disease, something that he does efficiently, but he can easily discern the lapses of judgment of his commander. At the end, viewing the catastrophe, the collapsed bridge built with such extraordinary effort, and the dead men, he utters, "madness . . . madness." In a long shot, he descends the hill, while a hawk flies above him, both symbols of objectivity, summing up a viewer's impressions of the absurdity of human endeavor.

Troy (2004); Director: Wolfgang Petersen

Wolfgang Petersen's Troy both fits and defies the classical mold, and does so with a certain amount of dignity, despite its lack of real depth and its failures in plot and design. Petersen directs with Germanic precision that seeks out the roots of tradition and regards the original sources (Homer mainly) with considerable respect, even referring to his compatriot's, Heinrich Schliemann's research to find the ancient Troy in his nineteenth-century excavations, thus seeking to ensure some historical basis for his epic. At the same time, Troy defies Homer's portrayals of both the events described in The Iliad and the characters presented in it, thus depriving a technically excellent movie of real distinction, failing to tell the story of this notorious ancient war as a unified event in terms of time and action. Examined from the point of view of its formal properties, Troy demonstrates why these play a significant role in the success or failure of a modern epic attempting to preserve the classic lines of plot and characterization, for it is in defining these that one discovers the mythic dimensions of a story that has survived in collective memory for as long as it has. When archetypal myths are emblazoned in a people's memory for millennia, their visible counterparts in film must achieve their status within the dramatic parameters of an equally compelling tale. Formally, it is impossible to tell a story without the use of a plot, although "episodic" stories have often achieved acceptable levels—as artifacts.

Inspired by Homer's poem, The Iliad, Troy explores the classic epic form in a number of ways: it avails itself of the structure and the theme of ancient epics, in this case drawing from the Greek classical tradition itself and its most famous war, which is featured in most schoolbook texts and familiar to most Western schoolchildren. The story of the fall of Troy, as universal a war story as any in world history and literature, was not drawn from the Roman and biblical tradition, on which the epic cinema has fed for an entire century, thus shifting the focus of the action to a new ground hitherto unexploited by Hollywood (at least in terms of significant output). At the same time, *Troy* can be seen as an attempt to link antiquity with modernity and its concerns, war being one of them, and epic film can bring its menace as close to our consciousness as any medium can. War, with its uncertainties, conflicts between heads of state, the hegemony of a superpower with its pitfalls, bravery in battle, heroism, guile, romance—these are the subjects that the epic in general and *Troy* in particular explore, a difficult task, given the vastness and complexity of these subjects.

Troy also builds on a familiar archetype formula, using the magnetism of a Hollywood superstar, Brad Pitt as Achilles, to portray the greatest war hero of antiquity, whose feats were sung by Homer and many other poets. Achilles, fated to die in battle and gain glory rather than live and be forgotten, as his goddess mother told him, is the archetype of valor—arête, or excellence, as the Greeks called it—a fearless demigod, unbeatable in battle, though still vulnerable, who can be seen as the war hero of today, and, for these reasons it was deemed that only a Hollywood superstar could play him. For the epic to succeed, it is a given that its formal qualities must strive to make it as perfect a work as possible, but its archetypal hero must also have the necessary star quality about him, must be a powerful figure such that he can invoke in the crowd a desire to vicariously experience his deeds.

Judged by the above criteria, *Troy* succeeds only modestly in achieving these aims. Despite its technical excellence and some very good performances, *Troy* is still a flawed epic for a number of reasons, but two, both related to its formal qualities, are singled out here. First, the movie in its entirety has a loose, episodic plot, which was borrowed from various sources, though, as stated, it was inspired by Homer's *The Iliad*. Here, the plot stretches over the expedition of the Greeks to take Troy, after the Trojan prince, Paris, seduces and abducts Helen, wife of King Menelaus of Sparta. The Greeks set up a siege of Troy, and it takes them ten years of hard fighting before they capture it, after using a ruse; it was cunning, not valor, that won them the day. When they do succeed, they kill every major figure (except one who escapes to found Rome—Aeneas—a fact not mentioned in the movie), and enslave the women. Achilles, in the movie, is killed by Paris in the final battle, as the movie correctly gives this final confrontation. The movie also draws material from the events described in *The Iliad*, but borrows rather freely from other sources, some from *The Odyssey*, which describes episodes of the sack of Troy in flashbacks, and mainly from Virgil's *The Aeneid*, the second book of which describes the sack of Troy in detail. The writers may also have had access to other historical and archaeological sources, including numerous other works on the Trojan War written by other authors during antiquity, such as Lesches of Mytiline, author of *The Little Iliad*, and Agias of Troezen, who is credited with *The Return of the Heroes*, a continuation of *The Iliad*.[30] The plot of *The Iliad* is tight, its duration is only nine weeks (or so), and its theme is exclusively the "wrath" of Achilles and its effects on the Greeks, who were losing without his power. *Troy* is true to some of this, but it broadens the plot by attempting to cover the whole period of ten years plus, and the result seems somewhat improbable, for no one gets visibly older in a ten-year stretch. Thus, the plot turns out a chronological sprawl, although the writers cleverly avoid mention of the duration of the war—cinematically it does not matter—or other factors, such as the total absence of the gods, so prominent in *The Iliad*. In the movie, the gods are only seen as oversized statues, their power invoked (mostly by the Trojans), but their involvement omitted. To modern audiences this may seem an advantage, for this omission frees the filmmakers from having the added burden of describing deities of long ago, though in Homer's world they function as divine intermediaries between man's works and his unalterable fate.

A more serious drawback is that the plot of *Troy* is not only episodic and somewhat slow moving but also attempts to combine two strands: the revenge theme, the Greek campaign against Troy to reclaim Helen, the abducted queen of Sparta—a theme that is generally given as the cause of the Trojan War (the other being the ambitions of Agamemnon for world dominance); the other strand being the clash between the two strongest leaders of the Greeks, the arrogant and conquest-minded Agamemnon and the proud strongman Achilles, a clash that is responsible for the near defeat of the Greeks, for at a certain point Achilles refuses to fight, and the result is a standstill. When he does fight, he kills the leader of the Trojans, Hector, after the latter kills his "cousin" Patroclus. The problem here is that the screenwriter of *Troy* (David Benioff) could not quite make these two strands of plot merge smoothly. On balance, the Paris-Helen plot is the weaker one, for the romance is a tepid affair, hardly worthy of motivating a large army to go after the missing woman—at least not in the Hollywood terms outlined here. The first third of the movie suffers because of the lack of sparks between the two lovers, while the older folks—gruff and warlike as they look—cannot outline a real reason for the war they are about to embark on. Then the movie details, rather sluggishly, the sailing of the Greek fleet to Troy, its sudden appearance there, and the first battles. There is no sense of time, and the ten-year period the war supposedly lasted is given in sporadic episodes, with crosscutting and telling of the stories from both sides—the Trojans making sorties from their fortified city, the Greeks responding in kind, unable to get through and win the day. There are several confrontations, the main ones being the confrontation between Paris and Menelaus, the latter absurdly being killed there by Hector (untrue in the Homeric story, where Menelaus not only survives the war but returns with trophies to his wife after seven years of wandering and gathering riches) after Paris is wounded and withdraws. The killing of Patroclus by Hector is given correctly, as is the duel between Hector and Achilles, during which Hector is killed and dragged around the city, as Homer tells happened. Troy is finally taken through the ruse of the Trojan Horse, Paris kills Achilles and in turn is killed. The story ends with the destruction of Troy and the burning of the body of Achilles in a pyre (again Homer does not mention this). Agamemnon is also killed in the final battle, a fact that remains ahistorical, for it is well known by all ancient narrators—including many tragedians—that Agamemnon returned home and was killed by Clytemnestra, his wife, who had taken a lover.

In this sprawling, episodic epic structure, the clash between Achilles and Agamemnon is intermittently given and fails to be the center of the action, as in the Homeric poem. Thus the plot becomes a mishmash of themes, drawn from different sources, and hardly meshing into an organic whole. By contrast, *The Iliad*, despite its size and many diversionary stories of the gods, is noted for its terse action, quick pace, and powerful central theme—the anger of Achilles and its destructive effect on the Greek campaign in Troy, an idea that is expressed in the first few lines of that poem: "Sing, goddess, the anger of Peleus' son Achilles, and of its devastation, which put pain thousandfold upon the Achaians."[31] This key phrase—the singing of the catastrophic anger of Achilles—in the first line of this epic is the catalyst for the main events that unfold. The narrative does not waste space, but falls quickly into the rhythm of war episodes that follow their initial premise in logical order. The anger of Achilles precipitates a quarrel between him and Agamemnon, the fighting stops, and the war slips into a dangerous lull, taken advantage of by the Trojans, who rally and nearly defeat the Greeks. A council is called of all the warrior leaders, and a delegation, led by Odysseus, is sent to Achilles, imploring him to reconsider; the latter relents but does not fight himself, rather he sends Patroclus, his friend (a cousin in the film) wearing his armor, but Hector easily kills him. Now Achilles is seized by a second "wrath," a desire for revenge for his friend's death. This second wrath reveals a more savage (but even so nobler) Achilles, who overwhelms the Trojans, kills many without mercy, and scatters the rest into hiding behind the walls of Troy. Ancient critics admired *The Iliad* for its focused action and unity of theme. In his *The Poetics*, Aristotle praised Homer for not attempting to make the whole of the Trojan War his theme, a task too large, and, in fact, impossible for any writer. Instead, he sections one portion of it, its ninth year, and concentrates on one thing only, the rage of its best warrior and the resulting wrangle among leaders—not many of whom he paints favorably—with its catastrophic results. Thus, a chain of events linked by believable causes brings about the climactic scenes of the death of Hector, the foreboding prophesies of the death of Achilles, and the looming destruction of a city. *The Iliad* becomes a metaphor (synecdoche) of the war in its entirety, a summing of its human failures, and the resulting evils. Horace, in his *Ars Poetica*, speaking to Roman neophytes, commends Homer for dispensing with preliminaries, starting his action in *medias res*, and proceeding to create an organic whole noted for its excellence of composition.

In modern times, Homer has more or less become the subject of archaeologists who parse his words seeking history behind fiction. But Homer's is a fictional world and it must be judged by aesthetic and humanistic criteria. War is the greatest hell humans can create for themselves, but it also brings out the noblest and the best moments. Achilles, recalling that he too has an old father, listens to an old man asking for the mutilated body of his son, breaks down and cries, pitying his enemy. To its credit, *Troy* shows Brad Pitt in, possibly, his best moment, crying over the body of the dead Hector. Can Brad Pitt play Achilles? If for a moment, he can. Add the magnificent portraits of Priam and Hector given by Peter O'Toole and Eric Bana, and you get a sense that the modern makers, despite their difficulties with form, were at least conscious of the awesome tragedy of a conflict without a cause—or a cause which was pretense, the abduction of a woman, a disguise of the real reason of conquest and imperial greed.

Suggested Films for Study

Gone with the Wind (1939); Director: Victor Fleming

Netting ten Oscars and $77,600,000 in box-office returns, this beloved American epic of the Civil War is not free from flaws in formal structure: it suffers from excessive length (222 minutes), and its two parts are dissimilar in thematic development, for the story drags on as a romance, while its main theme, the Civil War and its aftermath on the South, is relegated to a lesser status and practically abandoned. Thus, due to its lack of organic cohesion, a great epic loses some of its power, for its second part dwells almost exclusively and at great length on the fortunes of two adversarial lovers.

Lawrence of Arabia (1962); Director: David Lean

Written by Robert Bolt, *Lawrence* is regarded by some as the greatest epic ever made. Splendidly photographed in the deserts of Jordan (and in Spain), *Lawrence* tells the fortunes of English scholar T. E. Lawrence in the Arab campaign during World War I, as he leads the Arab revolt against the Turks. The first part of the epic is an absorbing adventure, as well-knit and fast action shows Lawrence leading a unit of Arab warriors across the Nefud Desert to capture the important strategic port of Aqaba. But the second part breaks into an episodic structure, showing Lawrence in various stages of the continuing campaign, blowing up trains, or conferring with important officials as they wrangle on their way to capturing Damascus. If seen as a study of the personality of Lawrence, this film succeeds despite its episodic nature; but as an organic whole, its break into two parts impedes its rhythmic development and narrative movement toward a powerful ending—as the one seen in *The Bridge on the River Kwai*.

The Godfather: Part II (1974); Director: Francis Ford Coppola

This sequel to the universally admired gangster epic, *The Godfather* (1972), is perhaps a greater work than the first one (many viewers thought so), not only for its development of the theme of vendetta and its tragic overtones, but also for its daring experiment in form, telling two parallel stories, a device that in this case works admirably. While the story of Michael Corleone, now the head of the family and more ruthless with the acquisition of power, develops, another tale takes shape: that of his father, Vito Corleone, in his youth, as he arrives from Sicily, an exiled boy, and through cunning, toughness, and his ability to assess and wipe out his opponents, gradually gains strength and rises to the status of "godfather," head of a family clan that competes effectively in the jungle of mob warfare. As the director cuts back and forth from one tale to another, the two lines of narrative dovetail perfectly, continuing to build suspense until each reaches its shattering, ironic climax.

Barry Lyndon (1975); Director: Stanley Kubrick

Barry Lyndon suffers somewhat by its deliberately slow pace, its break into two parts, and its change of tone in the second. The first part describes the exploits of an Irish adventurer, Redmond Barry, who, thanks to his wit, bravery in battle, and alliance with a cardsharper, also an Irish exile, rises to wealth and status by marrying an aristocratic lady, Lady Lyndon, after her husband's death, for which he is partly responsible. But, as the second part of the film shows, he is unable to hold on to his good fortune, living a life of dissipation and engaging in a feud with Lady Lyndon's Hamlet-like son, young Lord Bullington, losing a leg when he refrains from killing him in a duel. Crippled and impoverished, Barry is obliged to leave England for good, exiled to Europe. A slow pace and lack of cohesion of the two parts blemishes a potentially powerful epic, which still has some admirers.

Notes

1. Quoted in Aubrey Williams, ed., *Poetry and Prose of Alexander Pope* (Boston: Houghton Mifflin, 1969), 433.

2. Charles Kaplan and William Anderson, eds., *Criticism: Major Statements*, 3rd ed. (New York: St. Martin's, 1991), 27.

3. Quoted in Terry Eagleton's "Marxism and Literary Criticism," in Charles Kaplan and William Anderson, *Criticism: Major Statements*, 3rd ed. (New York: St. Martin's Press, 1991), 565.

4. Kenneth Burke, "Psychology and Form," in Kaplan and Anderson, *Criticism: Major Statements*, 466.

5. Aristotle, *The Poetics*, quoted in Kaplan and Anderson, *Criticism: Major Statements*, 22.

6. Aristotle, *The Poetics*, in Kaplan and Anderson, *Criticism: Major Statements*, 22–25.

7. Aristotle, *The Poetics*, in Kaplan and Anderson, *Criticism: Major Statements*, 25–26.

8. Aristotle, *The Poetics*, in Kaplan and Anderson, *Criticism: Major Statements*, 27.

9. The above points are discussed throughout *The Poetics*, but the main argument on the similarities between epic and tragic are found in books 23 and 24, which offer summations of Aristotle's observations on the epic. See Aristotle, *The Poetics*, in Kaplan and Anderson, *Criticism: Major Statements*, 46–49.

10. Aristotle, *The Poetics*, in Kaplan and Anderson, *Criticism: Major Statements*, 47.

11. Aristotle, *The Poetics*, in Kaplan and Anderson, *Criticism: Major Statements*, 48.

12. Siegfried Kracauer, *Theory of Film: The Redemption of Physical Reality* (London: Oxford University Press, 1971), 266.

13. This term has a variety of meanings, all explored in *The Poetics* (Book 26), from knowledge of body marks (as the scar in *The Odyssey*), to logical steps, to natural means. The best knowledge is self-knowledge, the kind Oedipus obtains when he discovers his identity.

14. Aristotle, *The Poetics*, in Kaplan and Anderson, *Criticism: Major Statements*, 32.

15. Aristotle, *The Poetics*, in Kaplan and Anderson, *Criticism: Major Statements*, 37.

16. Aristotle, *The Poetics*, in Kaplan and Anderson, *Criticism: Major Statements*, 38.

17. Aristotle, *The Poetics*, in Kaplan and Anderson: *Criticism: Major Statements*, 29.

18. Aristotle, *The Poetics*, in Kaplan and Anderson: *Criticism: Major Statements*, 29.

19. David Lean's *The Bridge on the River Kwai* took a year and a near brawl; *Cleopatra* (1963) nearly wrecked the fortunes of Twentieth Century Fox because of delays; and Francis Ford Coppola's *Apocalypse Now* was bogged down in the Philippine jungles for more than a year.

20. Susan Sackett, *Box Office Hits* (New York: Billboard Books), 27–28.

21. This is discussed in the introduction.

22. Examples include *Memento, Dark City,* and *A Beautiful Mind.* See chapter 6.

23. One such example can be opera, which thrived on its extravagant stage shows. A specific example is Mozart's *The Magic Flute* (see Bergman's filmed version, 1975), which displays magic dances, monsters on the stage, flying human groupings, and masked demons, not to mention the appearance of a Masonic chorus in the second act.

24. Audie Bock and Rob Edelman, "Kurosawa, Akira," in *The St. James Film Directors Encyclopedia,* ed. Andrew Sarris (New York: Visible Ink, 1998), 255.

25. *A Lion in Winter* (1968), directed by Anthony Harvey; *A Man for All Seasons* (1966), directed by Fred Zinnemann; *The Godfather* (1972) and *The Godfather: Part II* (1974), directed by Francis Ford Coppola, are among such epics with tragic or flawed heroes.

26. Kurosawa's work inspired American directors John Sturges, who directed *The Magnificent Seven* (1960), almost an exact remake of *Seven Samurai*; and George Lucas, who acknowledges his debt to *The Hidden Fortress,* the format of which he used as a basis for his plot in *Star Wars.*

27. For a study of this film's technique and language, it is useful to follow Michael Jeck's running commentary in *Seven Samurai,* Criterion Collection DVD, 1998.

28. Steven C. Earley, *An Introduction to American Movies* (New York: New American Library, 1978), 157.

29. One can cite *The Fall of the Roman Empire* (1964), directed by Anthony Mann; *Lord Jim* (1965), directed by Richard Brooks; *Dr. Zhivago* (1965), directed by David Lean; *2001: A Space Odyssey* (1968), directed by Stanley Kubrick; and the popular *Towering Inferno* (1975), directed by John Guillermin.

30. Henry Nettleship and J. E. Sandys, *Dictionary of Classical Antiquities* (Cleveland and New York: Meridian Books, 1964), 219.

31. Homer, *The Iliad,* translated with an introduction by Richmond Lattimore (Chicago: University of Chicago Press, 1962), 59.

CHAPTER TWO

The Mythological Epic

As many anthropologists have claimed, myths are universal and ubiquitous but they are also inextricably bound with communal interests specific to each time and place. Myths are constantly created by historical circumstances, social movements, migration, and conquest, while the invention of new mediums of expression gives rise to the forms myths take. American cinema not only gave expression to myths already embedded in its historical past, but it soon created new ones by projecting images on the screen that reflected the realities and social trends of the last two centuries. Moviemakers quickly understood the tremendous potential of myth and turned to well-known stories as the most appealing subjects of the new medium. Such figures as D. W. Griffith, Mack Sennett, and Charlie Chaplin became, according to one film historian,[1] the first mythmakers of the American screen, establishing archetypal figures that paved the way for emerging heroic figures. Despite the controversy surrounding his first great epic, *The Birth of a Nation* (1915), which cast a shadow on his cinematic legacy, Griffith is known for his exploration of historical data derived from ancient cities that perished (Babylon), the Renaissance, the American Civil War, and the present—all seen by him as morally bankrupt societies that allowed such evils as war and injustice to threaten or destroy them. In his films, controversial and unacceptable as some of his subject matter might be, the good people (or those he presents as good people) are victims of injustice and are either murdered or barely escape with their lives. The high moral tone of Griffith's movies was counteracted by the comedies of Mack

Sennett and Charlie Chaplin, who amused audiences with the creation of comic figures in the context of broader social conflicts. Sennett invented the highly amusing sight gags and car chases with the bumbling Keystone Cops, while Chaplin gave the world the archetype of the homeless tramp who survives despite the world's neglect or cruelty. Soon more archetypes were added: the romantic lover, the femme fatale, the adventure-seeking western hero, the biblical leader, and the female polished socialite.

As American film progressed from its genesis through the twentieth century to the present, heroic figures of all kinds emerged—war leaders, western lawmen, scientists, sea captains, space explorers, detectives, super spies—coming in all shapes and forms, populating the screen universe and winning audiences with their daring exploits, personal allure, and the embodiment of values peculiar to America. From gunning down outlaws in the plains, to saving populations from disasters, fighting the Nazis in World War II, or engaging in intergalactic struggles to fend against invaders from outer space, American heroes energized audiences with their daring, ruggedness, individuality, and the inborn sense of setting things right in the world. A string of larger-than-life screen personas dominated not only American life, but also projected images of courage, daring, rugged individualism, inventiveness, and self-sacrifice throughout the world. Hollywood owes a great deal to the glamour of its heroes, who nearly at all times won the lady, or reduced the villainous opponent to dust, or both. It was the dichotomy of hero-villain that nourished Hollywood melodramas, and the epic followed suit. Take the likes of John Gilbert, Douglas Fairbanks Sr., Charlie Chaplin, Errol Flynn, Clark Gable, Jimmy Stewart, John Wayne, Gary Cooper, Burt Lancaster, Steve McQueen, Tom Hanks, Clint Eastwood, and many others in recent times—figures who, in one way or another, embody American values in American movies.

The epic, the most dominant form in movies, by and large expresses positive values and the nobler side of humans, rather than their darker side, something that is left to the domain of gangster movies and westerns. The hero is the savior of humanity in one way or another, while the villain remains the hunted one. That epic format worked in many instances where the hero became the energetic force of the action. The James Bond epics (one must see these as derivatives of the epic forms), for instance, coming into existence at the height of the Cold War, feature a central figure as the hero, always the same person (though not always the same actor), battling megalomaniac villains who scheme up ways to try to destroy the Western world. The hero, Bond, a British secret agent, operates "at Her Majesty's service," while villains are of international origin, and the country defending itself against them is often America (wasn't Auric Goldfinger, in *Goldfinger*, foiled by Bond and his American allies when attempting to raid Fort Knox?) and Bond fought against enemies of the West. The Bond films, appearing in the latter part of the century and continuing to this day, feature an assortment of villains, power-hungry monsters, and lunatics, usually with polished manners, coming as close as a hairbreadth to destroying Western civilization. Armed with all the means of showmanship it could muster, Hollywood rose to the occasion by instilling the feelings of invincibility to an audience that witnessed an epic hero confronting a dastardly villain though knowing full well that the spectacle offered was no more than a fantasy. The epic, quite capable of being serious, is perhaps the greatest conduit of fantasy ever invented. And Hollywood producers fully understand this point and exploit it to maximum effect, offering escapist fare that nevertheless stirs up feelings of invincibility during difficult times in American history. Myth is embodied in a larger-than-life story that serves as the context, the value system projected subconsciously, for the heroic image to arise, take flesh and be worshiped— while the opponent is abhorred—by the masses. Audiences love heroes and are said to "love to hate" villains; yet both heroes and villains comply with archetypal patterns. Mercenary as Hollywood is, it manages to get hold of the basic communal instincts and transform them to images projected on a screen, thus appealing to the national psyche while piling up greenbacks. Rich in tradition despite its relatively short life span, American epic film has created a mythology through its Hollywood screen heroes almost unequaled by any other medium: from the Revolutionary War, the Civil War, immigration and urbanization, racial struggles, presidential assassinations, social conflicts, economic upheavals, to today's war on terror, America has given shape and form to its cultural drives and national instincts in the numerous images created for the screen whose presence reverberates throughout the world. The string of epic heroes is noted for its variety, for epic films present adventurers, famous war leaders past and present, naval heroes, western gunslingers, secret agents, lovers, religious leaders, and even notorious gangsters. Producers of epics were known to make careful assessments of the public mood and to choose their heroes accordingly.

Rudolph Valentino: The Romantic Archetype

The Sheik (1921); Director: George Melford

Rudolph Valentino (1895–1926) was the first great romantic lover on the screen, and he inspired and defined the lover's persona, establishing its format and function for the string of male epic/romantic heroes that filled the

screens (and still do) in the coming century. He had energy, animal magnetism, and a striking physical presence, expressing his virility with a trademark
smirk of self-assurance that unnerved his opponents and captivated female
worshipers. In his first epic hit, *The Sheik*, directed by George Melford, the
sheik is Valentino, playing Ahmed, an Arab prince, who practically abducts
an English woman, Diana (Agnes Ayres), the daughter of an English peer,
who had ventured into Arabia for thrills, against her brother's advice. In
those post-Victorian times an English lady venturing unescorted into the
land of "savages" was asking for trouble, especially when the lady borrows the
costume of a dancer in order to peep in on an Arab club reserved only for
men (as in England?). Ahmed soon discovers that she is a white woman, and,
within hours, if not moments, he is madly in love with her. At first she resists
him, calling him a savage, but soon relents when she learns the prince had
been educated in Paris, and has with him a French servant, Gaston, who soon
becomes Diana's guard. One of Ahmed's invited guests, a doctor/novelist
(Adolphe Menjou), arrives from England and reveals a few interesting details
about Ahmed. The prince, the son of an Englishman and a Spanish woman,
had been brought up in Arabia but he is by birth a European. In her attempt
to escape, Diana is seized by a bandit and taken to his fort, which soon is attacked by Ahmed and his tribesmen; Diana is saved, while Ahmed receives
a near-fatal wound, but recuperates thanks to the attentions of Menjou and
Diana. The end is happy, for the lovers are united.

In *The Son of the Sheik* (1925), directed by George Fitzmaurice, the son follows in the footsteps of his father, destined to be a lover first, then a leader.
(Rudolph Valentino plays both the son and the father.) Young Ahmed falls
in love with Yasmin (Vilma Banky), a dancing girl, who lives with a band of
derelicts who capture and torture Ahmed when he tries to take her away. He
is freed by some of his friends, and then he tries to force Yasmin to love him,
but she resists. His father (Valentino was deplorably madeup to look older),
disapproves of his son's wildness, but Ahmed's mother, played again by Agnes
Ayres, soothes the older Ahmed by telling him his son is behaving no more
wildly than he did when he was courting her. The action ends with a horse
chase, young Ahmed pursuing the villain who would harm Yasmin; there is
swordplay over the sand dunes, and a happy end when the lovers are united.

In these two films, Valentino is shown at the beginning and at the height
of his career, playing a lover from the Orient (he was Italian by birth), en-
trancing first a Western woman and then an Eastern one, exhibiting his irresistible sexual charm, but in both cases being a cross between a barbarian and
a half-polished civilized man, arrogant and sure of his magnetism over
women. Grinning with self-assurance, he never doubts his overwhelming

masculine charm. One has the impression that his grin is all he can do as an actor. At moments, he recites Arabian verses of love, and he can also scowl, look puzzled, angry, dejected, or ecstatic. His role does not demand serious acting and the plot is simple. But his efforts to save a wounded Gaston and the use of his doctor friend for humanitarian purposes reveal his good nature. Dashing, amorous, compassionate—and passionate—looking entirely the part of a lover, Valentino triumphed as a consummate image of what is known in Hollywood parlance as a heartthrob of the screen. Carl Jung saw him as the "male animus projection," the personification of the female fantasy. He groups him with Shelley (the poet), Hemingway, Gandhi, Tarzan, and Lloyd George[2] all of whom represent the male animus in one form or another. According to Jung's theory, "A woman falling in love with a picture (or film star) is clearly projecting her animus into the man."[3] In the silent era, Valentino personified this idol of romantic lover—as much as Shelley and Byron had in the nineteenth century as literary figures as well as adventurers and dashing lovers—images that Hollywood appropriated and cashed in on with male screen heroes such as Clark Gable, Errol Flynn, Robert Taylor, Elvis Presley, Robert Redford, Mel Gibson, and Brad Pitt—all of whom are, to some degree, genuine descendants of the ill-fated Valentino. Valentino was at the height of his career in 1922 when *The Sheik* was released to the public, and *The Son of the Sheik*, released in 1926, was his last film. Valentino died at the age of thirty-one of a perforated ulcer in August 1926, plunging many of his male and female fans into untold grief and even, unbelievably, suicide. His funeral in New York City almost caused riots. That event is surpassed in glamour and mass grief only by the Kennedy assassination—which, incidentally, created its own myths: the mass conspiracy theory in Oliver Stone's *JFK*, for instance, or his heroic status in the recent *Thirteen Days*. For Kennedy, even as president, was a Jungian "animus." Grief over his death was not only for a slain head of state, but also for a romantic hero.

Tarzan: The Archetype of the Jungle

***Tarzan and His Mate* (1934);**
Directors: Jack Conway and Cedric Gibbons
This jungle epic is as good an example as any of its sequels in reinforcing Jung's point that Tarzan (as played by Johnny Weissmuller) was an animus for women,[4] a type that attracts the female as the anima attracts the male, becoming a symbol of mass wish fulfillment of both sexes, for males too wish to emulate his screen persona. In fact, it is possible to argue that Tarzan represents what men believe women desire rather than what women actually

desire. Tarzan is a wild man, but in a noble way, for his good qualities have remained unspoiled by civilization's accumulated vices—greed and wealth, for example. Tarzan knows nothing about money, never takes from the environment more than he needs, lives in harmony with nature, and does not hurt anyone or anything, animal or plant, though he knows how to survive and defend himself. He loves a woman naturally, as she is in her present state, for she has willingly chosen to live with him, having rejected the elaborate accouterments and the makeup that civilization had thrust upon her. She thus becomes his equal in the battle of survival in the jungle. Nudity for both is a natural state only disfigured by gowns, perfume, and other cosmetic trifles her friends have brought her, things she has left behind. If Tarzan is the animus, Jane is easily the anima, the personification of the female form at its most enticing, for males will be attracted to the noble woman of nature, and Jane is fully conscious of what she has chosen to do.

The attraction of the Tarzan movies, still in force for us today, rests on the romantic nineteenth-century notion that civilization has corrupted the natural human, uprooted this being from nature, and transferred it to the cities, placing artificial obstacles in its development. A story that offers sheer adventure, attractive leads, and ostensibly not much for the mind is, of course, a projected fantasy of this idea, and a Tarzan movie fits this pattern. Because the popularity of this series was unmatched in the 1930s, it deserves some notice.

First, it is pure escapism, with all the trappings that this word implies. The movie was made at the time of the Great Depression, when people craved some form of diversion from their troubles. And sound had come in a few years earlier, so one could actually hear Tarzan's (and Jane's) yodel, and marvel that human lungs could produce such a stunning utterance; a sing-song yell that was used as a warning, alarm signal, or pal-to-jungle-pal greeting. Then, it was the allure of the jungle itself. Though the shooting of most Tarzan movies took place in Florida (Silver Springs), the jungle scenes looked as authentic as one would want them, thick foliage, trees with hanging vines, swampy areas, wild beasts—name it, it was all there. And of course, the principals: Tarzan, with the tall, sculpted body of Johnny Weissmuller, and the tantalizingly and scantily clad Jane (Maureen O'Sullivan). What was there not to like in these half-primitive creatures? Add a couple of villains who want to steal the ivory stored in elephant burial places—a sacrilege—and some hostile, attacking tribes, together with a few uncooperative lions, and you get a small-scale epic with all its wild attractions. Of course, Tarzan and his mate are a loving couple, and they cavort practically nude in the pond, taking deep breaths when they surface. After endless underwater footage, you think (and you do) that the world has left its ugly civilization and gone back to paradise with Adam and Eve. But evil lurks, even there: a monstrous rhino kills Cheetah, the intelligent ape, and almost Tarzan, who then does battle with a crocodile ten times his size. But Tarzan's real wound comes from a treacherous bullet fired by white intruders.

Edgar Rice Burroughs's novels were the models for the creation of the Tarzan type, and they evidently came from the nineteenth-century notions of the "noble savage," in circulation since the times of Jean Jacques Rousseau and Herman Melville (a term now of course defunct in the era of political correctness). The ivory hunters in some superficial ways resemble Kurtz and his cohorts in Conrad's *Heart of Darkness* (though the similarities stop here), for it is again about the greed of the raiders of the jungle who become bestial in their pursuit of wealth. Luckily, here we don't need to go to such depths or lengths. There is an element of romanticism in the story—innocents pampered by nature and escaping its deadliest perils can live happily ever after, or until the next episode. Hollywood knew how to exploit adventure-loving audiences, and these stories held up then, and still do today.

John Wayne: America's Western Hero

The Shootist (1976); Director: Don Siegel

John Bernard Books (John Wayne): "I don't think I ever killed a man that didn't deserve it."

Bond Rogers (Lauren Bacall): "Only the Lord can judge that."

No one in American film history has quite emulated John Wayne's screen presence as the foremost mythical western/adventure hero. Myth requires a larger-than-life persona, one not simply enlarged by the screen, but one that appeals to the instincts of the community in its search for ideal strength, endurance, and dominance in the physical world, qualities that spring from inner confidence as much as from physical size and demeanor. Though the American Hollywood screen fed audiences for decades with well-groomed heroes that met those criteria—Clark Gable, Gary Cooper, Errol Flynn, Kirk Douglas, Henry Fonda, Harrison Ford, and many others—no one projected as powerful an image of an epic hero of the old West as John Wayne, who was seen knocking baddies, helping the downtrodden, meting out justice for all, while harboring malice toward none but the most despicable. The Duke, as he was popularly called, was an American original, sharp in mind, independent to the point of absurdity, stubborn, even vindictive at times, but supportive of those who had use for his fists, understood his scowl (just as intimidating), or had enough respect for his gun-slinging skills. He became a legend in his own time, his career lasting for decades despite bouts with cancer, which eventually killed him. Together with John Ford, the director who helped mold his screen persona more than any other, Wayne became the archetype of the western hero in such western epics as *Stagecoach* (1939), *Fort Apache* (1948), *She Wore a Yellow Ribbon* (1949), *Rio Grande* (1950), *The Searchers* (1956), and *The Man Who Shot Liberty Valance* (1962).

Directed by Don Siegel, and based on novel by Glendon Swarthout, *The Shootist*, Wayne's last movie, brings to the fore both his persona as a brave hero and as an actor, who comes as close to playing himself as in any of his previous films, something that was much commented upon by critics—that Wayne simply played Wayne. The Duke's robust persona showed through despite attempts by various directors to disguise it in his various roles—most of which had him playing a western hero of the plains or a naval officer. In *The Shootist*, Wayne plays a dying gunslinger. The movie was made three years before Wayne's death (1979) and his health was already deteriorating. Wayne fit the image of the man he played, and the movie begins with a montage that features some of the best-known moments of John Wayne's movies.

The action begins soon after the turn of the century, on January 22, 1901, the day Queen Victoria dies, a piece of news that appears in headlines in local western papers. That is the day when J. B. Books, a notorious gunman, (the "shootist") arrives in Carson City, Nevada, to consult a friendly doctor, who saved his life once and whom he trusts to tell him the straight truth. Books, who had been alternately an outlaw and lawman, has a reputation for toughness in the most indisputable manner: he has gunned down thirty men, and he is still alive. He has survived the tough western frontier with its countless perils, has grown old but can still hold his own, and considers himself nearly invulnerable, "as strong as an ox," as he tells Dr. Hostetler (Jimmy Stewart). But suffering from unexplainable pains in his lower back, he visited a "sawbones" in some unidentifiable city and, wanting a second opinion, he comes to Carson City, Nevada, to consult Hostetler, who soon tells him that he is suffering from "a cancer,"[5] and that his days are numbered. He has six weeks give or take, two months at the most, and he will die in terrible pain. He can ease the suffering by taking laudanum, a concoction of opium and alcohol, used as a popular remedy before the age of illegal drugs and painkillers. Books finds quarters at the home of Mrs. Rogers (Lauren Bacall), a recently bereaved widow, to whom he gives the name of William Hickok,[6] as he doesn't want his own revealed to the townsfolk, for obvious reasons. But Mrs. Rogers's son Gillom (Ron Howard) soon learns the identity of Books and, awed by his reputation and proud to have a "man like him" in his own house, spreads the news. Word soon gets out that J. B. Books is in town, and the shootist receives visits from the local newspaper man who wants to write a piece on him; and by the local sheriff, the ludicrous and talky Thibido (Harry Morgan), who is at first intimidated on hearing who he is dealing with but soon regains his spirits when he learns the man is near death. Men in the local saloon, the Metropole, are agitated to learn who is in town, and some get ready for a fight. The local toughs include Dulford (Hugh O'Brian), a gambler; Cobb, who runs a creamery business and who plans a trap for Books; and Sweeney, a vengeful and seedy looking Richard Boone[7] who vows to kill Books in retaliation for his brother's death. In pain and obviously dying, Books gets his house in order, sells his horse, settles his accounts, has a suit cleaned, orders a tombstone with his name and year of death chiseled on it, then gets a haircut. An undertaker (John Carradine) gleefully plans to have his body exhibited for a fee after his death, and a jubilant barber collects Books's hair from the floor of his shop to have it displayed and sold later. Rather than face a painful and undignified death, Books chooses to let his opponents know that he is going to be at the Metropole at a certain hour—early in the morning on Sunday, January 29, the seventh day of his being there and his birthday. He asks Gillom to spread this information, but not to tell each of these men that he also told the others. There is a final confrontation during which Books, after a drink, calmly disposes of Cobb, who foolishly draws first; then Sweeney, who is advancing holding a table in front of him (also foolishly); and finally Dulford, whose approach he detects reflected in his glass. But the wounded Books is gunned down by the saloon proprietor, presumably wanting to collect the glory of finishing off Books, but who is in turn shot by Gillom, at last entering the fray.

The Shootist is different from the typical Wayne movie in a number of ways. For one, it lacks the usual format of pitting good guys against bad guys, the typical action in most Wayne vehicles. In those, Wayne was busy cleaning up towns from greedy cattle barons (as in *Chisum*) or hired gunslingers, who terrorized communities and got away with murder by being seemingly unbeatable (*The Man Who Shot Liberty Valance* is one). In this one, Wayne's last film, the shootist has come to town to die. His enemy is not "the bad guys," but death, something he confronts as a certainty for the first time in his life. When questioned by young Gillom as to how he has managed to stay alive, Books replies that what gave him the advantage over equally fast adversaries was his being "willing" to face death. He never blinked nor took a deep breath, but had the willpower to look at death with no hesitation. That readiness, not the fast draw in itself, preserved him. He triumphantly outlived all his opponents, but he could not prevent time from passing him by. Emblematically, he resembled Queen Victoria, who too had outlived her times. Time, the arrival of a new and mechanized century—these were the things that signaled the gunman's extinction. As he comes into Carson City, with its gamblers and remnants of the old West, he—and the viewer—can see the changes. Telephones ring, electric lamps on lampposts light the streets, the town generally has a peaceful air about it, and streetcars still drawn by mules are to be "electrified" next year. The gunman, a symbol of invincibility, of nobility—for Books brags of never killing unprovoked—of courage and daring, all these are coming to an end. Gamblers still exist but they may never live to see another day; and little ludicrous figures like Sheriff Thibido (who is perhaps Wayne's opposite with his lack of libido) are going to run the western towns. Wayne, now visibly older and worn at the edges, is perfectly attuned to this role and, not unexpectedly, so is Jimmy Stewart. Both were heroes of the old Wild West, both fought similar battles to make inroads for the peaceful folk to follow. Not having an adversary to gun down—for nobody was really bothering him—Books prefers to rake up some old resentments or to provoke others to gain glory by killing him as a means of being killed. Cancer is for the civilized man who is a town dweller. In a sense he battles cancer, not allowing it the privilege of killing him. The western—at least in its original Hollywood formats—essentially died with Wayne. Wayne knew this, and his weathered features mirrored his inner anxiety, borne with grace and courage. The Duke—and that was the name of his dog—was never replaced.

Epics with Mythic Patterns

The Greatest (1977); Director: Tom Gries

Cast in the epic mode (though not of epic length), *The Greatest* presents Muhammad Ali certainly not as an actor (of admittedly limited acting abilities) who can play himself, but as the one person who can *be* himself. His is a figure that transcends athletic abilities and achieves the mythic quality that emanates the aura of a national hero, for he embodies America's values, its mixture of cultures and races, its tendencies to both vilify and glorify its heroes, its strengths and weaknesses. Ali, sick now (in 2007) while approaching his sixty-fifth birthday, continues to enthrall our imagination, and this movie, even though it was made thirty years ago, captures some of that, even as awkwardly as it does, and as ineptly as it is put together. The action is episodic, the appearances of various actors and celebrities in cameo roles lack coherence and even purpose, and Ali's lackadaisical handling of himself as himself is somewhat embarrassing. But the Ali who fights in the ring is for real, and those moments alone almost compensate for the shortcomings of this mishmash of a movie. Clips are inserted as the action progresses and the Cassius Clay of the early fights transforms into Muhammad Ali, the kid with the big bad mouth that no one took seriously earlier, but one who became a great fighter in later years. The movie also documents Ali's induction into the army and his refusal to serve, his confrontation with the army brass, his statements of his conscientious objections to the Vietnam War, and much more—all rather awkwardly staged, despite the decently written script by Ring Lardner Jr., himself a victim of discrimination during the McCarthy era. The clips from the fights are judiciously edited, and the older viewer of today relives moments of Ali's greatest fights, his confrontation with Sonny Liston, his defeats by Joe Frazier and Ken Norton, and his triumphant comeback in Zaire against George Foreman. The movie ends on that note.

What this movie chronicles, however, is a deeper sense of what a figure that transcends the mere athlete means. The athlete is a twentieth-century phenomenon, for he came in when professional sports—and of course the modern Olympics and their amateur champions—arrived. Professional sports in England and America in the latter part of the nineteenth century—soccer, football, baseball—and the beginning of the twentieth, and the advent of the modern Olympics with the Athens Olympics in 1896 and following mark the beginning of the modern athletic persona with his/her special mystique, his/her ability to inspire the crowds, and the shaping and nourishing of an archetype at once distinct and representative of worthwhile human qualities. The Olympic athlete is not a warrior, but an agent achieving distinction in a peaceful context; in fact today's Olympic athlete pursues distinction for personal and social reasons, national pride being one. The professional athlete is a variation, working for his team, his city, and for personal distinction and wealth. Athletes excel, attempt to score more or higher than their opponents, and beat the competition. But to inspire and have a following, they must also have other qualities. They must be seen as fighters for ideals, as defenders of their own convictions, as fighters for the right cause. Jesse Owens achieved such a distinction in the 1936 Berlin Olympics by winning four gold medals but mainly his victory was seen as repudiation of Hitler's Nazi dogmas. Lou Gehrig (played magnificently by Gary Cooper in *The Pride of the Yankees*, 1942) became legendary because of his moral stamina in enduring a deadly disease. And Muhammad Ali has come to symbolize the man who rose to victory after the setbacks of civil disobedience, racial hatred, bitter defeat, and who made a triumphant comeback that defied all the odds. He has been called the greatest athlete of the twentieth century, but now, older and frail, he has been described (by his daughter, also a boxer) as a great humanitarian—a man seen as a symbol of his race and of America.

Gangs of New York (2002); Director: Martin Scorsese

Gangs of New York is a carefully documented and meticulously crafted epic film about a hitherto neglected period of American history that begs to be re-examined.[8] It is a myth of New York, a topic explored by Scorsese in a number of his earlier major movies, many of which play on the same motif: New York City as a microcosm for America. In his earlier works, *Mean Streets* (1970), *Taxi Driver* (1971), *Raging Bull* (1980), and *Bringing Out the Dead* (1999), Scorsese offers a single hero who dominates the action, with the background he lives in providing the rationale for his actions and shaping his mental orientation and decisions. By contrast, in *Gangs of New York*, New York City becomes the key metaphor, and, in a larger sense, the hero of the story. Using it as the backdrop, Scorsese sketches a world in perdition, a hell on earth, where forces battle out each other, and where the strongest (not necessarily the most moral or righteous) survive. Scorsese claims that the history of New York in the middle of the nineteenth century is a trope for the history of America as it strove to take shape—and is still shaping—in the first century of its existence as a nation.[9]

The film, based on Herbert Asbury's book, *Gangs of New York*, covers the period of pre–Civil War America, roughly between 1846 and 1863, which was the time of the arrival of Irish immigrants who left Ireland in great numbers during the potato famine, and who came in large groups, causing the antagonism of the so-called native Americans, those who had come earlier, fought in the Revolution and left descendants who were reluctant to share their hard-won freedom and its rewards with new arrivals. The film centers on the clash between these two groups, the Natives and the Irish, both of whom were divided into gangs that dominated the streets and fought each other in bloody battles of extermination. The film uses a central location, the actual battleground of these conflicts, a neighborhood called Five Points, where the immigrants and other cheap labor classes, including freed slaves who escaped from the South, were housed. Five Points was located in the southeastern end of Manhattan, not very far from Chinatown of today, and only a few blocks from where the twin towers of the World Trade Center stood before the terrorist attacks of September 11, 2001. Five Points, originally a swamp called "Collect Point," drained by the Dutch and eventually used as a housing area for new arrivals and cheap labor residents, was an intersection of five streets, Gross, Anthony, Little Water, Orange, and Mulberry, all of which converged on Paradise Square, where most of the movie's action is centered. This was possibly the worst slum in the history of America, whose living conditions "shocked and appalled both Walt Whitman and Charles Dickens."[10] Its poor living conditions became a breeding ground for disease, street fights, and the battleground of various gangs that struggled for dominance. The gangs with their weird names—Dead Rabbits, Bowery Boys, Broadway Boys, and Plug Uglies—acted as muscle in various disputes for turf between various factions in neighborhoods, or favored opposing factions that divided the area and New York in general. The Natives, as the Americans already born in America called themselves, split into various gangs (some of those named above) and they were all led by Bill Cutting, the "Butcher," a character based on an actual person, William Poole,[11] a powerful and influential gang leader who considered the Irish immigrants to be intruders and fought for their destruction. The film character, played by Daniel Day Lewis, is portrayed as a cruel and sadistic knife thrower, who clashes with Priest Vallon (Liam Neeson), who represents the Catholic Irish. Vallon is killed, but his young son Amsterdam (Leonardo DiCaprio), placed in a house of reform for fifteen years, emerges from there as a young man seeking revenge and redemption for his people.

The two main figures that represent the conflict are given in the context of the two opposing groups. One group, the Irish led by Priest Vallon, lives underground, in the vaults and underpasses of New York City, from where they emerge to confront Bill the Butcher and his bands of Natives. In a brutal battle, Vallon is killed, his tribe defeated, and his young son, Amsterdam, is taken to an orphanage, from which he emerges fifteen years later to form a new band and avenge his father's death. Amsterdam's odyssey forces him to blend with other gangs, follow their paths of violence and plunder, but he seems to be the only one who retains a moral consciousness of the enormity of injustice done to his tribe and the social chaos that prevails. He sees no way to achieve his end except to conceal his intentions, as he harbors a plot to confront the Butcher by ingratiating himself with him, gaining his trust, and becoming his adopted "son." The individual story was a story of revenge, Amsterdam being a kind of Hamlet, with whom he shares certain generic characteristics; he seeks revenge both for his father's murder, and as a leader of his people, the Irish immigrants, who suffered repression during the dominance of the Butcher, the archetypal villain. The latter is either related, or opposed to certain other elements in the city, having both connections with the various gangs, who look up to him as a leader, and the leader of Tammany Hall, "Boss" Tweed, who favors the Irish, whom he sees as voters in his political schemes. But the Butcher soon learns Amsterdam's identity, and the much-awaited final confrontation takes place amid the violent draft riots, during which mobs ravage the Uptown section of New York, threatening to overrun everything, until the navy cannons fire on them from the harbor. In the ensuing carnage, the Butcher is fatally wounded by shrapnel and begs Amsterdam for a mercy stabbing, which the latter delivers with horrifying reluctance. This brings an end to the strife, and presumably a new beginning for the torn city of New York. The Butcher dies while saying, "I am an American."

America's conflicts are presented as the country deals with the problems of immigration, racism, and ethnic identity in the most representative of American cities. Nineteenth-century New York was in the process of being molded, and still is; it is a city in constant creation and turmoil, and, as a mythical entity, it is the spinal cord of the entire nation: it contains the genesis of a society, created through merging and strife, and it is yet to acquire its final form and balance. Thus, *Gangs of New York*, historically based, becomes primarily a metaphor of a city's struggle to amalgamate its diverse elements, to survive during the country's most intense crisis, and to gain its unique identity.

Seabiscuit (2003); Director: Gary Ross

Horses, like human beings, have been epic heroes, and there are plenty of horse film epics: *A Day at the Races*, with the inimitable Marx Brothers; *National Velvet*, with a young Elizabeth Taylor; and *Black Stallion*—to mention a few. But *Seabiscuit*, directed by Gary Ross, may be the definitive horse epic, for it is placed in the context of human struggle and achievement. This is an American story, about the American dream, which says that you can start anywhere and still achieve your goal. If you have a handicap and you overcome it, the victory is even sweeter, for yourself and for those around you. If you are the underdog and you win in a race against tremendous odds, the crowds will love you too. In *Seabiscuit*, a horse owner, played by Jeff Bridges, is compassionate enough to take a youngster under his wing, a redheaded boy named Red whose father had sent him out into the world with a single commission: "You have a gift," though it wasn't clear what that gift was. Red tries boxing, gets injured trying to outdo huge opponents, and is practically in the streets when he is given a chance to ride a horse—one that, like him, had been given up by its owner as too small, too prone to injury, and too poorly trained (to always come second to the bigger horses). A horse trainer comes into the picture, one also handicapped by neglect and failure to win anything big, and one who is compassionate to injured horses (usually shot after an injury). This is a "feel-good" movie, designed to show how Depression-era audiences could be uplifted by the story of a winning horse—a time when audiences needed uplifting.

One horse that was considered a hero in real life is Smarty Jones, who had won the Kentucky Derby and the Preakness and was trying for the Triple

Crown at the Belmont Stakes on June 5, 2004. Only eleven horses in the history of horse racing had achieved the Triple Crown, the last in 1978. It was a huge day in the world of horse racing and the day would become strange—and significant—for another reason. The same afternoon as the race at Belmont, about 4:00 ET, former president Reagan died at the age of ninety-three, and eulogies from all quarters began to deluge TV screens. Which event was more newsworthy? Well, if you were watching the race unfold on ESPN, you witnessed the mass hysteria at the racetrack: TV commentators couldn't say enough in praise of this horse who had pulverized the opposition at the Preakness, winning there by almost twelve lengths. There had been no Triple Crown winner for twenty-five years; the scene was set for this extraordinary victory; there was no doubt Smarty Jones, a noble horse that had never lost, would deliver. Expectations were high, and the crowd went into frenzy as the horse appeared on the track. He lost by a length to Birdseed. The defeat of Smarty Jones seemed to cause more grief in the hearts of some Americans than the death of a president whom many called great. Now, why was that? Why would a crowd worship a horse, treating it like a deity, a savior almost? Why this mass wish fulfillment for a winner? Why treat a horse, an unknowing animal, like a hero? The answer—in symbolic terms—is that the horse is a hero. Heroes are needed for the mass psyche, especially when disasters, bad news, wars, terrorist fears, and other calamities, real or imaginary, prevail in the news. The praises for a dead president who was a hero to many, would fill that function. But the horse winning a final race to achieve the elusive Triple Crown would have been an even greater victory. Heroism, the visible expression of a hidden collective desire, is the essence of the archetype. And it makes no difference if that evasive image is a human or animal. (Incidentally, the death of Barbaro in January 2007, a horse that won the Kentucky Derby the previous year but broke a leg during the Belmont Stakes and survived for eight months after numerous operations, also caused grief reserved only for heroes who had died for a cause.)

Master and Commander: The Far Side of the World (2003); Director: Peter Weir

Master and Commander features Russell Crowe playing a hero of the British navy, Captain Jack Aubrey, who is chasing a phantom French ship called the Acheron through the South Seas. The director, Peter Weir, elaborates on interestingly placed personas that have more than one side. Sometimes, these sides are contradictory, but Weir manages to balance them out, so that they do not appear as unresolved conflicts. At first, Crowe as Captain Aubrey appears to be a cross between Captain Bligh (Mutiny on the Bounty, 1935) and

Fletcher Christian, a ruthless disciplinarian with the charisma of a matinee idol—but soon that impression is dispelled, for Aubrey turns out to be altogether likeable, a born leader of men, a patriot dedicated to duty, intent on his mission, a hero in the best sense, a sensitive man placed in a situation where the slightest appearance of weakness is a fatal flaw. Conscious that his dilapidated ship and motley crew are not a match for the superb French frigate he is pursuing with orders to destroy it, he knows he must use cunning to overcome a superior adversary, who usually attacks during a fog and slips away, only to shadow him. As the line between mutiny and obedience hangs in the balance, Aubrey has to play a mental game as well, leading his men by implanting in them the belief that he is invincible and fair, but also a stickler for discipline; above all, he abhors weakness in his officers. He is a disciple of Admiral Horatio Nelson, having served under him in his youth, and that in the British naval ethos defines the archetypal nineteenth-century naval officer, a leader of the high seas whose men had to endure life in cramped quarters, eating rotten food and being subjected to primitive medical conditions.

A naval story breeds a special kind of hero, for in the naval hero's small universe he is an absolute ruler, nothing short of a god. He is worshipped, feared, and hated, all at the same time. But he must not be despised. Any failure of principle, any deviation from the course he has carved, even the slightest hesitation in his set course of action will be seen as a weakness, and at once his tightly knit unit will break apart. Aubrey draws from his inner strength, and holds back compassion in order to reprimand a wavering midshipman (Hollam), and metes out corporal punishment on a man who fails to salute him. There is a larger point in the conception of this archetypal hero, however. This is not a case of villain versus hero, as in Bligh and Christian of *Mutiny*, where a completely villainous captain sadistically punishes his mutinous officer; nor is Aubrey the vile and evil Claggart of *Billy Budd*, whose victim is a hated innocent, incapable of striking back (but one who eventually does). Rather, we hear the reasoned voice of a friend—Dr. Stephen Maturin—testing the principle of absolute authority, which the naval captain is obliged to uphold. This argument is reminiscent of the Ahab/Starbuck conflict in *Moby Dick*, where the first mate advances the argument that it is a sin to take revenge against one of God's creatures—as the perverted logic of Ahab dictates.[12] For a moment, Aubrey sounds and behaves exactly like Ahab; he seems to ignore the ship's poor condition, his men's suffering, and the futility of a pursuit of a superior enemy. Aubrey and Maturin clash when the HMS *Surprise* is headed for the Galapagos Islands, where Maturin makes an argument in favor of observing rare animal species while there. Aubrey stubbornly rejects the notion that any act in the advancement of science is more important than his war mission. A classic argument ensues: the conduct of war is more important than any other pursuit—more urgent than science or humanity, or any other peaceful pursuit. Aubrey is not without understanding of the arts—he is a considerably talented musician and plays duets with Maturin in their spare moments, but to Aubrey, his naval discipline is of the utmost importance. Does any of the crew, he argues, want to live in a London occupied by the French? Do they want to be subjects of Napoleon? In the end, his persistence in his mission/goal—to find, destroy, sink, or burn the *Acheron*—defines the mindset of this naval hero. He is an example of an utter patriot, a military man of the age of Enlightenment. Men like this could handle the violin as well as the saber; they could lose an arm (Aubrey just gets scratches) and dismiss it as a minor deformity; they could watch the greatest cruelty on their ship—a battle on a ship is indiscriminate slaughter—without wincing; and they could empathize, but stay calm and cool under the greatest pressure. These are not inconsiderable virtues, evident in the military, navy or other institutions today.

Director Peter Weir is Australian, an easterner/westerner with polish, whose concept of a master and commander is one of a totally civilized human being under extreme stress; one who will not lose his humanity in the midst of war and who is a warrior with an understanding of the world of art and science.

King Arthur (2004); Director: Antoine Fuqua

Produced by Jerry Bruckheimer, *King Arthur* is typical of today's epics, which have separated themselves from the great epics of the 1950s and 1960s, epics that, with all their commercial character, often gave subtle characterization, plot development, and great, larger-than-life archetypal heroes who resonated with the broader public. There were also epics made during the predigital era, at a time when violence on the screen was still muted, and the stories were benevolent, rich in illusion. Today's violent epic is a staple that divides audiences. There are those who abhor violence in its extreme forms and abstain from seeing violent films, while there are others conditioned by the numerous thrillers such as *Pulp Fiction* and *Reservoir Dogs*, and follow them avidly.

Bruckheimer films more or less fit the mold of violent action/epic film, from *The Rock* (1996), to *Armageddon* (1998), *Pearl Harbor* (2001), *Black Hawk Down* (2002), and *Pirates of the Caribbean* (2003)—all large spectacles in which violence is routinely offered. Precious few of these received nods from critics, or won Oscars, but Bruckheimer aimed for popularity, with stock characters never developing beyond a certain point, and making no attempt at subtle messages. It is a cartoonlike cosmos that he presents, more or less in the mold of the comic-strip epic, and he has achieved both skillful staging and relative success in exploring a popular genre.

King Arthur boasts a large cast of extras, action sequences on a big scale, battles staged with the utmost detail to look both period and real, sets digitally magnified to achieve realism, and decent acting with mostly English and European actors. *King Arthur* is a gritty, spectacular epic that, in addition to its well-staged battle scenes and romantic themes, claims to have discovered "new" historical evidence that changes the customary configuration of the King Arthur mythology. Arthur in this movie is not the fifth-century figure usually portrayed in both history and film, but a displaced young boy from Sarmatia, an eastern European country which the Romans took but, admiring the bravery of its warriors, incorporated into the Roman Empire. The abducted boy, then in his teens, grew up in England, became a Roman and a Christian around 452, and undertook to defend England against Saxons from the north and unite England as a free country. This version of Arthur, however, does not command the magnificent palatial environments so usual in previous productions, and his queen, Queen Guinevere, is not an opportunity to showcase a glamorous Hollywood actress (witness Elizabeth Taylor or Ava Gardner in similar Hollywood productions of the fifties), but is presented as a woman in love who is also a tough warrior. Clive Owen, who plays Arthur, is rugged in war armor, and Keira Knightley, then a young phenomenon of an English actress still in her teens[13] who plays Guinevere, shoots an arrow with credibility. Despite, or perhaps because of, their youth, these actors fit the mold of postmodern epic heroes—down-to-earth, sexy but not sexually involved, having learned the craft of playing rugged individuals, historical heroes who dealt with violence coming from unexpected quarters.

Arthur, however, is a universal figure, able to engage in violent battle with his adversaries and envision a future without violence, where families with numerous offspring can live in peace and quiet. The theme befits our time as much as the mythical Arthur's. It offers hope that we can fend off our enemies and establish a world of peace and harmony among peoples of all origins and religions. Though its historical basis may be shaky and Hollywood oriented, *King Arthur* attempts to de-center history, replacing the old with the new in its ever-repeated cycles.

Notes

1. Steven C. Earley, *An Introduction to American Movies* (New York: New American Library, 1978), 13.

2. Carl G. Jung, ed., *Man and His Symbols.* (Garden City, N.Y.: Doubleday, 1964), 194.

3. Jung, *Man and His Symbols*, 194.

4. Jung, *Man and His Symbols*, 194.

5. Modern explanations of such diseases are attributed to long years of western men in the saddle, causing prostate cancer, which was then impossible to treat.

6. James Butler (1837–1876), an American frontier scout and marshal.

7. Boone died of cancer soon after Wayne's death in 1979.

8. See Martin Scorsese, "Commentary," in *Gangs of New York*, DVD Disc two (Miramax 2003).

9. Scorsese, "Commentary," in *Gangs of New York*, DVD.

10. "Discovery Channel Special" in *Gangs of New York*, DVD Disc two (Miramax 2003).

11. Poole died in 1857.

12. David Edelstein, "Naval Gazing," *Slate* (online magazine), November 13, 2003, www.slate.com/id/2091195.

13. Keira Knightley played the lead role in *Pirates of the Caribbean* at the age of seventeen and was in *Pride and Prejudice* at nineteen.

CHAPTER THREE

The Religious Epic

The religious epics, starting early in the twentieth century and continuing into the 1930s and 1940s and culminating in the 1950s, were mostly set in the historical and geographical context of the Roman Empire, becoming the most common, most popular, and the most exploitative of the Hollywood epics, made almost solely for commercial purposes. They resonated with the general public, which was ripe for religious topics in the post–World War II era, an era fraught with fears of nuclear annihilation and communism. At a time when Joseph McCarthy's investigations were ongoing, when agnosticism and existentialism were among the prevailing norms in academia and elsewhere, Christianity seemed an appropriate theme to filmmakers, who, at least in the world of commercial enterprise, appear to be trend followers rather than trendsetters. The religious faith some of their epics inspired served as an antidote to the fears of the time, giving audiences stories of heroes of unshakable belief in the face of tyranny or betrayal and providing examples of pagans converting to the true faith—Christianity—or leading their peoples to promised lands. Religious epics, like most other epics, honed images of archetypes that played decisive roles in bolstering the aspirations of peoples in the midst of a crisis. Thus, the religious epic, despite its excesses in style or the crassly commercial motives of its creators, found its time and place in mid–twentieth century American culture—and one might say in the free world as well—and functioned as a palliative to fear, while doing good business as a vehicle of entertainment, a principle well suited to the American entrepreneurial temperament.

Most of these epics were drawn either directly from episodes in the Bible—Old and New Testament—or from accounts of the sufferings of Christians under Roman rule, and, although almost entirely fictional, some claimed historical authenticity. One of the best-known filmmakers, Cecil B. DeMille, maintained that he had embraced a religious purpose, to show the truths of the Bible, when he made *The Ten Commandments* in 1956.[1] There is no reason to doubt his sincerity. The Hollywood studio system did not consciously exclude, or try to demean, a religion or any other topic purposefully when making movies. But DeMille understood the attraction of spectacle and his film epics were primarily commercial ventures, with a moral tag attached to them, as, almost always in his stories, Christian virtues triumphed over Roman decadence, abundantly displayed on the screen in sex and violence scenes. He and other Hollywood moguls of that era knew that if they offered grand spectacle, large casts with recognizable stars, and, as time went on, color and wide-screen technology, audiences, lately lured away by TV, would sooner or later return to the big screen. In fact, the epic flourished partly because of its commercial rivalry with the new medium of TV. The stories of these epics were usually overblown Hollywood fictions, some borrowed (freely) from the Bible (DeMille's *The Ten Commandments*, 1923, 1955; *The Sign of the Cross*, 1932; *Samson and Delilah*, 1949) or other ancient sources, or from popular fiction (Lloyd Douglas's *The Robe*, 1952; Lew Wallace's *Ben-Hur*, 1959). These grand productions were distinguished by their reverential tone, the exclusion of any direct political statement, and a careful assessment of the public mood. Bringing audiences back to the theater from the comfort of their home where they watched TV dramas and live shows was the main motive of these filmmakers, a motive that did not exclude or vitiate any other motive, such as a sincere desire to inspire or provide spiritual guidance in troubled times. Spectacle came as a result of advances in technology and it was only a step that separated the black-and-white, square-screen movies of the 1930s and 1940s from the "miracle" of CinemaScope and Panavision, not to mention stereophonic sound. Filmmakers took full advantage (something they still do) of these technologies and created spectacles on a grand scale in order to impress their audiences.

In certain respects, these films adhered to the guidelines of the epic. Religious leaders portrayed on the screen by charismatic Hollywood actors—Victor Mature, Richard Burton, Robert Taylor, Paul Newman, Charlton Heston—were well suited as archetypal heroes that embodied the Christian ethos of piety, integrity, and faith. The epics featuring these heroes were well funded by the still-powerful Hollywood studios that were able to feature "casts of thousands" (in most cases this was literally true), lavish sets and costumes, music and dance interludes (*The Ten Commandments*) beyond the pale of a religious topic, and high production values in general. Their plots easily conformed to many of the classic epic guidelines: length (three to four hours), multiple strands (in most cases), unified action (in at least a few cases), panoramic points of view, shooting on location (though generally Hollywood back lots or the Cinecitta studios in Rome provided the settings), and impressive special effects in general. Some achieved tragic effects of pity and fear, though most were ordinary melodramas, featuring villains clashing with, and often defeated by, sympathetic heroes. A happy ending was a standard Hollywood practice that did not change until the sixties, when this type of religious epic waned; often these grand spectacles came with double endings, resulting in the fall of the villain, and the victory of the hero. They generally corresponded to modern characteristics (albeit in a shallow manner) of the epic offered by anthropology and psychology: Psychologist Otto Rank defines a hero as someone who undergoes long trials or initiation rituals (baptisms, conversions, desert treks), overcomes enormous odds, has a great-minded mission, avenges a personal loss (Ben-Hur, in *Ben-Hur*), carries out a divine plan, or brings people to the promised land (Moses, in *The Ten Commandments*).[2]

As noted already, the McCarthy era of the 1950s and the Cold War uncertainties accelerated this tendency to seek refuge in religious subjects (among other things), and the always-shrewd Hollywood executives took advantage of these popular trends and offered what was wanted, but with style and spectacular effects that in some ways remain unsurpassed. The religious epic, as known in the 1950s era, came to an abrupt halt after that era, and when it resurfaced, it became something entirely different or lost its glamour. An example is the tediously narrated production of George Stevens's *The Greatest Story Ever Told* (1966), which, despite its excellent production values, turns out a blown-up repetition of the 1950s epics that lacks their zest and fervor, ingredients which made some of them irresistible and Oscar winners. Religious epics after that time became rare, and when they came back, they turned out to be controversial tracts, dichotomizing audiences and causing more controversy than commercial success, such as Martin Scorsese's *The Last Temptation of Christ* (1988) and Mel Gibson's (considered anti-Semitic by some) *The Passion of the Christ* (2004). Of course, some made their points in a different note, such as Robert Duvall's excellent movie, *The Apostle* (1998), which forgoes controversial and unsolved (in film) theological issues and concentrates on a man's efforts to reform by practicing his faith.

Epics with Religious Topics

The Sign of the Cross (1932); Director: Cecil B. DeMille

Cecil B. DeMille was the first director to understand the commercial value of the religious epic and his productions are held by some as responsible for the poor reputation the epic film, aimed at large audiences, has attained as shallow spectacle with low artistic merit.[3] But DeMille understood the box office potential of religious spectacle as much as any filmmaker, and gave audiences what they craved: martyred heroes and heroines (especially the latter), colorful villains, the doings of dissolute emperors loosely based on history, tribal leaders divinely inspired, and, above all, clashes between good and evil, with plenty of miracles artfully photographed with special effects as to appear as awesome biblical events to the faithful. At the same time, he recognized that moviegoers wanted more spectacle than piety, so he threw in scenes of wild orgies, scantily clad women, and masculine military men attracted to lustful empresses—scenes common to that era, at least before the Hays Production Code, a self-regulating system studios used to avoid government censorship, took effect in the early 1930s (the Code lasted until the mid-1960s) and put an end to all this. *The Sign of the Cross* combines all these elements perfectly. Choosing a time in Roman history noted for its moral laxity, the prevalence of the ethos that might is right, and the birth of a new religion that was seen as a threat to Roman hegemony, *The Sign of the Cross* takes the audience back to the time of Nero burning Rome in order to amuse himself and compose a song. Christians were an easy target when he wanted somebody to blame, and Nero, on the advice of a corrupt Roman guard, raids the Christian quarters, arrests and kills its leaders, and throws the group in prison, later to become a spectacle to Coliseum patrons who feasted on the spectacle of humans being devoured by lions. Meanwhile, an intrigue is at work. His bravest and most loyal general, Marcus (Fredric March) has fallen in love with a Christian girl, Marcia (Elissa Landi), while he is the object of desire of his lustful and decadent Empress Poppaea (Claudette Colbert), who tries in vain to seduce him. He begs Nero to save the girl he loves, but the emperor, under the influence of the malicious empress, turns him down. He could save her only if she renounced her faith, something she refuses to do, forcing Marcus to follow her to her death. Naturally, he converts to Christianity just before he dies. Both will be united in heaven. This formula worked before, as well as in succeeding epics, for the crowd craves a hero who, if not victorious in his battle with evil forces, dies for his faith.

The film became notorious for its sinful Roman villains, however: Claudette Colbert is shown practically bare breasted while taking a bubble bath submerged in donkey's milk and about to indulge in a lesbian scene with one of her ladies-in-waiting; while Nero, flawlessly portrayed as a lascivious and dissolute emperor by Charles Laughton, complains of a "splitting headache" after a night of "delicious debauchery." Later at the Coliseum, he is seen eating grapes (and other delicacies), giving the thumbs down to the gladiators being carved to death underneath him. This scene was practically duplicated in a later epic, *Spartacus,* with Laurence Olivier, playing a Roman senator, coolly severing the carotid artery of a slave gladiator climbing a wall to reach his captors, while Roman ladies yelling for the "kill" giggle in the background. Hollywood had no compunctions about making the Romans villains—as the Roman Empire is a bygone entity (and nation, one presumes), and therefore unlikely to be defended by any concerned parties. Roman conquerors, especially those who killed Christians—not that this is untrue, some did—get what they deserve: a vilified reputation, but in the end this distorted history. Hollywood rarely portrays Romans as good (*The Fall of the Roman Empire,* 1964, does), and, for purely commercial reasons, has given modern audiences, especially during the early decades of cinema, an evil empire, disregarding the fact that the Romans produced some good emperors (Augustus, Herodes Atticus, Marcus Aurelius, among others), as well as numerous historians, philosophers, and poets (Livy, Tacitus, Cicero, Horace, and Virgil come to mind). The Romans were also responsible for an unprecedented period of peace that lasted almost six centuries and for the preservation of the Hellenic civilization and culture. (Though, of course, they were also responsible for the conquest of Greece and plunder of Greek art.) But the Romans, like the Huns, are history. Hollywood found it convenient to use Roman figures as villains, picking notoriously decadent emperors like Nero, Caligula, and Commodus (in *Gladiator,* 2000), or using fictional Romans of high rank, like Messala (in *Ben-Hur*), to spice up its epic yarns that needed bad guys to antagonize noble heroes.

Quo Vadis (1951); Director: Mervyn LeRoy

Though religious epics had been made routinely since the early days of cinema, nothing is comparable in scope, spectacle, size of the cast (literally thousands), or budget to *Quo Vadis* (hugely successful when first made in 1912), which was the first of the grand epics to be produced by MGM in the 1950s. Pompously announced as "colossal," and "industry's greatest spectacle" ever, and supposed to be even greater than *Gone with the Wind, Quo Vadis* was filmed entirely on location in Rome and the Cinecitta studios at a cost of seven million dollars,[4] a staggering sum in those days. Though featuring only one recognizable American star (Robert Taylor), *Quo Vadis* was studded with talented British actors of the stage and screen, Peter Ustinov, Leo Genn, and Deborah Kerr (whose "angelic" persona established her as a multifaceted epic heroine in American films throughout the 1950s), something that gave the epic unprecedented polish since the days of Charles Laughton's portrayal of the mad emperor in *The Sign of the Cross*. Both epics took advantage of their talented actors, but *Quo Vadis* boasted color and a greater spectacle—more elaborate sets, expensive costumes, thousands of extras in its crowd scenes, and even sixty-five lions from neighboring European countries for the man-eating scenes in the arena.

Based on a novel by Henryk Sienkiewicz, the film follows the last years of Nero's life, between 64 and 68 AD, when the notorious Roman emperor allegedly burns Rome in order to be inspired to write an epic song. Though the main characters are fictitious, the film makes allusions to facts of history— the murder of Nero's wife and mother, his accusations and torture of Christians, and, more specifically, Nero's relationship to Seneca and Petronius, two Roman authors with whom Nero had close ties, and who influenced his life. Seneca, the Stoic Roman philosopher who had been one of Nero's tutor's in his youth, makes only a shadowy appearance in the film, but Petronius is skillfully portrayed by Leo Genn as a polished but opportunistic flatterer who curries favor with the tyrant in order to protect his and his family's interests. To its credit, the film makes enough of this relationship to demonstrate the perils of fawning before an unworthy head of state as a means of self-preservation.

The film also makes much of Nero's lunacy, mainly thanks to a no-holds-barred performance by Peter Ustinov, whose unsettling portrayal of Nero as practically the anti-Christ must have struck home for its audience, especially at a time when Hitler's crimes were still a fresh memory and Stalin's control of the Soviet block a distinct threat. Ustinov's Nero is shown as a self-indulgent megalomaniac, utterly devoid of moral consciousness, whose only preoccupation seemed to be the exaltation of his artistic "genius." In fact, since the film has little action—there are no battle scenes and the army is shown only in parades—and the tepid romance between Taylor as a triumphant general and Kerr as a Christian slave fails to generate sparks, Nero's relation to his court, especially to his "arbiter of elegance" Petronius, author of *The Satyricon*, becomes the epic's main focal point. The epic is loosely based on the account of Nero's life by Tacitus, the Roman historian, thence making claim to historical accuracy, as always embellished by Hollywood scriptwriting. If nothing else, the film succeeds in demonstrating the obsessions of tyranny as well as its inevitable downfall.

The Robe (1953); Director: Henry Koster

When it was released in 1953, *The Robe* became an international hit and even reaped five Academy Award nominations, with two wins.[5] It was the first movie ever in CinemaScope, with an actual aspect ratio of 2.55:1 and stereophonic sound, a complete novelty at the time.[6] Audiences went to the theaters in droves to see it, and many even today remember how amazing everything seemed on the wide screen, which some critics claimed was three-dimensional, since that technique, requiring that patrons wear eyeglasses, was also an innovation at that time. Judged by later epics, like *The Ten Commandments* and *Ben-Hur*, *The Robe* did not have much action, or the awesome spectacle of the later movies, which boasted sea battles, chariot races, and the parting of the Red Sea. For spectacle, *The Robe* confines itself to a few scenes of palatial Rome, the storm during the crucifixion, and a sword fight, not so impressive in itself, between Marcellus Gallio (Richard Burton) and a Roman centurion.

Yet, *The Robe* was spectacular and action driven enough to pave a new way in moviemaking while further promoting the growing popularity of the religious theme. Wide screen became the prevailing mode in film technology, affecting all filmmaking that followed, especially action-packed productions and the epics. Religious epics, mostly ignored by television which preferred comedy and soap operas or news and documentaries, were about to approach their golden era. Though the epic had been around since the early days of cinema, the CinemaScope technique gave this film its distinctive character, combining with one stroke color, scenery seen on a wide screen (and seen differently), action, and sound, not to mention a new emphasis on costuming, art direction, and a new concept, the mise-en-scéne.

As an epic, *The Robe* was a product of its time in other important respects. Its most characteristic traits were its reverential theme and its pious tone in delivering its Christian message. *The Robe* was about the conversion of a Roman tribune, Marcellus, to Christianity after his execution of Jesus. He is charged with overseeing Christ's crucifixion, but he suffers a crisis of guilt when he wins the robe Jesus wore, saved by Greek slave Demetrius (Victor Mature), in a gambling game. Back in Rome, and now a Christian, Marcellus and his also-converted girlfriend, Diana (Jean Simmons), confront the evil emperor Caligula, who sends them marching triumphantly to their deaths. The film, based on the novel of the same name by Lloyd Douglas, was a vehicle of ideas that seemed compatible to church-going, middle-class, conservative audiences who thirsted for a return to, or a new emphasis on, Christian values. The slave's unshakable faith and the proud Roman's conversion, combined with their act of confrontation with

the evil emperor, gave audiences what they craved at the time: a hero re-
jecting riches and the glamour of high rank in the world's most powerful
empire in favor of the salvation of his soul. Perhaps too corny for the tastes
of today's audiences, *The Robe* became the vehicle of the epic's resurgence
and its dominance during the half century following, and though its spectacle is minimal compared to the great epics that followed and the performances of its leads (Richard Burton, Jean Simmons) were thought deplorable by some, it does have its share of glory in its time, and, for the
particular audiences it was addressed to, it accomplished its purpose.

Ben-Hur (1959); Director: William Wyler

Ben-Hur belongs to the biblical/Roman/religious epics so frequent in the
1950s but it surpasses all others in popularity, scope, and ambition. And it
won eleven Oscars. It follows *The Ten Commandments* (1955) in close
chronology and features the same major actor, Charlton Heston, who plays
the leading role here as well. Clearly, the theme of revenge, the return of the
son to find his mother and sister and to avenge their arrest and torture, is the
controlling theme in the action of this grand epic—grand, that is, by Hollywood standards. Such a theme also fits the archetypal qualities of a hero who
protects his native people, going through the rigors of humiliation and enslavement, and rising to power again to confront his enemy, the Roman Messala. Judah Ben-Hur is the scion of a noble Jewish family and a leader among
his people. He had a boyhood friendship with a Roman youth, Messala
(Stephen Boyd), now a powerful ranking official, who asks Ben-Hur's help to
find out and uproot potential local rebellion. When Ben-Hur, appalled by
Messala's audacity and callousness, refuses, the two former friends become
mortal enemies, especially after Messala orders Ben-Hur's and his family's arrest and enslavement. From the galleys no one ever returns, but Ben-Hur,
having saved the life of a Roman consul, does. This sets up the heroic theme
and action of the story.

Two major reversals in the movie's action fashion Ben-Hur's fate and turn
him from a potentially tragic to an epic hero: one reversal occurs when he is
suddenly thrust from a high social and national position into slavery; the second, when a galley slave, as if "by magic" (to use Messala's words), is transformed into the son of a Roman consul, Quintus Arius (Jack Hawkins). That
gives him the status to challenge a powerful Roman to a chariot race, which
he wins, and to have the authority to search for his mother and sister. He accomplishes both tasks, though his triumph is marred by the discovery that
the two women have been living in the colony of lepers. But Ben-Hur's greatest moment as a hero is not his overcoming of Messala, but his passionate

search and his great affection for his sister and mother, whom he rescues from their appalling condition and restores to family life and to dignity.

The heroic and the religious themes interweave throughout. In the early stages of the film, Ben-Hur is not a character of Christian virtue, as the film eventually makes him. Outraged by Messala's proposal to betray his nation and embittered after his enslavement, he is out for revenge, which becomes an obsession that abides with him until the chariot race when he destroys Messala. Needless to say, revenge is not a Christian virtue, although the film allows him to entertain his passion, for that is the heroic quality that will allow him to fight back. And though he believes it is his God that will save him, to the astonishment of Arius who sees the "hatred" in his eyes, it is only chance (or a homoerotic urge on the part of Arius) that saves him.

Still, the audiences of that time bought into the theme of revenge, allowing their sympathies to remain with the hero who is out to find and destroy his enemy, for they saw in him the fighter for a righteous cause. The film is also dramatically sound and thematically coherent, because the basics are there: a friendship goes sour, a son and brother witnesses the intended extinction of his family, and a former childhood friend is unmasked as a cynical and ruthless tyrant. It is revenge then (it works as a theme—it worked for Shakespeare and other Renaissance playwrights), for which the audience craves, and that becomes the major factor in the epic's dramaturgy. The emotional level of the movie remains high, which—to make an inevitable comparison—is not the case with *Gladiator*, a modern epic with a similar theme. But in *Gladiator*, the high intensity lies in the constant mayhem surrounding the existence of Maximus, also a wronged man. The similarities end there. In *Ben-Hur* we follow the hero's yearning for return and reunion with his mother and sister. Whereas the hyperkinetic Maximus ventures into one physical feat after another, becoming a fighting and killing machine, Ben-Hur stimulates us to feel his deep affection, his pride, his revulsion at a friend's treachery—in fact, his nobility. Maximus is a stoic killer; perhaps a true gladiator. Ben-Hur is a charioteer—who goes after the love of the sport, but with a purpose. It is at the emotional—not the intellectual or the artistic—level that *Ben-Hur* wins, still drawing us to watch it.

And, in the end, Ben-Hur becomes compassionate, not only to his closest relatives but to all in general. His fight with Messala cleanses him of his hatred while bringing about justice. After his discovery and rescue of the two women from a leper colony, Ben-Hur sees Jesus in his agony carrying the cross, and for a moment he helps, without realizing he is repaying a favor— for when he was being led to slavery and in distress, a figure, whose face is never shown, offers him water. In the ensuing storm after the crucifixion, his mother's and sister's faces are cleansed of their deformities, just as the blood mixed in the rainwater symbolically represents the soul's cleansing. Without quite saying it, the movie implies that Ben-Hur is a convert from a nearly agnostic and embittered Jewish nobleman to a devout Christian. His mother and sister are, in a way, beneficiaries of his newfound compassion.

Seen from a certain vantage point, this epic movie could do without this somewhat contrived interweaving of themes—that of a vengeful man who becomes a Christian. But in the 1950s—an era of skepticism brought about by a brutal World War II and the Cold War that followed—the religious theme played an important role. Psychologically, *Ben-Hur* suited its era as no other epic film did: it saw a great leader of his people, staunchly defending their interests, opposing an insolent conqueror, and undertaking a trek of incredible suffering before he returns to avenge his humiliations—his and his people's—and crush his insolent enemy. *Ben-Hur* was an epic tailor-made for the mentality and aspirations of the fifties—brilliant despite its flaws, seen as the ultimate projected image of a savior who can lift the spirit of a community at times of spiritual confusion and political chaos. From that point of view, *Ben-Hur* seems dated today. However, its action scenes and the core of humanity radiating from the hero's trek and his overcoming of tremendous odds to reach his goal—these are perfect examples of the epic film in its heroic mode. Seen from an even more remote (chronologically speaking) point of view, the film reveals two ironies, both perhaps unintentionally placed: the first irony, with its political implications, lies in Messala's arrogant tirade as he outlines his proposition of "collaboration" to Ben-Hur; the sum of it being that Rome will grant freedom and justice only to those who go along with its grandiose, and imperialist, plans of conquest. There is no world outside the Roman Empire, and one has a place in the sun only if one cooperates. "The emperor looks at you!" Messala says to Ben-Hur. The second irony, perhaps the more poignant one, is when the horse trainer, who is an Arab, joins forces with a Jew in preparation for the chariot race, for Jews and Arabs are depicted as allies and are united against their common enemy. Whether the screenwriters of *Ben-Hur* meant this irony to resonate in their time (1950s) as it certainly resonates in ours (2000s) is something that can be left to one's own interpretation. Placed in a larger, political frame, seeing *Ben-Hur* today might be a worthy experience for those two ironies alone. But it's a heroic epic in every other sense, for a hero and leader is seen confronting a former friend's treachery, is arrested, and is thrown into slavery, recovering against enormous odds and returning to vanquish his enemy, restoring the honor of his people and family.

Suggested Films for Study

The Ten Commandments (1923, 1956); Director: Cecil B. DeMille
Both directed by Cecil B. DeMille, these two versions of the same story differ in content and outlook. The 1923 version, much shorter at 146 minutes, contains two stories: the first is the biblical tale of Moses, leading his people from Egypt, parting the Red Sea, receiving the Ten Commandments carved on a rock in a spectacular scene of divine revelation, then witnessing and scattering an orgy staged by his people turned pagan and worshipping a golden calf. The second part of the story abruptly turns into a contemporary tale of amorality, one mother and two sons loving the same vamp woman, with the more righteous winning in the end. The 1956 version is a much larger epic endeavor, at 220 minutes, featuring Charlton Heston as Moses, and a group of glamorous Hollywood stars, including Yul Brynner, Anne Baxter, Edward G. Robinson, Yvonne De Carlo, Judith Anderson, and Cedric Hardwicke. An expert hand at delivering spectacle of great dimensions, DeMille stages scenes of unsurpassed grandeur, including the construction of a giant statue in honor of the pharaoh by Moses, his transformation as he visits Mt. Sinai to hear the voice of God in the burning bush, his leading his people out of Egypt in a massive scene of the Exodus, and the parting of the Red Sea, where the armies of Ramses drown in a cataclysm. Still worth watching, as it is perhaps the best example of a species of epic film no longer possible to make and it is the quintessential religious epic of its era.

The King of Kings (1927); Director: Cecil B. DeMille
Starring H. B. Warner as Jesus, *The King of Kings* was the first grand epic to win wide popularity both in its time and in subsequent decades, being shown on television regularly at Easter time. This biography of Christ still holds up as a compelling visual spectacle. A movie of the same title, in color and of epic proportions (widescreen, 168 minutes) was made in 1961, directed by Nicholas Ray and starring Jeffrey Hunter, far outdistanced its predecessor in scope, spectacular scenes, and emotional depth. It is held by many to be the best biography of Jesus ever made.

Demetrius and the Gladiators (1954); Director: Delmer Daves
Rather shallow but still watchable for its spectacular fight sequences, *Demetrius and the Gladiators* is a sequel to *The Robe*. With Victor Mature as a Greek gladiator fighting in Roman arenas and wavering between his shaken faith and his passion for the promiscuous Messalina (Susan Hayward), wife

of the malevolent Caligula, who tries to shake off the curse of *The Robe*. Typical of the pious epics of the fifties, *Demetrius and the Gladiators* was made exclusively for cashing in on previous religious box office hits. Victor Mature's heroic persona (he played Samson in *Samson and Delilah*, 1948) compensates somewhat for the lack of a sturdy plot or other dramatic qualities.

The Greatest Story Ever Told (1965); Director: George Stevens

The Greatest Story Ever Told is perhaps the most ambitious epic on the life of Christ made in the era when grand epics with religious themes still held the upper hand. Directed with assured mastery of spectacular scenes by George Stevens and featuring Max von Sydow (the great Swedish actor) as Jesus, this epic boasts magnificent spectacle, including the crucifixion scene, but on the whole, it is considered a loosely structured narrative that barely holds together, despite the plethora of Hollywood stars in it, including John Wayne, Telly Savalas, Claude Rains, Charlton Heston, Angela Lansbury, and Sidney Poitier.

The Gospel According to Saint Matthew (1969); Director: Pier Paolo Pasolini

This film at 135 minutes is not strictly an epic, but it is considered by many to be the definitive film about the life of Christ, though based on only one gospel—thence it contains archetypal patterns known to the epic. Photographed in black and white, with nonprofessional actors, the film won many international awards, including a Special Jury Prize at the Cannes Film Festival, and it is singled out by the Vatican as the most revered film biography of Christ ever made. It still holds its power and makes an emotional impact on believers and nonbelievers alike.

The Last Temptation of Christ (1988); Director: Martin Scorsese

Martin Scorsese's version of the novel by Nikos Kazantzakis (1955) was condemned by both the Catholic and the Greek Orthodox churches and generated a storm of protest by mostly fundamentalist Christians in this and other countries. It takes the strange view that Christ was in love with Mary Magdalene (no longer so strange an idea after *The Da Vinci Code*—book and film) and wanted to marry her, start a family, and live a peaceful existence rather than undergo the torture of crucifixion for the salvation of mankind. Scorsese's film is loyal to the original novel, showing Christ receiving a last visit from the Devil in the form of a young girl, while on the cross, the temptation is finally rejected by Jesus, who cries, "it is finished!" and dies. With scenes of violence and sex, it was deemed repulsive by many of the faithful, although the film also had its loyal followers—not necessarily all non-Christian.

The Passion of the Christ (2004); Director: Mel Gibson

Produced as well as directed by Mel Gibson, *The Passion of the Christ* is not strictly an epic (Gibson himself called it a "small movie"), but its theme is embraced by epic elements—such as a wide communal response—common to epics of the previous eras on the same subject. This latest biography of Christ also generated some controversy when it first appeared, with segments of viewers considering it anti-Semitic. It concentrates on the last forty-eight hours of Christ's life, with flashbacks of his teaching, and centers on the scene at Gethsemane; the arrest and torture of Christ, in very graphic terms; and the crucifixion. In contrast to Scorsese's movie, *The Passion* was recommended to the faithful by both the Catholic and the Greek Orthodox churches, and had spectacular returns at the box office when it first opened. Now fading from memory, the film is a significant piece in a string of movies on the life of the West's greatest religious leader.

Notes

1. "Special Features" in *The Ten Commandments*, DVD Disc two (Paramount Pictures, 2006).

2. Otto Rank, *The Myth of the Birth of the Hero* (New York: Random House, 1959), 65.

3. Steven C. Earley, *An Introduction to American Movies* (New York: New American Library, 1978), 147.

4. Susan Sackett, *Box Office Hits* (New York: Billboard Books, 1990), 92.

5. Nominations: Best Picture, Best Actor (Richard Burton), Best Cinematography. Wins: Best Art Direction/Set Decoration, Best Costume Design.

6. Unfortunately, it has become Dolby Digital 4.0 in the current four-disc DVD edition (Warner Brothers, 2005), which does not render full stereophonic sound.

CHAPTER FOUR

The Historical Epic

The historical epic is consistent with the general aims of the epic, consciously or unconsciously expressed, of portraying a great leader with the archetypal qualities found in all epics—in this case a historical figure. Within the heroic context, the historical epic can also portray a conflict, such as a war, a natural disaster, or any other significant event in history cast against a large canvas. The realities of making a historical epic, however, are different from those faced in making other epics, for here filmmakers are faced with the responsibility of representing the facts of history—a difficult task under the best of circumstances. Thus, in dealing with the historical epic, filmmakers encounter many problems, two of which can be easily singled out: First, historical fact itself has laid a heavy obligation on any filmmaker who aspires to reproduce history to do so as accurately as possible in the relatively short span of a film—even an epic film, which is normally longer than average. This is especially true of biographical epics of well-known historical figures whose lives have often been minutely recorded and documented, such as Lincoln, Napoleon, John F. Kennedy, Malcolm X, Gandhi, Queen Elizabeth I, Queen Elizabeth II, and many others, male and female, whose biographies often become film subjects. Historical accuracy is also of premium value for historical epochs and related events, war easily being one of them; also stories of migrations, natural disasters, or social conflicts, including racial struggles and political events, are all topics that epic film has often drawn upon for its material. Exploration and space travel are also historical events presented in epics. In all cases, factual correctness is considered a prime factor, especially if the historical epic in question claims historical accuracy. Liberties are taken, of course—"poetic license," as such freedoms are often called—usually justified as necessities of dramaturgy. But important events in history, such as the story of the Holocaust, cannot be tampered with. Commenting on this point, Steven Spielberg finds David Lean's *Lawrence of Arabia* an epic admirable for its aesthetics but shaky on historical grounds, for both Lean and his screenwriter, Robert Bolt, took liberties with the original source, T. E. Lawrence's *The Seven Pillars of Wisdom*, that would not be admissible today.[1] The filmmaker must undertake extraordinary efforts, make delicate decisions, and even resort to the use of disclaimers if some concerned parties of his audience might take exception to what he claims is true.[2] This point has not been entirely and satisfactorily resolved, and the historical epic film, despite the scrupulous efforts of many filmmakers, remains of questionable value as a history source in many quarters, though valuable in some others.[3]

The second problem, much related to the first but not quite the same, arises from exaggerations implicit in attempting to reproduce for the screen the life of an eminent historical figure, especially one that has already achieved mythical or legendary status. When great figures of the past are featured in film, fact has a tendency to become myth while myth is often confused with fact. Of course, exaggeration is frequently seen as anything but a flaw in poetic compositions, and poets (in this case filmmakers) are notorious not only for making up facts, or distorting them, but also for investing their heroes and heroines with flattering traits, both physical and character related. Film cannot take sole responsibility for such distortions, for poets have used them to their advantage for centuries. Ancient poets, generally, took tremendous license with the portrayal of their heroes and heroines, relying on hearsay for their source, and decidedly adding freely to the fictional dimensions of their characters. Such figures as Gilgamesh, Agamemnon, Achilles, Odysseus, Helen, Oedipus, and many others in antiquity and later, were anything but historical figures as given by the poets, and, in fact, many poets gave entirely different interpretations of their personas, actions, and historical contexts. Orestes and Electra (often seen in film), for instance, are entirely dissimilar figures in the hands of Sophocles, Aeschylus, and Euripides. Modern playwrights, such as Sartre and Camus, have revisited these figures and others from antiquity (Orestes and Caligula being two), and recast them as modern heroes with existential traits. Epic film and historical film in general have, for understandable reasons, notoriously adhered to this formula, adding the glamour of a star to that of the historical figure represented. Hollywood, especially, exploited both stars and the myths of historical figures with abandon, mostly for commercial reasons, and often all pretensions to truth were cast aside, and historical figures were thrown into the mix of fantasy and truth (or half-truth) for the sake of box-office returns. Examples abound: How many Napoleons have been brought to the screen; how many Elizabeths, Cleopatras; not to mention biblical figures such as Moses, David, and Paul, or the bewildering interpretations and striking differences in approach when casting Jesus? To its credit, epic film has often taken pains to represent some historical figures, heroes or villains, with considerable documentary evidence; examples include *Gandhi*, *Patton*, *Schindler's List*, and recently, *Ike: Countdown to D-Day* (May 31, 2004), a TV epic miniseries.

Accurate historical representation has become easier in modern times, because the plethora of information in today's world—war archives, films, videos, personal recollections, diaries, biographies, and other forms—enables filmmakers to make sounder and safer choices in gathering facts to represent historical figures on the screen. Dramatization has its requirements—trimming, cutting, and simplifying, for instance—but an elliptical representation is not necessarily an inaccurate one. Aside from problems of accuracy, the historical epic film has been a subgenre of its own, distinct in its traits and aims, especially when limitations of the historical approach are recognized and pointed out.[4]

The main characteristics of historical epics are as follows: Historical epics are based on a historical era; a historical episode, such as a war or part of a war (always a popular topic); or on other events (or people) of significant historical compass, such as an exploration, a scientific discovery, a great cultural or popular event, such as the Olympic games,[5] and even space exploration (*Apollo 13*). Historical epics are set in periods which are considered historical (as opposed to prehistory or fantasy), more or less reproducing, or attempting to reproduce the historical period accurately. Very few historical epics have been documentaries, although this particular genre is possible.[6] Most directors who attempt historical epics will make claims that their films strive to reproduce historical reality, though admitting that fictional elements will be inevitable. Their attempts are based on history books, archives, letters, biographies, or archaeological sites, and their scenes are most often not filmed on the locations where events actually took place. A recent example is *Troy* (discussed in chapter 1), the shooting of which started in Malta, but production crews were moved to Mexico because preparations for the Iraq War (2003), then getting under way, might have interfered with filming. Historical film sets are built to reproduce scenes of historical reality; costumes are frequently modeled after existing historical designs of that era; and manners and even speech patterns, when these are relevant, are reproduced with accuracy insofar as it is possible. Historical epics often take full advantage of new technologies, such as color, surround or digital sound, and wide screens, which allow for a more inclusive mise-en-scéne and more realism in reproducing the various events described. Today, digital technology enhances the special effects needed to reproduce battles and landscapes with minimal cost, for computer images simulating reality can be multiplied ad infinitum. Not everybody is happy about this "falsification" by using virtual-reality techniques, but producers can save a lot of money. As mentioned above, historical epics, whether modern or of past eras, do not have to be entirely and painstakingly accurate. If the historical basis on which they rest is sound, the actions (or dialogue) of characters in it may be fictionalized, with the proper disclaimers. "Based on," or, in a broader sense, "inspired by,"[7] gives the audience a chance to enjoy a particular action knowing that the characters projected on the screen are myths in their details and "truths" in a deeper sense, echoing tribal wish fulfillments, as all epics must do. Flagrant untruths, however, will offend audiences able to judge and to make distinctions between fact and fiction.

Because of its potential for grand spectacle and ability to tap into the collective psyche, the historical epic is one of the most popular forms that film has produced. Many of the greatest epic films are historical, or war related, since history itself is one of the richest sources for narrative film, and filmmakers have taken full advantage of the access to free material. Well-made historical epics have been sure bets at the box office either because of their sheer entertainment value or the interest they manage to kindle in a certain historical period or person. Of course, not all representations of historical figures have been successful box office endeavors, as the two film versions of the life of Alexander the Great (1956, 2004) have shown.[8] But in most cases, the popularity of the historical epic seems assured, though artistic value may be questionable, depending on the era described, the intentions of the filmmaker, and the actual reproduction and authenticity achieved of an event. Authenticity, of course, does not guarantee box-office success or cinematic perfection. One still has to make a distinction between history described on the screen (as, for instance, in a documentary) and the formal qualities that narrative film as an art form requires. Still, narrative film can be at the service of history when fidelity and aesthetics coincide. In describing a historical event, the film epic may help clarify issues that have remained current or controversial (the Vietnam War, for instance), or prolong and revive interest in a historical or social occurrence whose historical perception may need reexamination. On the whole, historical epics have exerted a great deal of influence on audiences, either as entertainment tools or for their educational value, where such exists, and some have become excellent means of discussion and discourse in and out of the classroom.

It can be said that war epics have dominated the historical epic genre more than any other kind of epic film, for they provide scenes of action, so beloved by contemporary and historical audiences. The history of World War II, told numerous times in the last half of the twentieth century, continues to be popular in the beginning of the twenty-first century. As technology progressed through the decades, war movies became more realistic (especially in the description of actual war conditions), more historically accurate, and more thematically complex than the earlier war movies, some of which were mass-produced by Hollywood to boost morale both on the front line and on the home front. In later decades, beginning in the late 1960s and early 1970s, just as antiwar sentiment grew and the country became embroiled in the controversial and unpopular Vietnam War, authenticity became a more significant factor in historical filmmaking, either because audiences tired of eulogies or because data became more easily accessible. War heroes also underwent a change of perception in the depiction of their personas, and a controversial figure like George Patton, for instance, drew more attention from filmgoers, tired of the endless parade of straight patriots, like Dwight Eisenhower, who, up to that point, had never been the main hero in a war movie, except in minor roles and in documentaries. The movie biography of George Patton, on the other hand offers a general who is brilliant in battle but is an egotistical exhibitionist, insecure about his image. Above all, at least as he is interpreted by George C. Scott, he appears custom-made for audience entertainment, a hero who is self-destructive, a megalomaniac, and almost a villain. *Patton* (1970), directed by Franklin J. Schaffner and produced by Frank McCarthy, was based on authentic materials and biographies of the general, *Patton: Ordeal and Triumph* by Ladislas Farago in particular. Written by Francis Ford Coppola and Edmund H. North, this epic film features George C. Scott as General Patton and Karl Malden as General Omar Bradley. It was filmed in Spain and was probably the best war movie made during the late 1960s and early 1970s, an era that had already seen scores of good movies about the Second World War.

If one looks at historical/war movies in their totality, one will find that many other interests add or interfere—depending on how one looks at this—with purely historical film narrative, as, for example, the romantic element (as in *Pearl Harbor*, 2001), added to add interest in movies that otherwise might look too monotonous to patrons watching uninterrupted exchanges of gunfire and explosions, no matter who their heroes are or what they are fighting for. For any movie, the dramatic interest is of paramount importance and, for better or worse, producers and directors choose to enliven their narratives with love stories to counteract psychological tension, or for other reasons, such as entertainment value by featuring glamorous Hollywood stars, like Brad Pitt as Achilles in *Troy* and Angelina Jolie as Olympias in *Alexander the Great*.

Epics with Historical Themes

The Battle of Algiers (*La Battaglia di Algeri*, 1966); Director/Coauthor: Gillo Pontecorvo

Historical epics are not just recordings of memorable past events, or a means to glorify historical figures. They are also vehicles for expressing awareness of our own historical condition, a means of drawing parallels and discovering analogies that will help us not only to relate to but also to profit from the past. Many historians have pointed out that history is cyclic, that human events of note, especially catastrophes such as war, have a way of repeating themselves, pointing, sometimes with uncanny accuracy, at the causes of present trouble.

One example is the film *The Battle of Algiers*, made in 1966, more than forty years ago. It tells the poignant story of a rebellion and the methods used to crush it that bear a troubling resemblance to terrorism in our own day. Not that everything fits exactly; but analogy, usually an imperfect measure of accuracy, can help the viewer draw conclusions after a careful assessment of similarities and differences. Perhaps because of the obvious similarity to the present day, *The Battle of Algiers* was rereleased theatrically in 2004, and Criterion Collection followed suit with a three-disc restored edition of the black-and-white film, with plenty of extras, including comments by various critics and contemporary directors, all of whom attest to the film's relevance in today's world.[9]

That, in capsulated form, is the gist of the idea in calling such attention to a film noted for its tight plot, remarkable performances, and thrilling action. As soon as the early scenes unfold, a viewer today (2007) becomes aware of the fact that history is replaying itself. This film was bypassed by American audiences when it was first released in the 1960s (it was banned in France until 1971) because America was not directly involved in the conflict it describes. Today, America is preoccupied with its own problems resulting from terrorist threats, and not much thought is given to Algeria's struggle for independence in the 1950s. Ironically, the film is quite relevant today because it describes a historical period when terrorism was an important issue in France and certain historical parallels between that era and today may be drawn. The film's storyline illustrates these points amply. A resistance group, the National Liberation Front (FLN, short for Front de Libération Nationale) is organizing against the French occupation in Algiers, beginning about 1954 and continuing until 1957, when the main events occur, as the rebellion is crushed by a detachment of French paratroopers, led by Colonel Mathieu. That brought a period of uneasy calm, but in 1960, a popular uprising forced France to take another look at its colony, and two years later, in 1962, Algeria was recognized as an independent nation by the UN. The film concentrates on the crucial years between 1954 and 1957, describing the genesis of the resistance movement, the persons involved, the mechanism of its organization, and the methods used by the French contingent sent to defeat it. Saying again that this film is a reflection of the events of today is almost an understatement, for once more, and for the last several years, we in the United States have faced the threat and destructiveness of terrorism, and this film reminds us of what is still happening in several countries (aside from the events of 9/11)—Israel, Lebanon, Iraq, and other vulnerable hot spots around the world. The sides are reversed, for we, as residents of the United States, victims of terrorism, look at it as an evil that must be guarded against and resisted. The psychology, methods, and motives of the rebels in the movie seem to have an uncanny resemblance to those used today by terrorits. The forty years since this movie was made is enough time to allow the events to be viewed with some objectivity. Hopefully, some conclusions can be drawn about why humans are pitted against humans with such hatred, dedication, and determination to die for their cause. History tells us that these things have happened before. People have fought for freedom—all people, none excluded, whether "good" or "bad"—at some point in their history, and they have done so, giving up their lives and taking the lives of their enemies, often without remorse.

One irony (one of many) here is that when we are oppressed, we regard the enemy as brutal and savage, casting him in the most hideous terms possible; but when we are forced to protect ourselves and our interests, we become the aggressors and use methods as ruthless as our enemy might have used on us. The film does not say that there are only bad guys and good guys; it says that "bad" and "good" become relative terms, depending on whose side you are on, for what reasons, and at what time in your history. The French canonized Joan of Arc, who liberated their country, but the British burned her at the stake. That statement does not say everything about the pervasive ironies of this movie, but it says enough. The French fought fascism underground, creating networks of freedom fighters who were considerable help to the Allies once they arrived. After their country was liberated, within a decade, the French applied the same methods to the Algerians that the Nazis (and their collaborators) had applied to them. To their credit, the French

(*The Battle of Algiers* is an Italian/French production) showed in the film, in the most dramatic fashion, what they had done to the Algerian resistance. The producers thus revealed crimes committed against the resistance movement and against innocents caught in the crossfire.

The movie begins at the end of the conflict, in 1957, after the French interrogators have tortured an elderly man and forced him to give them the hideout of the four remaining members of the FLN, among them a woman and a boy of fourteen. When the French find them hiding behind a wall, they ask them to come out peacefully, to save their own lives and to assure themselves of a fair trial. The film then flashes back to 1954, and Ali La Pointe, one of those hiding behind the wall, is seen enlisting with the FLN. La Pointe is an ex-boxer and illiterate, with several arrests in his record. He is thrown in jail once more after he punches a French youth, breaking his jaw. Upon his release from jail five months later, La Pointe is approached by a boy who gives him a note, saying he is to meet a woman, who will give him instructions how to join the FLN. The woman, dressed in white and with a head cover, gives him a pistol and instructs him to shoot a policeman who is receiving information about the resistance from a bar owner. He follows the policeman and tries to shoot him, but the gun isn't loaded. La Pointe runs after the woman, and she takes him to the head of the organization, a man called Jaffar, who tells him that he was being tested, for informants infiltrate the organization, and one of them would never shoot a French policeman. From this point on, La Pointe becomes a key member, organizing the network and recruiting new members.

Following various acts of terror, the French retaliate by blowing up part of the native quarters, after which the FLN embarks on new acts of terror reminiscent of the ones that have happened in the Middle East. Three women don Western apparel, and passing for French, or modernized Algerians, carry bombs to three crowded places, a bar, a disco full of dancers, and a fish market, and set the bombs to go off within a half hour. Unbelievable carnage follows when the bombs explode and moments of chaos and panic prevail. The French send an elite corps of paratroopers to Algiers, headed by Colonel Mathieu, a tough, swaggering, and confident officer, who understands that the only way to dismantle the organization is through informers and so he undertakes a methodical search of the city of Casbah, having no compunctions about using torture as a means of getting information. When asked at a press conference about his method, he calls it "interrogation," and then proceeds to brief his subordinates telling them that the FLN is like a "tapeworm," which you can cut to pieces but it will regenerate if you do not crush the head. So he goes after the leadership of the organization, and gradually, using torture, he gets them, one by one. Methodically, he surrounds the places where he knows they hide and asks them to surrender; and some prefer to blow themselves up, including Jaffar. The remaining resistance fighters include La Pointe, Halima, another friend, and the boy who has been active carrying messages. When the four are ordered to come out from behind the wall, they prefer to stay and be blown to pieces. In the film it is now 1957, the FLN is dismantled, its members caught or killed, and the revolution seems at an end. But the film does not end there. An epilogue shows that two years later, in 1959, what seemed like a spontaneous demonstration in Algiers erupted into a violent riot, which caused the question of the liberation of Algiers to be brought before the United Nations, and finally the independent nation of Algeria was established at that time.

The action of these horrendous events moves along at a brisk pace in the film, while a directorial steady hand maintains its objective point of view, letting the viewer decide for himself how to judge the unfolding action. No attempt is made to mollify the sadistic cruelty of the interrogations, and no sympathy is elicited for the steely resolution of the rebels who explode bombs killing innocent people. The picture the film paints of slaughter and mayhem in the streets and buildings of Casbah is neither flattering nor condemning the persons involved—it just gives the facts as they occurred. The women who carry the bombs into crowded bars and fish markets cut their hair short (which is against their religion) and use makeup, transforming themselves to look like liberated Algerian women, and they do not show the slightest hesitation or remorse in carrying out their horrible missions. The war between the two factions is relentless, cruel, inhuman, almost unbearable to watch, but told lucidly and, as far as can be judged, accurately. The works of some contemporary filmmakers (such as new wave—*nouvelle vague*—French auteurs) look like child's play compared to this somber, unsparing movie which, though relatively unappreciated by its audiences then,[10] shows man's inhumanity to man on both sides.

Though the film obscures guilt and innocence, its making suggests the guilt of the French, and the filmmakers are aware and mindful of the fact that France fought for justice and liberation during the Second World War and is and has been a country that champions liberation causes, although a colonial power in the past. The sadistic French colonel, for instance, is the most repulsive figure in the movie, while the FLN members are the heroes, and La Pointe, despite his criminal record and seething hatred of the French, is given a sympathetic treatment. What one is to make of this story is that great powers, even the most generous and humane, even those that set the example for fighting for freedom, will not relinquish the same right to others. We ourselves deserve freedom, fought to gain it, and supported others who sought it, but when it comes to our own interests, we do not want to grant it as generously as we should. Algiers deprived France of the title of superpower after the Second World War. It broke away, and it had the right to do that. This movie acknowledges this right, but it is gutsy enough and big enough to also state at what price it achieved glory—or liberty. It is a human tragedy, described on an epic scale, but a movie as honest as they come.

Tora! Tora! Tora! (1971); Directors: Richard Fleischer, Kinji Fukasaku, Toshio Masuda

A joint Japanese and American production, *Tora! Tora! Tora!* is an accurate historical filming of the Japanese attack on Pearl Harbor on December 7, 1941, an incident that plunged America into the Second World War and a subject of much interest in the latter part of the twentieth century. The Japanese sections of this film were shot in Japan, with Japanese directors, while the American counterparts were filmed in Hollywood at Twentieth Century Fox Studios and in Hawaii. The historical events narrated in the film were based on minute research that involved examination of war records and the reproduction of exact replicas of aircraft and warships used during the attack. The characters, conversations between them, and communications were also based on existing records and 100 percent accuracy was sought in all aspects of this movie project. To their credit, the producers of both Japanese and American sides succeeded in putting together a cinematic artifact that could legitimately be called an actual historical document.

 Tora! Tora! Tora! can be described as a docudrama, that is, a film that takes the pains necessary to replicate a historical incident as accurately as possible in dramatic terms. Despite its affinity to a documentary, a docudrama is a narrative film, with a director, producers, and actors to play the various parts, using all the techniques and methods of filmmaking— montage, editing, art design, sets, lighting, and so forth. A documentary is a nonfictional form,[11] usually put together in chronological sequence through already existing archival footage (although filming new scenes is possible), while a docudrama maintains artistic freedom by being selective of materials used, employing actors to represent real persons, and, as in any other regular film production, attempts to establish narrative tension and point of view. In some ways, a docudrama is a regular drama/adventure film, only having the distinction of being largely true. As for the factual accuracy of *Tora! Tora! Tora!*, there is no reason to doubt the assertions of film historian Stewart Galbraith and director Richard Fleischer,[12] both of whom provide ample evidence of the willingness of the Japanese and American producers to put on film an objective storyline that documents as closely as possible what happened in those fateful days preceding the attack at Pearl Harbor and during the attack itself. Documentation of the preparations for the attack and of the deliberations between high-ranking officials on both sides is impressive. Since all Japanese warships were sunk during the war, exact miniature replicas of the huge warships were constructed; and, on the American side, a partial replica of the *Arizona*, which was destroyed and sunk in the attack, was made at Pearl Harbor. Again, since most warplanes of the time, especially the Japanese Zeroes, no longer existed, some American training aircraft were remodeled and used, with the full cooperation of the American air force and navy. The film can boast almost complete accuracy, and it is possible to use it—and it has been used—as a historical document in educational environments.

It is in the creation of narrative tension and point of view, however, that *Tora! Tora! Tora!* owes its continuing appeal, not only as a war document, but as a human story that brings home a message about the causes of war and its consequences. Without attempting ambiguity of theme or character equivocation, *Tora! Tora! Tora!* manages to blend the two strands, the American and Japanese, of the same war incident admirably, avoiding jingoistic statements at the expense of the other side, offering balancing points of view from the "winners" and the "losers," and leaving any lesson that could be learned from these experiences to the discretion of the viewer. Still, the two points of view remain distinct and identifiable from each other, told in contrasting colors and narrative styles. For the Japanese, this is a story of triumph, the moment in their national consciousness during which they felt great pride for attempting to bring down a giant, with whom they vied for dominance in the Pacific. For the Americans, this is a moment of bitter defeat, humiliation, hurt pride, self-reflection, and renewed determination. Two proud nations collided, one delivering a blow, while the other took it, was floored momentarily, only to regroup and go on to eventual victory. It is also a story of two culturally different sides, the Japanese, used to absolute discipline and obedience, owing its victory to the strength of its mind and heart as well as the skill of its pilots. On the American side, it is a story of folly, ignorance of both the enemy and the warning signs of danger, of miscalculation, laxness, even hubris. The film is scrupulously honest and it does not spare the blundering high-ranking officials, both in Hawaii and in Washington, nor the petty assurance of the low-ranking echelons (with the honorable exception of one or two) who either neglected to report or trivialized information—information that if transmitted to the proper channels could have saved the fleet and thousands of lives.

From the point of view of sheer narrative, the movie builds momentum re-
lentlessly for nearly an hour and a half, starting with the Japanese plan to attack Pearl Harbor, showing strategic deliberation on the one side and frantic
attempts to comprehend what is coming on the other, culminating with the
attack itself. The Japanese, as the Americans imagined, could not have mus-
tered enough naval and air forces to extend an attack as far as the Hawaiian
Islands and were thought to be planning attacks on nearby targets like
Malaysia or the Philippines. The plan to attack the fleet at Pearl Harbor was
placed in motion by Admiral Yamamoto, who saw that the only chance
Japan had to defeat the United States would be to deliver a telling blow that
would wipe out its fleet (some ships had been diverted to the Atlantic for the
war in Europe), thus maintaining naval superiority in the Pacific for a year or
so. After that, Yamamoto, who had spent time in America and had studied
at Harvard, predicted that eventual victory would sway to the side of the
Americans. But he saw no other alternative but to attack; if not, Japan would
be permanently delegated to the status of a secondary power in the Pacific.
It was a dangerous gamble, and as a man of vision, he knew what a counterattack would mean and accepted it with stoic resignation. Some junior officers in his staff, and especially some of the firebrand pilot aces, were assured
of final victory, especially after the bombing at Pearl destroyed the bulk of
the fleet, America's pride.

As it progresses through the events showing the preparation for the attack, the film manages its double point of view admirably, though not without difficulties in editing and blending the two styles as far as possible, cutting back and forth between the war rooms in Washington and the Japanese
headquarters, and to the fighting force afloat and already moving toward its
target by the end of November and early December. Tension is built as events
progress from the preparatory stages of the attack to the launching of the flying squadrons from the six Japanese air carriers on Sunday, December 7,
while intercutting in Washington shows the Japanese ambassador getting
ready to deliver an ultimatum and being delayed because of a slow typist. The
chief of staff, General Marshall, sends a message to Admiral Kimmel that an
attack on Pearl Harbor is imminent, but the message, sent though civilian
channels, arrives too late, after the Japanese planes have attacked and flown
away. Other warnings either failed to reach their destinations or were ignored, and when the attack came, it was a total surprise and a great shock to
both the troops and the generals. Three battleships—the *Arizona*, the *Oklahoma*, and the *Utah*—were totally destroyed and sank, and nearly every other
vessel there was heavily damaged. More than two hundred planes in a nearby
air base were destroyed, the fighter planes never having a chance to take off

and protect the fleet. Over three thousand men were killed and thousands were injured. The *Arizona* turned on its belly, after a dive bomb pierced its armor and hit its powder compartments, and an explosion killed hundreds of men instantly. The disaster was of staggering proportions, and President Roosevelt, in a speech to a joint session of Congress on December 8, called the attack "a day that will live in infamy." The film, however, keeps an objective eye on these events, dividing its attention between the participating sides and making no attempt at jingoistic sloganeering so common in the films of that kind made during and in the immediate aftermath of the war. It shows the Japanese assured, methodical, confident, even cocky, devising a plan of attack that worked to perfection, only raising doubts about the judgment of some of its leaders, who wanted a second attack—or the attack to continue—on the carriers that were not destroyed at Pearl. But the Japanese did not have any doubts about their triumph.

Coming on the thirtieth anniversary of the making of the film (or its release), the DVD edition coincided with another attack on America, which cost as many lives, and which has called for national introspection about safety, national security, and the need for vigilance. *Tora! Tora! Tora!* is a film that speaks to today's audiences with as clear a voice as it did when it was released, and it is as relevant today as it was then, aside from its pure historical value. History in film and film in history are not mutually exclusive terms. When filmmakers are both astute artists who know their craft and honorable historians bent on accurately telling a true event at the same time, film achieves its own distinction and has a place in school and public libraries.

The Kingdom of Heaven (2004); Director: Ridley Scott

The Kingdom of Heaven is presented as a revisionist version of the Crusades, which started at the end of the eleventh century (around 1095) under the authority of Pope Urban II, whose ostensible purpose was to recover the holy sepulcher from the Muslims, who were then expanding to the West. There were eight Crusades in all, but the most important were the first three, when Jerusalem was taken; when the Kingdom of Jerusalem, which included the principality of Antioch and the countships of Edessa and Tripoli, was established; and when the Kingdom of Jerusalem was lost back to the Muslims.

The film concentrates on the Second Crusade, which started in 1147, and ended in 1186, with the retaking of Jerusalem by the Muslim leader Saladin. It is only the last two years of this period with which the film occupies itself. All the major characters in the film are based on historical figures, with the exception of Balian, a young French blacksmith who feels the urge to travel to the Holy Land when his father, a knight, Godfrey of Ibelin, returns from the war to teach his son how to fight. Godfrey dies before reaching Jerusalem from wounds received during the trip, and Balian finds himself involved in the turmoil then prevailing in the kingdom. There are two camps vying for supremacy. The legitimate one is that of King Baldwin IV, who is supported by the barons of the kingdom led by Raymond, count of Tiberias. Baldwin is dying of leprosy, and his legitimate heir is his sister's son, Baldwin V, who is still a child. The king's sister, Sibylla, is married to an arrogant and weak figure, Guy de Lusignan, whose cohorts are a group of reckless local lords led by two extremely ambitious men, Reynald of Karak and Gerard of Rideford. When the king dies, these two stage the coronation of Guy de Lusignan, who, spurred by the others, undertakes an ill-advised campaign against Saladin, after they ambush a caravan of peaceful Muslims and kill Saladin's sister. Balian has in the meantime established a friendship with Tiberias and has also drawn the attention of Sibylla, whose lover he eventually becomes. Both he and Tiberias object to the expedition against Saladin, and Balian warns that it would not be wise to take the army, and all the knights with them, on a journey across the desert without water. Indeed, Lusignan's army, exhausted from heat and thirst, becomes easy prey to the forces of Saladin, who destroys it and takes its leaders captive. Reynald is slaughtered, but Lusignan is kept as a hostage. Meanwhile, Balian senses that Saladin will attack Jerusalem, now without defenders, for Tiberias, seeing defeat as certain, flees to the sea. Balian rounds up the male population, gives them a rousing speech, and "confers" knighthood upon them. His strategy proves brilliant, for when Saladin attacks with all his war machines and even manages to bore a hole in the wall, he is repulsed and forced to ask for terms. Balian agrees to surrender the city, and Saladin assures him that the city's entire population will be escorted to the sea. A massive exodus of the Christian population streaming out of Jerusalem is shown, and that, to Balian, is the "Kingdom of Heaven" established on earth—with a peace pact. Balian and Sibylla are now free to enjoy each other's love and their new life.

The Kingdom of Heaven is not a particularly religious movie, as older epics, Ben-Hur, for instance, were. It is a movie bent on showing parallels between older cultures and their wars, and their similarities with clashes today. The Crusades were launched ostensibly in order to recover the Holy Land, and there was undeniable truth in that, but in the process the West acquired many Eastern products—spices, sugar, silk, dyes for clothes, and, a bit later, gunpowder—all introduced to the West following the Crusades. It is hard to see how any of the persons named in this film were saved spiritually, defining the term as Christians would, except of course for Balian, who steadfastly remains humanistic in the broadest sense, for it is he who represents knighthood in its ideal form molded in the Middle Ages as its philosophers and poets—Dante, Ariosto, for example—conceived it.

Balian is only a blacksmith, but also the son of a knight, and, right from the start, he displays his concern for the downtrodden, a primary Christian virtue; in addition, he exhibits bravery in battle, war savvy, and a strategic mind. He also exhibits the archetypal qualities of the hero as a leader of his people. He is not subject to corruption, as some other conquerors are, and abstains from making love to Sibylla until her husband is captured and dead, and she is a mourning widow and sister, sincerely repentant. Balian's search is spiritual, but his mission changes as circumstances he encounters evolve. He fights with fury when he has to, but his larger purpose is to save the people of Jerusalem rather than to defeat Saladin. In essence, he is an embattled Christ figure. Many viewers (and reviewers) attributed the relatively lukewarm reception of this film to Orlando Bloom's performance as Balian, claiming that he does not possess the charisma and screen presence of Russell Crowe in Scott's previous grand epic, *Gladiator*. This comparison is unfair, and, if one places the two actors in the context of the films they were in, Bloom actually gains the advantage. Crowe was more muscular, more physical, more vindictive, and, when trained as a fighting machine in the Roman arena, as much of a killer as anybody else. He had no particularly distinguishing spiritual qualities or goals—aside from revenge. Bloom's Balian, on the other hand, gains on that point. He is a man in search of a soul and, in terms of cultural progression from antiquity to more modern times, a man with the distinct spiritual qualities of the Middle Ages. He has heard of compassion, meekness (he possesses a certain self-effacement, in contrast to the brassiness of a sword hero), and the obligation of a knight to help the helpless. This is all reflected in his face, which projects his inner world, emblematic of the transfiguration of a humble blacksmith into a warrior who is incorruptible and untainted by the flatulent, arrogant, ignorant, and brutal predecessors who were supposed to be doing what he actually comes to achieve.

The film also shows the tragically masked leper king, wise in mellow-toned voice, like a figure from Homeric Hades, foreseeing the decaying and betrayal of his kingdom by those who had usurped power in his name. And Jeremy Irons as Tiberias is excellent, a man who can read the decrees of fate, but is too weak to stand up to the pretenders, and, knowing the kingdom will collapse, at least as he perceives it, flees to safety, refusing to stand up and fight. Finally, Saladin, played with distinction by Ghassan Massoud, is a man above internal conflict, menacing and terrible in his revenge but serenely pragmatic and honorable, yielding to necessity and allowing the determined

Christian population to flee to safety rather than sacrifice his own army in a futile fight. Saladin represents the Eastern cultures, which in the bygone era of Hollywood movies were represented as the "evil" side the West had to conquer and drive away.

Director Ridley Scott is known for his attempts to treat serious socio-political and religious matters (and other subjects) in subtext fashion. Whether one accepts points of view that may tamper with history is another question, but a movie—and an epic one to boot—need not always present absolutely accurate historical truth in order to be effective. The movie/epic can be seen as a trope for contemporaneity. And as such, it will remain controversial, for this is a statement of opinion, tackling political and religious views that continue to afflict and torment the relations between East and West. The version of the Crusades given in *The Kingdom of Heaven* is presented as a metaphor for this conflict. There are so many interested parties among viewers, aside from historians, that it will be impossible to satisfy every one of them, let alone convince them to go to a theater to spend two and a half hours[13] to see a spectacular and rather tortured version of these remote events. The film aims, above all, to depict the ugly reality of the war, and in that sense it gives a grim view of all participants, for it was a violent, blood-soaked period of history that produced those events. Swords were prepared that could cut the human body in half with one blow (Godfrey, who is reputed to have done so, teaches his son Balian how to do this). Other weapons, like maces, were prepared to crush a human skull without spilling a drop of blood (which was sin!). Other weapons of mass destruction—like arrows for instance, or axes—were developed to destroy the human body with unbelievable efficiency and one wonders if the automatic weapons of today could do more damage (at least they kill more quickly and efficiently). Seen in that light, the movie must be viewed as a moral statement of the human capacity to deny others' natural human rights, sometimes in excruciatingly brutal ways, which continues today in one way or another, rather than as a discourse as to which side was right, or which culture superior.

Munich (2005); Director/Producer: Steven Spielberg

Munich is Spielberg's second major attempt to deal with a subject that is utterly and painfully serious and based on indisputable historical fact; the first being the Holocaust, in *Schindler's List* (1993). *Munich* is about the terrorist attack on Israeli athletes during the Munich Olympics in 1972. *Munich* deals not so much with the event itself, but with the aftermath, the attempt to assassinate those responsible for the massacre by the Israeli secret agency Mossad (equivalent to the CIA) which precipitated reprisals, authorized personally by Golda Meir herself, prime minister of Israel at that time. A squad of five operatives was dispatched from Israel to Europe, and the terrorists were eliminated, execution style, one by one, though their leader, Salamah, was missed. In the process, several innocent bystanders were killed, and also three of the group became victims of their own mission. The field of operations was Europe, but not in the Soviet block, and not in any of the Arab countries. The unit, assembled by a Mossad high-ranking operative, Ephraim, played by Geoffrey Rush, had to be a group of unknowns, of different backgrounds, looks, and personal traits. Carl is the "cleanup" man, who made sure schedules were kept, explanations to authorities were provided, and that the operation was a clean one, with no "collateral" damage (killing of innocents which was not avoided). Hans is responsible for getting the team across borders, forging passports, etc. Steve,[14] a "gung-ho" type, with an explosive temper and not too mindful of the finer moral points of his mission, is the caretaker driver, responsible for getting the team to the scene of the crime. Robert is the explosives expert; and Avner, played by Eric Bana, is chosen as the leader of the group, for reasons unexplained to him by his boss, Ephraim, who simply tells him he fits the role as well as anybody. Avner plays the leader of the well-knit group as an efficient, but not ruthless, young man who answers the call of duty unhesitatingly and conscientiously, but one who, more than any in his group, suffers from conflict of his conscience, being uncertain that the reprisal premise—the literal "eye for an eye"—is either morally justified or ultimately effective. In the end, he sees it as a chain, a cycle of violence, which will never close the book on a nation's ultimate survival. Adding to his conflict is the fact that he is newly wed to a woman he loves, whom he leaves seven months pregnant, and whom he will probably not see again for several years—for the mission will last for as long as it takes for all the targets to be eliminated.

In his commentary to the movie, Spielberg takes pains to explain[15] that his movie is not meant to be a criticism of Israel or its policies; nor does he wish his viewers to believe that it is a literal rendition of history, but that it was "inspired" by the events at the Munich Olympics and their aftermath. But he establishes that at least three facts are indisputably historical, and that his tale is firmly based on history: First, that several Israeli athletes were kept hostage and then murdered by fedayees, members of an Arab commando group operating against the Israeli occupation of Palestine, is a fact amply documented by news broadcasts (some of which the film includes) and other historical evidence. Second, Spielberg states that Prime Minister Golda Meir made a personal decision to counterattack with reprisals, fully conscious that this act would increase anti-Israeli sentiment;

and third, a team was indeed dispatched from Israel to assassinate those considered responsible for the Munich massacre. Spielberg also takes pains to explain in his commentary that his film is objective, that he did not take sides, and that he enlisted the services of well-known Broadway writers, Tony Kushner and Eric Roth, to ensure treatment of the subject not only with the requisite seriousness but also with the utmost attention to detail and to fact. Kushner explains that what drew him to the project was the premise that the film would not dwell exclusively on the Munich events but on the underground operation that called for assassinations, and on the effect that such an operation would have on the perpetrators themselves. The murky area of committing murder for a righteous cause thus becomes the central issue that the film deals with. Perhaps with the exception of Steve, none of the participants come out of it unscathed—or alive. This central theme remains the main challenge in interpreting this film, and not just its historical accuracy. Historical fact is the broader basis on which human actions, especially those that define the parameters of morality, will be judged.

The main point, of course, is the most challenging, whether it is ethical to seek revenge (the word was used for an earlier and rejected title for the film) once you have been attacked, thus showing strength to your enemies, not weakness or passivity. Thus, Spielberg takes his tale, based on actual incidents, one step beyond, and examines the principle of reprisal, entirely from the human point of view. Here, he faces a task much more difficult than the one he faced in *Schindler's List*. That movie stood on a firmly distinct and plain moral ground: it had villains—Hitler, Goeth, and the Nazis—who committed unspeakable atrocities; and it has victims who suffered what they did not deserve and thus won the total sympathies of the audience. It was a clear-cut case of good versus evil. Reprisal, though, is a different moral configuration. It calls for revenge, once an atrocity has been committed. Reprisal is a morally ambiguous ground; the Germans during the Second World War in occupied countries of Europe are reported to have shot thirty innocent inhabitants for every German soldier killed by the resistance. The purpose of reprisal is to discourage the repetition of an act of hostility against a nation or a group; but if reprisal generates more reprisal (or revenge) from the other side, the cycle is perpetuated, and nothing is resolved. For in most such cases violence, as the film's premise based on that principle assumes, will continue forever. It is a cycle that seemingly will not be broken, at least in the foreseeable future. Reprisal is futile and dangerous, if not in itself an immoral practice. The film *Munich* aims at elucidating that point—but not claiming to resolve its inherent dilemmas.

But the movie also shows an even deeper problem—the toll the practice of reprisal takes on those individuals committed to it, the squad itself and one of its members in particular. Avner, the leader of the squad, an Israeli raised in Germany, who leaves a pregnant wife behind to embark on his mission of finding and eliminating those responsible for the murders of the Israeli athletes at the Munich Olympics. He is a tortured man, though he does commit himself to his mission conscientiously and efficiently. Here a note is needed on the performance of Bana, who plays Avner, the leader of the group. Tall, athletic, handsome, he is on a mission that, in some ways, looks like a James Bond adventure, finding and eliminating villains who threaten humanity. Yet, Bond is never tortured by scruples. He coldly and coolly eliminates an assortment of thugs and no one is the worse for it. Bond is designed essentially as a cartoon hero, efficient, dashing, and unflappable—not to mention his insatiable sexual appetites—and he always gets his victim, often tossing a sarcastic remark on a newly created corpse. The underground Israeli squad—for no one has official knowledge of their existence—operates in the dark, has only a few contacts, often lacks sufficient support in resources, possesses none of the gadgets Q provides Bond with, and leads an assemblage of individuals often at odds with each other, for not all agree on or comprehend to the same degree the extent of the violence they have to commit in the name of their mission. Many innocents die. Avner is distressed by the fact that more people than their actual targets are killed, and he is deeply troubled by the killings themselves. Are not those killings acts of murder? When he asks that question of Ephraim, his official connection, the latter's answer is always the same: Israel must hit back when hit first in order to communicate the message that no attack on its citizens will go unavenged. Avner fully accepts the premise initially, but in the process of carrying out his mission qualms are generated in his mind, not because he doubts the soundness of the principle articulated by those who sit behind desks giving orders, but by the consequences to those killed by those charged to carry out the mission. Killing for any reason is a crime. And this realization grows worse when a mistake is made and innocent persons are killed. Even killing a hired gun—a hit woman's murder after she had killed one of his colleagues—is troubling to him. It is one thing to press a button on a remote device and explode a bomb, another to come face to face with one's victim and coolly dispatch him or her.

To its credit, the film dwells on this murky area of the morality of reprisal as objectively as its creators could make it. In his commentary, Spielberg also makes it clear that he is not taking an anti-Israeli stance. But his film shows, in live action, the conflict that reprisal, even if considered justified, will cause ordinary human beings exposed to its cycle of violence—damaging traumas and inevitable moral dilemmas from which they may never be able to extricate themselves. Avoiding the higher moral ground, Spielberg simply implies that only eventually stopping the cycle of violence, somehow, will solve the problem—a proposition known since Aeschylus, but something for which no cure has yet been found.

Suggested Films for Study

Khartoum (1966); Directors: Basil Dearden, Eliot Elisofon

Khartoum is based on a historical episode, the fall of Khartoum (capital of Sudan) to the Arab leader Mahdi, when William Gladstone was prime minister of the British Empire, in 1883. Khartoum is one of the last grand epics made between 1950 and 1970, when the spectacular films dominated the big screen, offering the typical Hollywood formula of a hero displaying valor in battle (and even in defeat), bravery, and generosity, while demonstrating the cowardice of those who refuse to help the hero in his great undertakings. Well acted by Charlton Heston and Laurence Olivier, playing Mahdi, the leader of the Arab rebels.

Patton (1970); Director: Franklin J. Schaffner

See the brief description provided earlier in this chapter.

Gandhi (1982); Director: Richard Attenborough

Gandhi reaped several Oscars, including Best Picture and Best Actor for Ben Kingsley, playing protagonist Mohandas K. Gandhi, an obscure lawyer who rose to be one of the great world leaders of the twentieth century and the key figure in the liberation of India in 1945 from British rule. Kingsley, an amazing Gandhi look-alike, gives a convincing performance as India's martyred leader but the film veers between historical accuracy and some fictionalized elements, especially in the portraits of some of Gandhi's disciples. Worth studying for its message, dramatic power (lacking somewhat in the second part), and especially for its challenge to the student of history who demands historicity in a modern epic.

Titanic (1997); Director: James Cameron

Titanic combines the intrigue of romance with a momentous historical event of epic proportions, thus broadening its appeal to modern audiences. While the sinking of the world's largest ship was the subject of the movie, it was the romance that actually sparked interest in the story, culminating in the tragic separation between two likeable lovers, Jack and Rose. Even so, it was the staggering special effects that helped modern audiences visualize the magnitude of this catastrophe at sea that cost the lives of nearly twelve hundred people.

Pearl Harbor (2001); Director: Michael Bay

Pearl Harbor once more repeats the story of the destruction of the bulk of the American fleet by a Japanese attack in 1941. Made in an era when special effects technology had risen to a new level, *Pearl Harbor* presents a much more graphic and closely photographed scene of the carnage and destruction produced by the attack than previous movies on the subject, and in that sense it might be called much more realistic and emotionally shattering. But *Pearl Harbor*, sprawling and meandering through its first half with a love triangle whose characters are played by glamorous Hollywood stars (Ben Affleck, Kate Beckinsale, Josh Hartnett), lacks the leanness of action and straightforwardness of *Tora! Tora! Tora!*, thus losing some of the latter's concentrated message and dramatic power.

The Last Samurai (2003); Director: Edward Zwick

The Last Samurai attempts to reproduce a historical era, the latter part of the nineteenth century, when the Japanese Empire was opening its borders to the West, particularly America, which attempted to expand the influence of its newborn industrial might into other countries after Civil War technology had improved its weaponry. America was enjoying a tremendous advantage, and the country could compete with the European powers for dominance in the East. Convulsions inside Japan produced the demotion of the shogun, the prime minister of the emperor, and the assignments of the training of troops to Americans and other Westerners. The class of the samurai, warriors at the service of feudal lords who had ruled Japan for centuries, was to be abolished, by force if necessary, and replaced by modern armies modeled after those of Western powers. Captain Nathan Algren, a fictional character, embarks on a mission with an extremely limited vision of the culture he attempts to invade and Westernize, contemptuous of their awkward efforts to learn and adjust to his Western methods. After his defeat at the hands of a samurai warrior, Algren, a serious and generous man, is capable of learning the ways of the East and reforms. Similarly, a Japanese star, Ken Watanabe, embodies the qualities of the samurai, now eclipsed, but enlarged by poetic—or epic moviemaking—imagination.

Alexander the Great (2004); Director: Oliver Stone

Alexander the Great was undertaken with total seriousness as a historical epic, judging from the remarks of its director, Oliver Stone, when he defended his movie in his DVD commentary.[16] This film's historical background was carefully researched, and scholars in the field—Egyptian, Greek, Baktrian, etc.—were consulted on even the most minor details, and what was presented on the screen was, in the large sense, correct.[17] The film is presented as a "frame story," with Anthony Hopkins, as Ptolemy, Alexander's friend, general, and founder of the Egyptian dynasty, appearing as a voice-over narrator and lecturer to a younger audience about the historical phenomenon that was Alexander. We hear of Alexander's childhood, oedipal relationship with his father and mother, his ambivalent sexual nature (which offended some audiences), his Persian campaign, his entrance into Babylon, his expedition to the East, the conquest of India, his return to Babylon, and his death (which was also shown in the beginning). The device—the frame epic—works up to a point, thanks mostly to Hopkins's performance, but the narrative tension, usually achieved at the outset of a story, is missing, and the epic, though based on fairly accurate historical facts, fails on aesthetic grounds.

Flags of Our Fathers (2006); Director: Clint Eastwood

Based on a book by Ron Powers and James Bradley (the son of an actual combatant), *Flags of Our Fathers* details one of the bloodiest battles of the Second World War in the Pacific, the invasion by American troops of the island of Iwo Jima, during which more than six thousand American troops died. The story is told from the point of view of three survivors, navy corpsman John Bradley, and two marines, Rene Cagnon and Ira Hayes, who raised the American flag on Mount Suribachi, Iwo Jima's highest peak. Avoiding a direct political statement, the movie nevertheless seeks a parallel with our times, pointing at the savagery and futility of war and the exploitation of war heroes by the media.

Notes

1. See "A Conversation with Steven Spielberg," *Lawrence of Arabia*, DVD Disc two (Columbia Pictures, 2002). Spielberg comments in detail about the historicity of this movie, which he calls into question, though he generally admires the epic's aesthetic qualities, the sweep of its action, and its heroic stature.

2. For example, a disclaimer appears on the screen at the beginning of Atom Egoyan's *Ararat* (2002) that states that the Turkish government rejects that the Armenian genocide by the Turks early in the twentieth century is historical fact. Thus, the film presents itself as a fictional event, allowing the knowledgeable viewer to make up his/her own mind whether the events narrated in the movie are true or not.

3. The History Channel often uses films, especially war films, to provide visual impressions of many historical events, but such showings are usually prefaced and analyzed and historical inaccuracies are pointed out. An example is the repeated show-

ings in the spring of 2004 of *Midway* (1972), an epic film that documents a decisive naval battle in the Pacific during World War II.

4. Responsible commentaries by directors and others on DVD editions have precisely that function. For instance, Martin Scorsese's acknowledgment of the historical basis for *Gangs of New York* (2002) in the *Gangs of New York*, DVD Disc two (Miramax, 2003). Included in the DVD's special features is a Discovery Channel special that explains that the film is based on Herbert Asbury's book, *Gangs of New York* (1963).

5. *Chariots of Fire* (1983) is a fictionalized version of the Paris Olympic Games of 1924 and *Munich* (2005) shows the effect of terrorism on the conduct of the Munich Olympic Games in 1972.

6. Leni Riefenstahl's controversial *Triumph of the Will*, detailing the infamous 1934 Nazi Party convention at Nuremberg, is entirely historical, but, strictly from an artistic perspective, it has had few imitators. And of course her *Olympia* (1938), describing the Berlin Olympics in 1936, is a film that many have praised for both its accuracy and artistic cohesion.

7. As in *Troy*, which was "inspired by" Homer's *The Iliad*, as is seen in the credits.

8. A good source for checking on the accuracy of historical films is Mark C. Carnes, ed., *Past Imperfect: History according to the Movies* (New York: Holt, 1995).

9. Disc two, in particular, contains a thirty-seven-minute director's commentary, and similar commentaries by contemporary directors Spike Lee, Mira Nair, Julian Schnabel, Steven Soderbergh, and Oliver Stone. Disc three has an extensive interview with former State Department counterterrorism coordinator Richard A. Clarke.

10. Of course, there was critical recognition of the first order: *The Battle of Algiers* won the Golden Lion at the Venice Film Festival XXVII in 1966; the International Critics Award for 1966; and an award from the city of Venice during the same year.

11. For further distinctions between the terms docudrama and documentary, see Frank E. Beaver, *Dictionary of Film Terms* (New York: McGraw-Hill, 1983), 96–97.

12. See the *Tora! Tora! Tora!* DVD Special Edition (Twentieth Century Fox, 2001), which contains a twenty-minute documentary, "Day of Infamy," as well as a running commentary by director Richard Fleischer and Japanese film historian Stewart Galbraith.

13. The original uncut version of this movie was nearly four hours at 222 minutes.

14. Interestingly, Daniel Craig, who plays Steve, played James Bond in the latest Bond caper, *Casino Royale* (2006), which demanded a rough-hewn character, similar to the character of Steve in *Munich*.

15. Introductory remarks in *Munich* DVD, Disc two, (Universal Pictures, 2006).

16. "Commentary by Oliver Stone," *Alexander the Great*, DVD Disc two (Warner Brothers, 2005).

17. "Go behind the Scenes of Alexander with Sean Stone Via 3 Documentaries: Resurrecting Alexander, Perfect Is the Enemy of Good, The Death of Alexander," *Alexander the Great*, DVD Disc two (Warner Brothers, 2005).

CHAPTER FIVE

The Women-Centered Epic

Though precious few epics featured women as leads during the classic era when epics were made, films with women heroes fitting most of the characteristics of the epic hero do exist. Nearly half of the Hollywood film productions or films made elsewhere in the world depict women in roles as powerful as those of men. Women have been part of the cinematic lore from the outset, and their presence has been not only crucial to film development but also essential to its success. Of known women stars one need only mention a few: Lillian Gish, Bette Davis, Greta Garbo, Vivien Leigh, Joan Crawford, Ingrid Bergman, Barbara Stanwyck, Meryl Streep, Hilary Swank, Kate Winslet, Cate Blanchett, Helen Mirren, Julia Roberts, and Annette Bening. One can cite dozens of others in the contemporary scene. Women as film heroes, whether in epic or drama (or in other formats), have abounded from the start and continue to do so today. In this sense, women actors have been the equals of men, especially in romantic roles, comedy, and melodrama or drama, familiar formats in which women as actors are unsurpassed. But in the epic genre, especially the lengthy and spectacular Hollywood epics of the 1950s and 1960s, the usual role of hero, at least in the majority of cases, was played by a man. The great epics made at the peak of the Hollywood studio era—*The Robe, Ben-Hur, The Ten Commandments, Spartacus, Lawrence of Arabia*—and even many of the later ones, like *Saving Private Ryan* and *Gladiator*—all starred men. Sporadically, a woman's name will be attached to a great epic film such as *Queen Christina, Cleopatra*, and *Elizabeth*, and some of them are distinguished movies. This chapter will examine some of the most significant of such movies, which bear in their general characteristics the epic form, and several categories, defined as archetypal patterns, will be explored here. Some of these epics feature women as the main protagonists; some feature women who share epic roles with men; and some feature women in epic roles within groups, including groups of women. These and other categories, however, are the outgrowth of known archetypal modes placing women in special relations with men, with other women, with various groups, or with the community as a whole. The main point of all of these archetypal patterns is that they all place women in a position of power or in a situation where they strive to achieve status through the various conflicts they encounter in their path to victory.

Often women's stories do not possess all the epic qualities that men's stories do. Strife of some type or other, rather than spectacle and action, is what defines a women-centered epic. She is frequently in a position of subservience in a patriarchal society, and her struggle is to achieve equal status with man, or to engage in social conflicts that entail economic power, personal and tribal freedom, and power over the opposite sex. Women-centered epic action is often perceived as a struggle to achieve economic and social status, political rights, and other benefits of equality with man, so pronounced in the women's liberation movements of the last three or four decades. But women's epic struggles, in whatever category, date from much older times, and in some cases their original struggles are contemporaneous with men's. As usual, film borrows from archetypal patterns offered in myth and literature, expanding on them and creating numerous variations, genres, and subgenres. As with men, the women-centered epic may feature women at war; in historical or religious conflicts; in amorous, dramatic, psychological, or social conflicts; or in other situations where the epic form comes into play. As with men, women in epics can serve as archetypal images that inspire admiration, spark debates on important social issues, serve in the cause of science or other pioneering endeavors (Madame Curie and Helen Keller, for example, whose biographies were made into excellent movies), or they can be leaders of nations during war or other national crises (Cleopatra, Elizabeth I, Catherine the Great, Queen Christina, Queen Victoria—most given in noted epics). They can even become models for their grace and beauty, whether in mythic lore or history, and inspiring artists, such as Aphrodite/Venus, Helen of Troy, Galatea, Queen Guinevere, Camille Claudet, Isadora Duncan, and many others.

Several archetypal patterns emerge in women-centered epics that place the heroine in a position of strength, giving her moral, psychological, intellectual, or at times even physical superiority over her male counterparts. In an epic film, a woman's role must be of epic proportions, that is, it must adhere to those characteristics and follow psychologist Otto Rank's similar adventure patterns: She must be of great birth (an aristocrat or princess of past ages), or must be brought into a set of circumstances or social milieu with great expectations for her; she must undergo momentous growth and initiation rites and must meet challenges proportionate to heroic expectations and actions; she must encounter monsters, in the actual, symbolic, or allegorical sense.[1] In today's world, she must be a woman who has achieved status by accomplishments or distinction in the corporate world or other field, rising in rank by effort, design, or even luck, such as the accident of being born wealthy or unusually talented. She must undergo stress that demands exceptional will power, intelligence, or mental toughness. As a consequence, she must undergo a transformation commensurate with her character and expectations, and through action, decision making, or other significant quality reach maturity, while her life and exemplary accomplishments must bring to bear on conditions that reverberate with or shape communal interests. In the modern sense, a woman can be a great author, scientist, explorer, filmmaker, artist, humanitarian, politician, or must have dedicated herself to a great social cause. She could be a hero at war or in a concentration camp, a rebel in a repressive system, an artist or fighter for a cause, or a woman with exceptional political or social aspirations. She must be a hero in the truest sense, as much as a man is, or even more so. As epic film does not necessarily represent reality but archetypal patterns, she must appear larger-than-life, glamorous or unusually gifted, and inspire audiences through example. Distinguished actresses, in the past or present, must play her, and examples abound.

In most cases, film, and epic film in particular, has inherited its themes, and often its plotlines, from literature (and that includes historical accounts), and thus it allows modern archetypes to share common links, traditions, and even predispositions, where the similarities are relatively easy to point out. One can mention briefly a variety of archetypal patterns regarding men/women relationships, such as the Nausicaa/Lolita archetype in *Lolita* (1956) by Stanley Kubrick, the Pygmalion/Galatea relationship in *Pygmalion* (1938), the beauty and the beast archetype in Cocteau's *Beauty and the Beast* (1946), the Cinderella myth in *The Prince and the Showgirl* (1956) and *Pretty Woman* (1990), and the battle of the sexes in *The Taming of the Shrew* (1963), *Who's Afraid of Virginia Woolf?* (1966), and *The War of the Roses* (1989). While these archetypal patterns are common to most genres and they are not particularly epic in nature, they do exist in films that feature women in leading roles by themselves or sharing the lead with men. An important factor in making these distinctions is whether the name of the woman in question is also the title of the film. Cleopatra, Elizabeth I or II, and Joan of Arc, to give a few examples, are well-known names that leave no doubt as to who has the leading role. But film epics like *Indochine* (1992) and *Out of Africa* (1984) give no initial clue and do not pretend to claim that a woman has the leading part—something that becomes readily obvious to the viewer. Male dominance in film titles is only too obvious to deny—as such names/titles as *Lawrence of Arabia*, *The Terminator*, and *Rocky* will attest—but women have had their share in grand titles, and at least two, *The Queen* and *Elizabeth I* (the latter a TV movie), both with the same actress, were released in 2006. Perhaps this is a sign of the times, but it is also a historical fact that film, and epic film in particular, had women with heroic archetypal qualities since the outset, as the following discussions will demonstrate.

Epics Featuring Women

Cleopatra (1963); Director: Joseph L. Mankiewicz

Though not the first movie to be made about Cleopatra (see the description of Cecil B. DeMille's *Cleopatra* (1934) under "Suggested Films for Study" later in this chapter), *Cleopatra* was nevertheless the first grand epic in the tradition of the 1950s epics with a woman's name as the title, and with an actress who had an enormous reputation for beauty and talent as the lead. However, unlike many epics named after characters, Cleopatra does not play the starring role as a hero on the side of righteousness. She is instead the hero's foil. Perhaps this caveat allowed audiences to accept a woman in such a powerful role. Elizabeth Taylor had been a child actress, who successfully progressed into adult roles and had already played a romantic heroine, Rebecca, in *Ivanhoe* (1952) and won an Oscar for Best Actress for *Butterfield 8* in 1960. Taylor had also lost her husband, Michael Todd, in a plane crash; earned the reputation of home wrecker by dating Debbie Reynolds's husband Eddie Fisher (Fisher left Reynolds and married Taylor), and nearly died of pneumonia in London, where the initial filming of *Cleopatra* had started at the Pinewood Studios. With all this, Taylor was at the peak of her career in the early 1960s, and it seemed appropriate that she would be the top candidate to play one of the most notorious female historical figures—bearing the name of a heroine already immortalized in the works of ancient authors such as Plutarch and Suetonius, in Shakespeare's *Antony and Cleopatra*, and in modern times in George Bernard Shaw's *Caesar and Cleopatra* (also made into a movie in 1948 with Vivien Leigh). Another strong factor in Taylor's favor (there were, of course, numerous other candidates who tested for the role, one of them being Joan Collins) seems to be related to the original intentions of Twentieth Century Fox president Spyros Skouras to create an epic where great spectacle and star glamour would be needed to salvage the financial straits his studio was in at the time. In the late 1950s, Twentieth Century Fox had experienced several flops at the box office, and *Cleopatra* would come to its rescue. And only an actress of Elizabeth Taylor's caliber, with a great cast and the most lavish production ever been seen would help straighten the fortunes of his company. Taylor cleverly negotiated a contract of one million dollars for her performance—the first woman actress to receive a salary of that magnitude—something that added to the mystique of her role and excited the expectations of audiences to see her on the screen playing the legendary queen.

In the film, Cleopatra, despite her eventual downfall, is presented as a true leader: Through her alliance with Caesar, she envisions a united West and East that would continue the conquests of Alexander the Great—an idea she tries to implant in the mind of Caesar—and thus create a truly powerful and great nation. But Caesar, bruised by his perception that a woman's plan of conquest was grander than his own, and embroiled in Rome's internal conflicts—and also an ailing epileptic—could not muster the strength to follow Cleopatra's grandiose plan and invited her to Rome only to show her to the Romans as his own triumph in annexing Egypt and bringing the queen there as his spoil. Whatever other plans he had are foiled by his assassination, and Cleopatra returns to Egypt, now a Roman province, only to be soon visited by another Roman suitor, one with greater passion but less reserve or political acumen than Caesar. Cleopatra now has a second great Roman crawling at her feet, and, as this liaison is perceived as treason in Rome, where Antony has left enemies behind him, war between the two sections of the Roman Empire becomes inevitable. But Antony, as history has also shown him, was a brave fighter but a weak man. At the most critical moment, when his presence was needed in the naval battle at Actium, Antony abandons his fleet and follows Cleopatra's retreating flagship, and they return to Egypt defeated and soon to commit suicide. A stunned Octavius finds his two dead foes, cowards in battle but brave in death, a fact that deprives him of his planned vainglorious grand entrance in Rome with both his opponents in chains.

When the epic premiered in June 1963, critical reception was mixed, to say the least, and the audiences, after a surge of attendance in the opening weeks, stayed away, though eventually the film managed to recover its enormous costs, and eventually even made a profit. More importantly, Oscar nods were limited to cinematography, art direction, and sound effects, and *Cleopatra* was perceived by many as a failed epic, marred by too many negatives and not equaling the accolades accorded to some other epics of its era. Delays in production, change of directors and producers, escalating costs, Taylor's near-fatal illness, and, above all, the scandal produced by her affair with costar Richard Burton—not to mention the mutilation the movie suffered when cut by nearly two hours by the producers to bring it to the manageable length of four hours, rather than the six-hour, two-segment movie envisioned by its director Joseph L. Mankiewicz.

The sluggish reception of *Cleopatra* could also be attributed to the fact that audiences, already saturated with male-titled epics—*Ben-Hur* (1959), *Spartacus* (1960), and *Lawrence of Arabia* (1962)—had had just about enough of Roman/historical costume spectacles, as cultural orientations shifted to social issues, racial conflicts, antiwar sentiment, and hip subjects such drugs and campus unrest, not to mention the foreign movies that at the time were deluging American screens.

Still, in the history of film epic making, *Cleopatra* remains one of the great epics of its era, worthy of renewed attention, especially since it is the only epic in the grand tradition with a woman as the lead. Joseph L. Mankiewicz's giant movie was mounted as an expensive project and its makers had ambitions that this would be the epic to end all epics. Besides Burton, it featured popular male stars, Rex Harrison as Caesar, Roddy McDowall as Octavius, and Martin Landau as Rufio, among many others—adding a special challenge for a woman actress to act opposite such a collection of powerful men. In fact, this is a configuration that makes *Cleopatra* so unique. For not only did Taylor dominate the screen with ease; she also shone brighter than any of her male costars, leaving no doubt in the minds of those imposing figures surrounding her that she was indeed the queen she was playing, having scenes demanding that both Rex Harrison as Caesar and Richard Burton as Antony, playing arrogant Roman generals, kneel before her. As a consequence, Taylor made history as a film epic actress, all scandal forgotten the moment one looks at this screen icon of her day. She manages to resurrect a historical woman figure who shaped the fates of great men as no other had in antiquity, not excluding Helen of Troy—a plaything of warring nations but possessing no state leadership qualities.

Cleopatra came at the end of an era, and it was indeed the epic that ended all epics of its kind: expensive, history oriented, a grand costumer that relied on glamour and star power, scenery, art direction, and magnificent sets. It was literate but undeservedly unlucky, for just about every conceivable obstacle inhibited its production. The epic was presented to audiences in a mutilated form, and it was never restored to its original length—as it was meant to be. Still, it is the only grand epic of its era whose lead is a woman, one who could stand her ground not just as the character she plays, but as an actress who shone bright in the constellation of men dominating the wide screen in those days. Even if one considers this only as a mere relic in the history of great epics of her time, Elizabeth Taylor stood the test of time as a female epic persona, perhaps the only one of her time that could have brought the aims of this grand production to fruition.

Out of Africa (1985); Director/Producer: Sydney Pollack

Based on Isak Dinesen's best-selling novel-memoir, *Out of Africa*, the film recounts the adventures of Karen Blixen, who in real life married her cousin from Sweden, Baron Bror Blixen, and went to Kenya with him to start a new life after a sentimental disappointment in Denmark. Dinesen of course is the pen name of Blixen, and the book is a leisurely and plotless narrative, in diary form, recounting her life in Kenya in minute detail. It is clearly the story of her adventures, told from a unique viewpoint, for it is not really herself she writes about but what she sees and experiences. The self emerges as the story progresses, and both reader and viewer of the film gather impressions of this woman, who, perhaps unbeknownst to herself has become a true hero of humanity, though she hardly fights any battles in the traditional sense of a movie heroine of epics. It is, however, an epic adventure, if one counts her inner metamorphosis from a rather innocuous European lady of manners to a hard-boiled but not hardened woman, who rises above circumstances that would have dragged her down and who does her part in the creation of a European identity in Africa. Hers is ultimately a story of defeat—in marriage and in love; but it is a triumph of her human spirit, for she struggles to retain her dignity, to learn to accept defeat, and, in the end, to have a deeper understanding of her adopted country than those who were there as conquerors and colonialists.

Rising above circumstances that could have dragged down a lesser person, Baroness Karen Blixen as played by Meryl Streep is a woman who is noble in every sense of the word. She is tolerant of her husband's excesses, even the fact that he gives her syphilis, forgives her lover Denys Finch Hatton (played by Robert Redford), who remains uncommitted to a lasting relationship, and bravely faces the governor of Kenya in her fight to secure a piece of land for those servants who had worked for her. Meryl Streep, then in midcareer, splendid looking, and sporting an enchanting foreign accent (that could have belonged to any European nationality east of France), surpasses expectations. There are two reasons for her success. One is the role and the other is her performance, which combines elements and traits only an extraordinary actress could possess.

It is all these elements combined that make her a heroine, and an epic female hero at that—though a lot of qualifications have to be made in such a definition. First, she is not the usual epic hero—male or female—who wins physical battles, as some of her female counterparts have done before and since. Karen Blixen is a female epic hero in the fullest sense, but in unusual and more profound ways. A woman with considerable personal wealth, from a small European country (Denmark), decides to travel to Africa to marry a nobleman, with a nobleman's affix—baron—to his name, and agrees to spend her money on a cattle-breeding venture in Kenya. But a surprise awaits her. As soon as she arrives, Bror tells her that they must marry immediately, something that she accepts, and that, instead of the cattle-breeding venture he had spoken about before, he had invested her money in coffee growing, an operation that would be less onerous for him, for the plants grow by them-selves, not needing tending. Grudgingly, she agrees to go along with his schemes, not knowing that he is carrying on with other women, something that continues after they are wed (though we never see his escapades). When she gets ill, her doctor tells her she has contracted syphilis and needs to go back home for a cure.

Meanwhile, she has met and fallen in love with a maverick English pio-neer, Denys Hatton, who lives with his friend, Berkley Cole, both men being wild animal hunters, adventurers, and committed bachelors. When Karen separates, without a divorce at first, from her estranged husband, who is ab-sent more than half of the time, she and Denys become romantically in-volved, but their affair does not last long and is confined to casual safaris dur-ing which they share quarters. He loves flying, acquires a plane, and soon gets killed on one of his expeditions.

When Karen's coffee plantation, which had thrived with the hired help of local Swahili natives, burns to the ground, she is left penniless and leaves for her country, leaving ruins and a homeless group of people behind her. She is finally chased out of Africa after a series of failures, in marriage, love, and business.

And yet, Karen is a heroine, and one of unusual dimensions. Her heroic status comes from her inner strength and inner nobility. There are no other words to describe her. In the face of her husband's blatant deceptions, she manages to avoid hating him, and they remain friends, and yet there is no trace of resentment or ill will toward him on her part. Bror is a cad and knows it. He also knows he does not deserve a woman of Karen's adamant qualities, and yet he callously, and without self-reproach, takes her money though he does not attempt to interfere with her extramarital affair. Karen also guards against resentment and, though she is not forgiving and forgetting, she bears his unscrupulous actions as best she can. Her lover is not up to her standards of commitment either. A loner, an animal lover (though he shoots a lion when he has to), a naturalist, a music lover who plays Mozart on his phonograph, and a free spirit, Denys lacks the ability to commit and the sense of belonging to another that makes marital ties meaningful—and permanent. Karen knows as much, but she expresses herself not in anger, but in sadness. She is capable of seeing Denys for what he is—a good man but limited to serving his own appetites, though, when occasion calls for it, he will help a friend in need. He is dedicated to Berkley, especially when he is dying of black fever, and he helps Karen after she kneels before the new governor of Kenya to ask for asylum for the homeless people who have served her.

Karen displays one characteristic that, above all, distinguishes her as a heroine of unusual dimension. She is an empire builder, but one who does not resort to ruthlessness to gain her ends—as is the usual practice of those who seek to build at the expense and exploitation of others. Herbert Spencer's law of laissez-faire or Charles Darwin's survival of the fittest, practiced universally in business, are not Karen's practices. She is a capitalist, yes; otherwise she would not undertake a trip to an unknown country, enduring marriage to a worthless man, and suffering the vagaries of wilderness and wartime turbulence. But all her moves toward businesslike practices are done in the spirit of fair play, as she behaves more as a philanthropist rather than an entrepreneur—taking care of a boy with a lacerated leg or fragile elderly people, respecting their traditions, and paying fair wages to her employees. She is the one that would build a school—if not a church—and a new society. She would seek stability in marriage. She would have children and descendants and would have respected an ancient country—using it but not depleting its resources or recklessly destroying it. Karen is the heroine of the spirit of goodwill and philanthropy—in the broadest sense. It is tragic that all her ventures fail. Her cad of a husband, her attractive but uncommitted escapist lover, and the greedy colonial environment that comes with the annexation of Kenya by the British crown—all contribute to her material downfall. She leaves the country, in compassion and sorrow, but not in indignation or defeat. She cares for the workers of the farm she acquired and secures them a portion of the land that "was theirs before it was ours," as she tells the new governor; and she leaves the place with love in her heart for all the things that she saw and experienced, but especially for the land.

Building such an image of a woman in a film becomes possible with the dedicated and technically excellent writing and direction of Sydney Pollack, his writers, photographers, and crew. But above all, it was the performance of Meryl Streep that made the portrait of Karen Blixen so compelling. She adopted a heavy foreign accent, which, with a lesser actress could have been a disastrous cacophony; instead, it is a melody, a rhythm, and cadence that matches the visual splendor of the photographed landscapes. Hers is an imitation of imperfectly spoken English. But here imperfection becomes perfection, just as a kneeling noble woman before the representative of a mighty monarch is an act of not just compassion but also of real dignity and superiority. Stooping before the boots of unworthiness makes the possessor of power worthy. Even so, it is the governor's wife, seeing a noble woman begging on her knees, who gives her word of honor for him. Heroism comes in many forms, but here innermost strength and real affection—a merging of acting with reality—defines its power.

Indochine (1992); Director: Régis Wargnier

Catherine Deneuve plays a rubber plantation owner in Indochina (modern-day Vietnam, Laos, and Cambodia, the entire peninsula formerly known as the kingdom of Siam [or Thailand]), when that country was under French rule in pre–World War II days. The action occurs early in the twentieth century, in the late twenties or early thirties, judging from the cars and costumes. It moves through several generations to the mid-1950s, just before the French lose control of Indochina in the Dien Bien Phu war, which looms in the background as the movie ends. In any case, the French are fighting a lost cause, since it is evident that corruptions, abuse, and cruelty toward the native people had begun to bear negative fruit, to say nothing of that people's desire for freedom. Revolution is in the air, and one easily connects this episode to stories of Vietnam, though this is really not a war episode as such. It is rather a story of the love found and lost between one of the occupiers and a native girl, Jean-Batiste and Camille; the love between a mother and her adopted daughter; and the love the mother has for her adopted country. The film is an epic because of the (ultimately doomed) empire building to which Eliane (Deneuve) is committed.

Here Deneuve plays Eliane, a plantation owner whose adopted daughter Camille (Linh Dan Pham), brought up in Western fashion, is caught up in one of the many skirmishes between the French police and the rebels and is apparently mortally wounded. When Jean-Batiste, a young French officer, rescues her and attempts to wipe off the blood from her bare chest, he discovers that she is only wounded, and he instantly falls in love with her. But the romance seems an affront to Eliane, who had already formed a liaison with the same younger man herself. After several emotional confrontations with Eliane, Camille leaves to join Jean-Batiste, who has been sent to an outpost, and ends up becoming friends with an Indochinese family who had escaped from bondage. When Jean-Batiste spots her in the prisoners' group, where she has been kept after she was arrested as a rebel (for befriending the native family), he rushes toward her and exchanges blows with another French officer.

Camille then grabs the officer's gun, and shoots him in the head. She and Jean-Batiste flee, live together with a group of fugitives, and have a baby, but eventually he is taken prisoner while christening the baby in a pool.

Though Deneuve's role seems somewhat limited, as the focus shifts to her adopted daughter, she still remains an integral part of the story and, ultimately, the story is about her. For one, she looks the part of an epic heroine. Once called the "most beautiful woman in the world," she is not just a beautiful face, but a graceful, commanding presence on the screen. Deneuve deserves to be called a "goddess," equal in "divine" graces to her predecessors of the silver screen—Garbo, Bergman, Hepburn (both), Joan Fontaine, Bette Davis (and others)—women whose acting abilities were matched by a special charisma, a beauty that possesses a "high seriousness" to it—to use the well-known term of Aristotle and Matthew Arnold. Both of these critics were talking of poetry, but there is a depth and resonance not only in the sound of music or poetry, but also in the human face. Screen "goddesses" possess that quality that consists of complex qualities: beauty that need not always be perfection; that ideal of high seriousness noted by the above critics and others; that special look of intelligence. All this is complemented with a special movement—a stately step, a gesture, a look—as well as the pronunciation of a word or phrase.

In some ways, Deneuve's Eliane parallels the images of movements and speech patterns as well as the heroism established in *Out of Africa* by Meryl Streep, the indomitable Baroness Karen von Blixen. Both women were heroines rooted out of their native lands; both dealt with intractable authority figures; both were compelled by circumstances (or conscience) to fight for the rights of native peoples and for the liberation of their own sex. Both were awakening criticisms of the evils caused by Western civilization in its blind and overbearing conquests of other cultures while at the same time complicit in the colonialist efforts of their time period. Though their stories differ in many ways, the central figures—both women—are heroes by acting out their inner convictions in the face of the brutal realities of rigid patriarchal and colonial systems. The female heroism, in this sense, is not expressed by acts of aggression—a characteristic of so many macho types, from Stallone to Schwarzenegger—but by words of compassion, arguments for human rights, and by female comportment. But Eliane is ultimately unable to rise out of the debris left by the French colonialists, to which, by extension, she belongs, to create a better society, and as such she is also unable to aid in the expansion of the French Empire—the project anyway, history reminds us, was already lost. Her adopted daughter recognizes the error of her mother's ways even before she does, to the point that the girl can no longer call her "mother." Eliane perhaps realizes the gap between her intentions and reality, thus resulting in her own internal struggles and dependency on opium. In the end, however, the movie gives us two strong female characters who play out the conflicts involved in intercultural strife, oppression, intergenerational love, motherhood, and the subjugation of women.

Suggested Films for Study

The Passion of St. Joan (1927); Director: Theodore Dreyer
The Passion of St. Joan, a masterpiece of the silent era, could be said to be among the most significant of women's epics, though not lengthy by ordinary epic standards. Concentrating on St. Joan's trial, her ordeal, and death, the film has the structure of a Greek tragedy, achieving epic proportions. The burning at the stake of Joan of Arc, the woman-martyr in the fifteenth century, is both a great event of history and a masterful piece of filmmaking.

Queen Christina (1933); Director: Rouben Mamoulian
The goddess Greta Garbo is Queen Christina of Sweden who loves Antonio (played by John Gilbert) and she relinquishes her throne for her lover.

Cleopatra (1934); Director: Cecil B. DeMille
With Claudette Colbert as the famous Egyptian queen, *Cleopatra* still holds the interest of the modern viewer thanks mainly to the opulence of the production and the intelligent performance of Colbert. One of the most spectacular black-and-white epics ever.

Joan of Arc (1948); Director: Victor Fleming
With Ingrid Bergman as the protagonist, this film, based on a Maxwell Anderson play, takes Joan into the actual fields of battle, her trial, and martyrdom. Ingrid Bergman, for once not a romantic heroine,[2] gives a memorable performance.

The African Queen (1951); Director: John Huston
The African Queen stars Katharine Hepburn and Humphrey Bogart, who won an Oscar for his performance. Hepburn shares duties with Bogart in one of his most colorful roles, but it is clear that it is as much her story as it is his. She transforms a scruffy boat owner into a hero, and she is also transformed by him (or by their mutual growing respect) from a dried-up spinster to a passionate woman. Going through incredible hardships during their trip, both become heroes when they manage to sink a German torpedo boat that was infesting the territory.

Saint Joan (1957); Director: Otto Preminger
Saint Joan features Jean Seberg and Richard Widmark; one of the most ordinary of these productions, based on George Bernard Shaw's play but still cast in the heroic mode.

L'Avventura (1960); Director: Michelangelo Antonioni
Antonioni's masterpiece can be considered the epic of a woman who undertakes an inner search for her true identity, as she finds herself in denial of her guilt for having betrayed a friend who has mysteriously disappeared. This is an odyssey of psychological disaffection which is the result of the heartbreaking discovery that a betrayal, regardless of the extenuating circumstances that may have caused it, is bound to have repercussions that are as destructive as they are redeeming.

Cleo from 5 to 7 (1962); Director: Agnes Varda
Agnes Varda, hailed as a prominent French "new wave" director, directs the "voyage of death" of a young singer, Cleo (Corinee Marchand) who thinks she will die of cancer and who, in the space of two hours (the film's duration), shows growth and regeneration as she acquires qualities of character that transform her from a spoiled celebrity to a mature woman. A fine woman's story, this movie can be considered a "minor" psychological epic, for it recounts a journey from death to renewal, a story of darkness emerging into light—a trip known to male epic heroes since Orpheus and Odysseus.

Bonnie and Clyde (1967); Director: Arthur Penn
A classic Hollywood movie of two outlaws—the first ever made of a male-female team—based on a real-life story. The film's episodic plot (with several classic reversals nevertheless) details the adventures of two bank robbers whose lives march toward a tragic end. Bonnie, played by Faye Dunaway, shows the traits of an "underground" heroine, turning to violence and achieving notorious feats that she never could have achieved as a waitress.

The Lion in Winter (1968); Director: Anthony Harvey
In this powerful, history-based epic, Katharine Hepburn won an Oscar (her third), as Eleanor of Aquitaine, wife of Henry II (Peter O'Toole), imprisoned in a castle for years by her husband but able through sheer willpower to influence his three sons in their brutal struggle for dominance over a stubborn, unyielding, and power-hungry monarch. As Eleanor, Hepburn shows strength, compassion, an indomitable spirit, and an ability to tame the conflicting ambitions of her sons and the excesses of an unscrupulous tyrant.

Ryan's Daughter (1970); Director: David Lean

This is the story of Rose Ryan Shaughnessy, who marries a local school-teacher (Robert Mitchum), whom she idealizes. But, unsatisfied with her marriage, she takes a lover and that causes a wrecked marriage and a near lynching by a local mob of villagers who think of her as an adulteress and traitor. Shot magnificently in western Ireland by David Lean, this became one of his least-liked epics, yet the story, framed within the events of the Irish rebellion in 1916, and modeled after Flaubert's *Madame Bovary* by screenwriter Robert Bolt, is told with an assured hand and has made a comeback with select audiences.

Julia (1977); Director: Fred Zinnemann

Julia describes an episode in the life of Lillian Hellman, in which she is presented as a contentious, temperamental, young writer who does not bear failure easily and whose relationship with Dashiell Hammett, her friend and mentor, soon catapults her to Broadway fame. But the film is also about Lillian's relationship with a young woman of English peerage, Julia, with whom she had formed a relationship in her adolescent years. Now, in 1937, Julia is in Berlin, involved in rescuing Jews and other threatened minorities from Nazi Germany. She sends a message to Lillian, who is in Paris and traveling to Moscow, to carry a large sum of money which will help hundreds to escape. Not epic by the usual standards—length or spectacle—the film shows Lillian's heroic decision to undertake this perilous mission, her train ride given as a "dip" into the underworld, as the Nazis have discovered her scheme and follow her every step. Through flashbacks and expert parallel editing, the film shows a woman's struggle with her conscience as she makes a fateful decision to follow its dictates.

Octopussy (1983); Director: John Glen

This is the only Bond film that bears the name of a woman, albeit a symbolic one. Maude Adams plays a woman who, despite her obvious mafia connections, is running a school in India that trains young women to be independent. It is Octopussy's group that defeats the villain in pitched battle between these modern Amazons and a batch of villains. Though a cartoonlike character in this deplorable script, Maude Adams shows strength, dignity as a head of a woman's establishment, and the ability to handle baddies equal to that of her famous counterpart.

Queen Margot (1994); Director: Patrice Chearau

A French-Italian-German production, *Queen Margot*, notorious for its sex and violence scenes, demonstrates that women's (and other) epics were not the exclusive province of Hollywood. Isabelle Adjani plays Marguerite de Valois, a Catholic who marries a Protestant prince, Henri of Navarre, an action that causes bloodshed and civil strife in sixteenth-century France.

Titanic (1997); Director: James Cameron

This classic epic can also be considered a women-centered epic, for it is the female protagonist, Rose DeWitt Bukater (Kate Winslet), a passenger on the doomed ship, who tells the story in old age, recalling and reconstructing the events as they took place. She was a rebellious young debutante who, during the course of the trying adventure, falls in love and becomes the one person surviving the disaster who gains perspective on the immense catastrophe that cost the lives of thousands.

Elizabeth (1998); Director: Shekar Kapur

Though the life of Queen Elizabeth I has been retold several times, arguably this is the best and most historically accurate movie of epic proportions (if in a limited sense) of that distinguished and much-talked-about queen in her early years. Imposing as a queen in her first important role, Cate Blanchett handles her role with great aplomb, stamina, and sheer showmanship, exhibiting her dominance over weaker men in a poisonous royal environment.

The Messenger (2000); Director: Luc Besson

This modern women-centered epic uses various film techniques (wide lens) to enhance the battle scenes, showing not just Joan of Arc's adventures but also the brutality of war. Milla Jovovich gives a powerful, realistic performance as St. Joan, a woman warrior, although she is not too convincing as the woman heroine/saint who brought France her freedom.

The Time of the Butterflies (2001); Director: Mariano Baroso

This movie is about the life of a woman, Minerva Mirabal, played by Salma Hayek, resisting one of the twentieth century's most notorious dictators, Rafael Leonidas Trujillo—a ruthless dictator in the Dominican Republic—with the murders of more than thirty thousand people to his credit. Mirabal is the leader of a local resistance group, which includes a significant number of women, and it is clearly epic by definition, since it involves—though only in highlights—the entire story of a woman in the context of a national struggle.

The Lady and the Duke (2001); Director: Eric Rohmer

An epic romance set in France during the French Revolution, *The Lady and the Duke* questions the ethics of the "philosophes" of the French Enlightenment movement, as practiced by the leaders of the Reign of Terror. In the midst of murder and mayhem, it is a woman, Grace Elliott (Lucy Russell) who, in a series of lucid dialogues with a Scottish duke living in France, defends the rights of innocent humans executed by the Jacobins only because they happened to be born aristocrats. A rarity for director Eric Rohmer, this movie's action is entirely digitally photographed, something that allows the viewer to focus on dialogue and nuance, which defines Lady Grace's revulsion for war and critique of the abuses of those in power.

Million Dollar Baby (2004); Director: Clint Eastwood

This is the story of Maggie Fitzgerald (Hilary Swank), an unskilled boxing trainee, who becomes an aspiring female prizefighter who wins a championship under the guidance of reluctant trainer Frankie Dunn (Eastwood). She is paralyzed from a blow to the head from a vicious opponent whom she had already defeated. Almost a female Rocky, Maggie shows heroic qualities similar to those of an epic heroine—indeed her rise to fame is a heroic journey of life and tragic death.

The Queen (2006); Director: Stephen Frears

With Helen Mirren as Queen Elizabeth II, this film shows the struggle of England's very traditional royal family to adapt to modern reality. Taking place at the time of Princess Diana's tragic death, the film focuses on the Queen's absolute refusal to mourn Diana in public, thinking such action unroyal, but in the end she relents under growing public and political pressure and addresses the nation—an act that humanizes her in the eyes of her people and the world.

Notes

1. Otto Rank's heroic patterns, here applied to female heroic figures, are mentioned in the introduction and explained in some detail in chapter 2, "The Mythological Epic."

2. Ingrid Bergman also gives a fine performance as a fighter in *For Whom the Bell Tolls* (1943), a Spanish civil war epic based on the Ernest Hemingway novel. In this, though, it is Gary Cooper who has the lead role. Incidentally, Katina Paxinou, the Greek actress playing Pilar, won an Academy Award for Best Supporting Actress for her powerful performance.

CHAPTER SIX

The Comic Epic

At first sight, a comic epic seems like a contradiction in terms. It cannot have a hero who is noble and one who commands respect or awe among his or her tribe with his or her exemplary actions. In addition, comic works, whether of stage, film, or literature, generally have been shorter narratives with minor casts whose personas' main function is to induce laughter in an audience in response to some ridiculous gaffe they have committed. Comic works first appeared as stage plays and continued as such through antiquity and into modern times, though some prose works have also had comic characteristics.[1] When films first appeared, comedy came along almost immediately in the form of a short feature (one or two reels), or a less-than-two-hour feature film. More importantly, the hero, or heroine, in a comic film is, as in the earlier stage plays, usually conceived as a buffoon, a fool, or a coward, a persona designed to evoke laughter in an audience, laughter at the expense of the protagonist, who is ridiculed and demeaned by his/her own actions. Thus, comedy can only be epic by default, by satirically echoing or reflecting the grand manner of the epic in diminution, by bringing it down from its height and reducing it to a base human activity that is meant to be ridiculed.

Yet, comedy, whether as ancient or modern stage play or as film, has occasionally borrowed characteristics from the epic and used them on its own terms. This was not done by extending the length of a play—or narrative in general—but by expanding the moral parameters of a work to include epic elements. If the epic's function is to extol the hero and his role is to advance tribal interests, then the comic hero's function is to cauterize the tribe's foibles and to provide, often through self-ridicule, a barometer of social be-havior and a barrier against misconduct. A comic epic—or "mock epic" or "mock heroic," as it came to be known in the works of Geoffrey Chaucer (*Nun's Priest's Tale*), Edmund Spenser (*Muiopotmos—The Death of the Fly*), Jonathan Swift (*Battle of the Books, Gulliver's Travels*), and especially of Alexander Pope (*The Rape of the Lock*)—can only exist by contrast, by adopt-ing the epic proper as its companion and being fed by its companion's con-ventions. If the epic hero is an achiever, then the comic hero is a failure, so-cially and individually, though sympathy for his misadventures is often kindled, as in the films of Charlie Chaplin, or other lovable losers. His fail-ure, though, is not painful (or tragic), but laughable; he suffers no real calamities; his pitfalls are there to entertain, and, at best, to teach those who watch—and are by association ridiculed—a lesson.

Comedy has always had a moral tag attached to it since antiquity,[2] and thus the comic epic finds in failure an element of didacticism. Some modern playwrights, George Bernard Shaw for instance, insisted that the aim of com-edy (and all art in general) should be didactic.[3] The overt purpose of comedy is entertainment; its covert aim is to impart a moral lesson—or a lesson of some kind, even at the expense of tearing down something else. Savage satire (as in the case of the Roman satirist Juvenal and of the English Jonathan Swift) is an outgrowth of the comic genre and has its roots there. Its aims are similar (in a broad sense), for they include a catharsis not through laughter only but also through seemingly malicious criticism. It is not just laughter that is induced in satire, but scorn poured upon hypocrites, pompous politi-cians, or other high-ranking officials, and generally on those who profess but do not follow morality. Comedians and satirists mix well in film as well as in any other literary genre, as we shall see.

Comedy has its roots in antiquity, developing along the same lines as the epic, though it produced fewer authors than the epic or tragedy. Aristotle in his *The Poetics* claims that Homer, who had been the originator of both com-edy and tragedy, had written a comic work, *The Margites* (*The Dolt*), which fits that category.[4] This example indicates that some of the writers of the epic had branched off into what was later called comedy, although the origins of the word "comedy" are derived from various etymological interpretations of "κωμαζειν" (to lampoon) and possibly "κατα κωμας" (against the town) where revelers roamed during various festivals in honor of Dionysus.[5] A lam-poon differs from comedy in that it is directed against specific social mores or individuals, but the aims of lampoon and comedy are similar—to castigate social ills. There is also evidence that the notion that the comic and the tragic forms (which derived from the epic) were related had gained some currency in antiquity. In his *Symposium*, Plato relates that Socrates wins an argument with Aristophanes, maintaining that a poet who composes comedy is capable of composing tragedy as well, and vice versa.[6] The Romans, generally imitators of the Greeks, found no expression in comic works outside the plays of Plautus and Terence, which were imitations of the plays of the new comedy (as distinguished from the old comedy of Aristophanes) Greek writer Menander, who lived in the fourth century BC. Romans Horace, Juvenal, and Lucan composed comic works that were called satires (*saturae*), which they claimed were forms they invented (*satura nostra est*); these were generally verse compositions whose intent was to castigate specific social foibles, rather than to entertain, though Horace is famous for having combined the two concepts (*utile et dulce*), pleasure and morality, an idea that left a mark on subsequent writers in the eighteenth century, when satire was reborn, and in the modern era.

Comedy on the stage continued through the Renaissance in the plays of Shakespeare, some of which (*The Comedy of Errors*, for instance) were derivations from plays of the Roman Plautus (*The Menechmi*). But the idea of a comic epic or mock epic, having circulated since the times of Chaucer, as stated above, did not become an accepted literary term until the works of Rabelais (*The Gargantua*) and Cervantes (*Don Quixote*), works that appeared in prose form, with narratives that attained great length. *Don Quixote* may deserve the name "comic epic," from a number of viewpoints, for its hero, despite his noble aspirations fails to fulfill them, and his comic adventures carry him to extreme and ridiculous acts that could have been worthwhile social goals had he not been suffering from delusions. From that time on the comic epic had an easy ride, and found expression in various comic novels of the eighteenth century, Jonathan Swift's *Gulliver's Travels*, for instance, and Henry Fielding's *Tom Jones* (which translated into an entertaining film in 1963). At that point, the comic epic had assumed the form of the picaresque novel, whose hero is a vagabond roaming the world more or less aimlessly, undergoing various adventures, or encounters, making contact with various social classes—villagers, aristocratic enclaves, warriors, religious groups—that shape his own relationships to these social milieus. The picaresque novel reigned during the eighteenth century and found expression in the nineteenth in only a few works, such as Mark Twain's sprawling and episodic *Huckleberry Finn*, which has the characteristics of the comic epic form.

The two genres, comedy and mock epic (or mock heroic), had more or less the same aims—to entertain, teach moral lessons, or mock social or literary conventions; the difference is that the mock epic was created as a deliberate attempt to parody, attack, and denigrate the epic proper and all pompous compositions in general. Its concept was elucidated in Alexander Pope's satirical essay *Peri Bathous* (or "The Art of Sinking in Poetry"), which was published in 1728, and purported to rid poetry of "false taste," "bad writing," and "commercial values" that dominated contemporary literature.[7] *Bathos*, coined by Pope,[8] became an accepted literary term used to describe the author's intent during the eighteenth century, when the satiric genre was revived, to ridicule pomposity in writing that had become prevalent during late antiquity[9] and the Renaissance. Bathos is the essence of the mock epic. To borrow a modern expression, the writer of the mock epic, by using bathos, deconstructs (or "de-centers") the epic proper. Ideas that seem noble and high-minded actions are brought down from their height to pedestrianism and ridicule. Some of the best-known mock epics in literature are works that tried consciously to parody the epic form, Pope's "The Rape of the Lock" being the prime example. In it a young peer offends a young lady by cutting a lock of her hair, causing a feud between two families; the intent of this short poem (only five cantos—about eight hundred lines) is to ridicule not only Pope's contemporary society that prepared to fight a interfamily feud for a trivial reason, but to parallel and drag down from their heights epics like *The Iliad* that had dominated Western literature and had set the standards for writing lengthy and (for the most part) overblown poems. In many ways, Byron's *Don Juan* (1818), coming about a century later, is a lengthy mock epic that serves a similar purpose: to tear down heroes—whether war heroes (like Lord Horatio Nelson), heads of state, or literary giants: Byron had a special hostility for the emotionally charged but (to him) pompous poetry of the Lake Poets—Samuel Taylor Coleridge, William Wordsworth, and Robert Southey—whose shallow verses Byron ridiculed. *Don Juan* was the mock epic that put an end to the verse epics species, and in many ways it succeeded, for the epic verse form has since then become moribund. The novel has produced such works as Mark Twain's *Huckleberry Finn* (*HF*), which debunks the works of Walter Scott—epic novels in scope—and the American mania for imitation of European manners; the famous "feud" between two aristocratic southern families in *HF* is an example. In twentieth-century literature, the mock epic waned considerably as a genre, fitting neither the existential mood of the century nor the preponderance of the psychological novel and the mainstream novel with its reliance on action and romance.

In the twentieth century, the comic epic novel is found in only a handful of major authors, whose aim took a decidedly satirical or ironic (and even allegorical) form: Aldous Huxley's *A Brave New World*, George Orwell's *Animal Farm*, and Joseph Heller's *Catch-22* are a few of the most prominent examples. These satiric works, often translated into film, sometimes have common characteristics with the epic, such as length, complexity of plots, and spectacular effects, though always minor in scope compared to epic proper.

Versions of the Comic Epic

Though film produced great comedies from approximately 1915 through the 1920s and 1930s, and later decades, only a handful of giant movies can be legitimately called comic epics, for comedy entails a smaller compass of action than the classic epic, fewer principal characters, less spectacle, and no great length. The films of such luminaries of the comic genre as Charlie Chaplin, Buster Keaton, Harold Lloyd, Laurel and Hardy, W. C. Fields, and the Marx Brothers, almost all of them slapstick comedians, were generally devoid of heroic elements, and their comedies reflected ridicule of bourgeois social mores rather than daring action. Initially, comedies were shorts, and the feature films of most of the above comedians are few by comparison and came in the later stages of their careers. Chaplin, Laurel and Hardy, and even Keaton made few full-length films that barely reached two hours—most of them were of average length, ninety to ninety-five minutes. When screwball comedy arrived in the mid-1930s, the lower-scale buffoon was eclipsed by the presence of aristocrats—the wealthy class of America—who engaged in tomfoolery, with plots centering on flopping romances and marital disputes (*Bringing Up Baby*, *The Philadelphia Story*, for example), all ending up in some kind of reconciliation between wrangling parties but at the expense of their dignity and upper-class upbringing. The screwball comedy used no regular comedians but leading actors and actresses (Cary Grant, Jimmy Stewart, Clark Gable, Claudette Colbert, Katharine Hepburn, among others) who found themselves in ridiculous situations, acting the part of clowns and degrading their own regular screen personas and the social mores of their class,[10] though such antics were welcomed by audiences and did not hurt box-office receipts. Comedy has thrived on self-ridicule, and aristocrats can be as self-abusive as any other class, while their external luster may add a note of hilarity to their debasement. Comedians of later generations, such as Abbott and Costello, Jerry Lewis and Dean Martin, Danny Kaye, Red Skelton, Bob Hope, and Steve Martin, made only farcical movies, noted for their gags and innocuous plotlines rather than their length or heroic episodes. Comedians revel in self-disparagement, aiming at provoking laughter by demeaning themselves before an audience that constantly assesses its sense of superiority. With the possible exception of Chaplin, who sought to evoke pathos, the comic hero refrains from actions seen as painful or tragic. Modern comedians have often complained of "lack of respect,"[11] a condition that seems to have afflicted the comic persona since antiquity. That of course is a result of their mockery of society's highly valued and pompous icons, something that leaves them vulnerable to ridicule, in turn.

But film took a greater advantage of the mock-epic form than modern literature did, producing a number of distinguished films that were created not merely for their comic effects but with deliberate intent (as far as this can be proven) to debunk the epic form. The spoof, an outgrowth of the mock-epic formula, came to aid its efforts, and some comedians and directors of comedy prefer that mode of debunking the epic by parodying a specific form of it; the western for instance, was shredded in the hands of an outrageous comedy, *Blazing Saddles* (discussed below), by Mel Brooks. The spoof takes a specific hero and cuts him down to size, ridiculing him, and showing his vulnerable spots or exposing his social standing. Its aim, like that of the mock epic, is to show how shallow the persona of the hero projected on the screen can be, and how hazardous the business of building up icons for public consumption is. Some examples of these subgenres of comedy are Preston Sturges's *Sullivan's Travels* (1941); *Casanova's Big Night* (1954), with Bob Hope as Casanova; Billy Wilder's *One, Two, Three* (1961), mocking executives of big corporations; and Stanley Kubrick's *Dr. Strangelove* (1962), which features a paranoid American general ordering a nuclear attack. If the aim of the epic hero is to serve the national interest, then the aim of the mock-epic hero is to derail or ridicule it. Pompous heroes or high-placed villains are cut to shreds by a comedian's vicious attacks, as Chaplin's mad Hynkel in *The Great Dictator* (1941) demonstrates. But the mock epic launching an attack on the heroic genre itself, rather than the persona it embodies (though it can do both) does not arrive on the American screen until Woody Allen consciously imitated it in several of his films, *Love and Death*,[12] *A Mid-summer Night's Sex Comedy*, and *Deconstructing Harry*. Others like him—and also very unlike him—are the Coen Brothers (Ethan and Joel), who in some ways can be considered champions of a new brand of screwball comedy that bears similarities with the mock epic in the modern era, mainly because they employ both comedians and lead actors.

Though it might be considered a distant relative, the comic strip epic might also be a version of the comic epic as well as its logical extension, as it shares some of its characteristics with the mock epic and the adventure story. Its main line of narrative has borrowed elements from newspaper comic strips, cartoon-type heroes like Dick Tracy, Batman, and Superman, all of whom ended up either as TV series, movies with sequels, or both. The comic-strip hero has a more positive image than the comic hero, for he embodies some of the main characteristics of the leader of his tribe, being ei-

ther a very smart detective solving crimes or a guardian of the weak and de-
fenseless due to his superhuman qualities. He is known by his double personality, his fighting spirit and physical stamina that enable him to prevail
over a host of villains, and, most importantly, his fight for the right causes,
usually patriotic or universally human—as, for instance, Superman's slogan
expressed in his fight for "Truth, Justice, and the American Way." His double persona is a must, for he is compelled to appear in disguise to justify his
existence among ordinary people (Clark Kent in *Superman*), and also in order to deceive his adversaries. He is not a character that suffers from self-
doubt or existential angst, and, though he likes a certain kind of girl, who
often shares his adventurous ways, he is not deeply involved in romance:
he is brave, hard-boiled, tough to beat, capable of nearly miraculous feats
(flies with the speed of a bullet), and has the capacity to outmaneuver his
villainous opponents. He has similarities with the James Bond character,
but not the latter's pretense of seriousness. The comic-strip hero is believable on the plainest level, the common run of humanity, and he never
tampers with irony, sarcasm at the expense of his adversaries, or with friv-
olous jokes, though at times he indulges in well-meant and rather plebeian
humor. He just fights villains to help you and me; he fights simply, with his
fists if he has to, and does not have at his disposal the elaborate gadgetry of
Bond; nor does he have the latter's playboy glitter and insatiable appetite
for sex. For him, women are respected as companions and coworkers, sharing his perils and his triumphs, not his bed.

The comic-strip hero is one-dimensional, but he does not need to be anything more, for his persona works to carry out tribal wish fulfillments, or the
dreamlike mass wishes of humanity. The Western popular imagination is full
of these cartoonlike characters, most of whom have come to us from great literary works of the past and popularized in modern times in schoolbooks, children's literature, cartoons, TV, and the daily newspaper. Hercules is known
for his labors, David is the underdog against Goliath, and King Arthur
searches for the Holy Grail, while Don Quixote, Lemuel Gulliver, and Sinbad the Sailor fill the gap between early and recent modern times, until Walt
Disney introduces Mickey Mouse and the countless heroes of animation that
have entertained humanity since movies were invented. Between animation
and feature film several comic-strip heroes had an intermediate step—TV.
Batman and Superman appeared in movies that began in the 1950s and
1960s. The movie *Superman* (1978), with three sequels, broke the mould by
introducing the "Man of Steel," who came from the distant planet Krypton,
disguised himself as the mild-mannered Clark Kent, but could, in a moment,
change his garb (to an outfit with the letter S emblazoned on it) and rush to

the rescue of hapless victims, or fly to defend humanity from the villains. More than any other, Superman fulfills America and humanity's wish for a one-dimensional savior, who has no real flaws, can do no evil, and has armed himself with a compassion for the weak that equals the greatest epic heroes of the past. Superman appears as a defender, not as an aggressor; for his stance is entirely American, and, like America, he has no selfish designs on the conquest of other nations or lands; he simply wants to help selflessly, restoring and keeping justice in the world. Simplistic and one-dimensional, he is likeable (especially in the person of sympathetic actor, the late Christopher Reeve), compassionate, quick to act, and nearly invulnerable, though at times he must face extreme peril. Superman, like the other cartoon heroes (and the villains) is a product of fantasy, embodying humanity's undying wish to protect itself from the evils that surround it, whether these are cosmic in origin or the products of earthbound humans. The threat is perpetual, so the hero must never die, either being immortal by nature (as the gods of Olympus are in *The Odyssey*), or indestructible, fortified by magic (as Sinbad is) or superhuman qualities. Suspension of disbelief is crucial here, but audiences are knowingly deceived, appreciating the fact that their subconscious wishes for self-preservation are carried out, even in the realms of a fantasy world.

Comic Epics

The Navigator (1924); Directors: Donald Crisp, Buster Keaton

Of all film comedians, Buster Keaton comes closest to the comic archetype of a hero who bulls through to his goal—and wins the girl in the end—despite formidable obstacles, whether natural or self-inflicted. In his independent phase (in 1928 he was absorbed by MGM), Keaton did not use a script, preferring to improvise on the spot, performing incredible antics with his entire body, such as wiggling past traffic, scampering down hills, and being chased by boulders (or barrels), while his ever-unsmiling face with his hypnotically expressive large eyes spoke a different language: that of a man undeterred by setbacks, set on a goal, going steadily forward, and disregarding any physical force trying to stop him. In fact, Keaton's body was his instrument regulating his resistance to fate: with it he could do things that most humans can't, such as darting like a bullet to make an appointment or standing up to the forces of nature, if provoked. Once, in a hurricane that tore down trees and carried away everything in its path, Keaton stood against the gale, bent by its force, but not totally uprooted. His resistance seemed foolhardy, for who can stop a hurricane with his body? Yet, it is his body that is constantly doing unpredictable and astonishing things, but we know it is his mind that is in control. It is this mental strength, apparent in his actions, where Keaton comes through as a comedian who does not ridicule himself, as Laurel and Hardy do, and one who does not seek the audience's pity, or evoke pathos, as Chaplin does, for the idea of pathos is alien to him. Not that he cannot elicit sympathy, but that is an entirely different emotion, for we sympathize with his endless futile pursuits without really feeling sorry for him. Chaplin wants the audience to pity him, or the little tramp he plays. He scorns the world he lives in, and avoids it if he can. Keaton is constantly in the middle of it, and his most frequent activity is chasing something that always eludes him. He goes on with his pursuit undaunted, allowing nothing to stand in his way—though everything conceivable does—but he bulls ahead, as if he judges the world to be an obstacle course and the path of life a series of bumps placed there by some kind of secular fate. He is pretty stoic about it all, and he keeps moving, not looking at you in the face, saying, "what kind of trouble I'm in?" Oliver Hardy, after an abysmal fall in a puddle, looks at his partner, Laurel, who has caused it, and then he looks at the camera as if to say, "World, how do these things always happen to me?" But Keaton is in motion, already busy superseding another obstacle, and he doesn't even seem to mind being swept away on a flying tree in a gale. His undaunted attitude seems to say, "you, nature, and you, man, have invented obstacles for me, but you are not going to daunt me."

Keaton often presents his comic hero as a person with no brainpower, no common sense, and no skills for plain jobs, and yet he is able to cope both with his own ineptitude and all the calamities that seem to pile on him, never losing his stamina or drive, emerging victorious no matter what the situation. The comic hero is not known for his good sense or practical ability, but for his determination, sheer bullheadedness, and ignorance of danger. He knows no fear. He accomplishes feats that even a skilled hero is unable to, and, of course, finally wins the girl. In *The Navigator*, Keaton plays a reluctant sailor, who has to deal with an equally inept female, an abandoned ship in the middle of the ocean, fending off an attack by cannibals, and facing a myriad other contingencies. The reluctant sailor is millionaire Rollo Treadway, who, after proposing to Betsy O'Brien (Kathryn McGuire), a rich girl whom he loves, and being unceremoniously rejected, embarks alone on what would have been his honeymoon trip on a ship that is targeted by "foreign agents" for destruction. At the same time, Betsy is escorted to the same ship by her father and gets on board, ready for a luxury trip. Rollo and Betsy both unknowingly board the wrong ship by mixing up the piers, and in the morning they find themselves alone together on the ship that is, for some unexplained reason, adrift on the ocean, with no one else onboard. After the first shock of recognition, Rollo attempts to play the hero and provide the lady with food—but his kitchen skills are minimal and the lady remains unfed and drenched after an unwilling dip in the ocean, where both of them almost drown. Soon they catch sight of cannibals on a sandy beach, where the ship runs aground. Rollo dons a diver's outfit and dives underwater, where he tries to free the propeller by cutting a wire with the claws of an obliging lobster, an image that ironically reminds one of the famous T. S. Eliot lines, "I should have been a pair of rugged claws/Scuttling across the floors of silent seas."[13] As the cannibals board the ship, and after several scuffles, the outnumbered duo falls into the ocean and swim for a while, then find a boat, scramble on it, but it begins to sink, and then they are rescued by a . . . submarine! Well, the two marry afterward. Blunderbuss as Keaton is as Rollo, the acrobatic little man does miraculous short work of villains and chance itself. Not brains, but courage and stamina win in the end.

It's a Mad, Mad, Mad, Mad World (1963); Director: Stanley Kramer

In the annals of film comedy, only one movie has made it to epic status due to its formal epic qualities: length, spectacular action, large cast, and massive adventure. And that is Stanley Kramer's It's a Mad, Mad, Mad, Mad World, a movie that set standards for comedy never again followed, at least not on that scale and magnitude. It presents mass action, rather than a lone comic hero, featuring a group of people pursuing a foolish goal, and failing in the end. This unique, massive film comedy takes on an allegorical character, becoming a parable for greed that drives to potentially disastrous results—except that it's all done for laughs. Kramer assembled just about all of the well-known comedians of his time—Jonathan Winters, Ethel Merman, Milton Berle, Sid Caesar, Phil Silvers, Jimmy Durante, Buddy Hackett, Mickey Rooney, among many others—and even assigns a famous straight actor, Spencer Tracy, a rare comic role.[14] This was the epic comedy to end all comedies—and, in its unique way, it did. It is a giant movie, containing everything, from slapstick madcap action to verbal sparring, wild car chases, minor explosions, road rage mayhem, a subverted plot to steal, and above all, mad behavior—to borrow the word from its title. It's an epic all right, not of heroism but of human folly, a story of a mad rush to find hidden stolen treasure, illustrating the principle that the pursuit of happiness boils down to the pursuit of money in its most Darwinian extremes. Mad World is a comedic "catch-as-catch-can" game, funny and crude at the same time, shameless and hilarious, but moralizing all the while, showing that neither the would-be thief nor the vain pursuer has, in the end, anything to show for his efforts. The motto "finders keepers" has a moral attached to it—that keeping someone else's money when found is an immoral practice, as the movie illustrates.

Here reason is shattered and the principle of self-enrichment, found in every single human (the movie implies) is paramount, especially when luck interferes and brings potential riches to you. If you try to steal, that's an immoral act; if you try to obtain something that someone else has stolen—money in this case—then you are only left with his claim that what was stolen was his, therefore it's a justifiable find, which should belong to you. Well, it doesn't. If the possessor of the money stole it and went to jail for fifteen years, then having repaid his dues for his crime to society, does the stolen money now belong to him? A tangled question, both morally and legally. But the eight people who have obtained such information from a dying thief (actually only five of the eight do so) don't for a moment hesitate to rush to the place indicated, a park in Santa Rosita with a "W" as the sign of its location, nor do they doubt the legitimacy of their claim. The money was left to them; they are not going to report it to the authorities—who inquire about it—and the only question that plagues them is how to share it among themselves. In one of the wildest comic scenes, during which they try to devise ways to divide the loot, they fail to agree on what is "fair" for everyone, and the result is a splintered group who rely on their individual efforts to get to the money first. They split into three smaller groups in three cars, and a lone driver in a truck. One car contains three individuals, J. Russell Finch (Milton Berle); his wife, Emeline (Dorothy Provine); and his mother-in-law, the loud and obnoxious Mrs. Marcus (Ethel Merman). The second car contains two drivers who are going "to Vegas" (that's all we know about them), Benjy Benjamin (Buddy Hackett) and Ding Bell (Mickey Rooney); the third car contains a dentist, Melville Crump (Sid Caesar) and his wife Monica (Edie Adams); and finally the truck with its driver, Lenny Pike (Jonathan Winters). To these eight, three more are added during the mad rush to the park: one is Otto Meyer (Phil Silvers), a conniver who picks up the secret from a naive Pike who asks for a ride after his truck is demolished in a collision; another is a bizarre Englishman, J. Algernon Hawthorne (Terry-Thomas), who is returning from the desert with a jeep full of cactus specimens he collected; and the third is Mrs. Marcus's son, Sylvester (Dick Shawn), a resident of Santa Rosita, too dumb to understand his mother's frantic instructions to get to the park first and instead is coming to meet her. More people are added to the cast, most having just cameo roles, but an important figure is the Santa Rosita chief of police, Captain C. G. Culpepper (Spencer Tracy), who has been waiting for years for the convict who stole the money, Smiley Grogan (Jimmy Durante), to escape or complete his sentence, so that he can trace him, find out where the money is, and appropriate it for himself. While the mad drivers are rushing to the park, causing property damage and road mayhem, he slowly forms a plan to let them get there first and find the hidden money. Then he will take it away from them on some pretense or other, and escape to Mexico. He had been planning to retire on a small pension, but, after a wrangle with his wife, he decides to take advantage of the race for the stolen money.

As the various groups split, pursuing the same goal, crosscutting shows where they are and what they are doing: the dentist has hired a dilapidated 1916 plane, flies over the traffic, arrives in town, and ends up in a hardware store, which closes just after he and his wife enter, and he practically blows himself up trying to get out by dynamiting the steel door. Bell and Benjamin also get a plane, but their pilot, played by Jim Backus, is knocked out trying to get a drink, so they manage to fly the plane themselves, miraculously avoiding a crash and finally landing. Pike, meanwhile, has demolished a gas station, stolen a truck, and now allies himself with Mrs. Marcus and her daughter, while Finch and Hawthorne are seen in a rental car and being chased by an enraged Sylvester who has no idea where he is going in trying to find his mother. There are comic incidents here to fill several comedies, but finally the groups are reunited at the park, some driven there by two cabs, and, after some searching, they find the treasure buried under two diagonally interlocked palm trees, that form the sought-after "W" sign. Just when they start dividing up the money, Culpepper, who followed them there, sees them uncover the treasure, takes it from them, and instructs them to "turn themselves in" voluntarily in order to influence a judge in their favor. They discover his ruse, go after him, climb up an abandoned building, and end up on a collapsed fire escape platform, where they see the money flying to the ground while they try to grab it. They all, save the women, end up in the hospital, among them Culpepper, who bursts into laughter when Mrs. Marcus slips on a banana peel and falls on the floor.

In the midst of such extravagant silliness, director Stanley Kramer manages to maintain some organic coherence, tying up the various strands of the plot, as he lets his characters fall victims to their own folly. His tale can be seen as an allegory—of the sheer failure of the group to coalesce into a common goal. The story shows the collective transformation of commonsensical, ordinary humans into greedy lunatics wreaking havoc in various communities when the prospect of a large amount of money is in sight. It is like pressing an electric button and turning dull characters into racing maniacs. What is it that effects such a transformation? It is the prospect of an unexpected fortune of $350,000, a huge sum of money at the time,[15] that will supposedly put an end to a doldrum existence. It is similar (and dissimilar) to the craze generated by the prospect of a large lump of money a lotto promises—when crowds cross state lines to buy tickets hoping to win against staggering odds. A hidden treasure is an even greater allure, for, as in this case, it revives the spark of possession with unexpected and shattering suddenness. It's a universal phenomenon, for no one is exempt from the temptation of sudden riches: "They all went for it," the dentist tells his wife knowingly. He is the only one in the group who sees more clearly than the others that the effort to reach a reasonable conclusion ("I tried to reason with them," he tells his wife) had no chance of succeeding. Instead, the group adopted the motto that hidden treasure belongs to whoever gets to it first. An ethics committee might dispute that idea, but a disorganized group of casual strangers easily abandons reason in favor of the motto: "Every man (or woman) for himself," a phrase that one of the characters, Benjy Benjamin, shouts as the group stops discussing how to share the treasure and rushes off to find it. Any veneer of reason is given up, and an irrational glee—one could call it sheer mania—at the prospect of gaining an advantage against the others prevails. What this mania is exactly is something anthropologists might wish to explain—and probably have. These passengers who start out in four vehicles do not just want to get to the money; they want to get there first, and take it for themselves. Sharing is a civilized instinct, for in most cases communities will share both wealth and adversity. The movie does not parade its message with dictums of civilized dialogue, except at the beginning, when reason fails; it lets the action speak for itself. But humans are also laughing beasts, and in the end, bandaged and stretched out on hospital beds, they laugh in self-mockery, forgetting for a moment justice and broken bones. Comedy shows human folly, even if it comes in "heroic" proportions. Would such heroes drive that fast, or take such risks, for a "good" cause?

Mock Epics

Love and Death (1975); Director: Woody Allen

Love and Death, a relatively early work by Woody Allen, provides a good example of a parody of literary manners, a satire of modern intellectuals, and it is a film mock epic in its own right. As said above, a mock epic is an exercise in bathos; its main device being literary, behavioral, or philosophical allusion. By alluding to a certain work, preferably an epic (or any form of it), the mock epic attempts to tear it from its pedestal and reduce its ideas, words, or philosophical positions to ordinariness and ridicule. The audience laughs, often maliciously, as the balloon of an honored work bursts and drops.

In *Love and Death*, Woody Allen cuts a broad swath of objects for ridicule, alluding to a staggering number of literary and philosophical, if not musical, works, though not one specific epic. His targets are literary masters of the nineteenth century, Tolstoy and Dostoyevsky in particular, philosophers of optimism in general (parallels exist even with Voltaire's *Candide*, itself a prose mock epic), and other Western grandiose beliefs and values: the belief in immortality, moral truth, love, marital sex, the Bible and Christianity, Greek philosophers, and a host of others. His periscope surveys authors of the twentieth century, parodying existentialism and its angst, and the great film-makers Bergman and Fellini (whom he admires), to whom he alludes with ir-reverence. It is astonishing that a movie of such short duration can work on all these levels at once, but Allen manages this while delivering a compelling (in comic terms) story of love, war, and adventure.

Allen plays a Russian, Boris Grushenko, at the time of the Napoleonic wars. He takes a glance at his past life the night before he is to be executed by firing squad for having made an attempt on the life of Napoleon. He is one of the three sons of a Russian serf who owned a piece of land no more than eight inches in circumference, a comic vignette offering the film-maker a chance to take a little stab at the institution of property owning, precious during czarist Russia. His two brothers, Ivan and Mikhail, are ro-bust fellows, excelling in squat dancing and favorites of women, while Boris is short and scrawny. He loves his cousin Sonja (Diane Keaton), who is an intellectual who indulges in ideas about life and death; but she is also flip-pant, promiscuous, unfaithful, greedy, and, naturally, beautiful. She calls herself a cross between a whore and a saint, an obvious reference to Dos-toyevsky's heroine, Sonja, in *Crime and Punishment*. Pursued by several suit-ors, she chooses a herring merchant, whom she weds and readily cheats on. Boris is reluctant to enlist in the armed forces when Napoleon invades, but of course his wishes are ignored and he is drafted, goes to war, and proves an inept soldier and an extreme coward. Despite that, he is decorated for an act of valor when he is accidentally shot from inside a cannon and cap-tures a French battalion. He becomes an attraction in Russian society, woos an aristocratic lady to whom he makes love, and subsequently fights a duel with one of her suitors. He returns to the war; reunites with Sonja, whose husband has died; meets Napoleon after a guise, pretending he is a Spanish ambassador; is arrested and thrown in prison for attacking the emperor, and is executed. He does not go to heaven, but ends up a ghost, paying a visit to Sonja, to tell her about the afterlife.

The story is an exercise in allusion. Through imagery, quotation, dialogue, costumes, and other means at his command as a filmmaker (montage, for instance) Allen mocks every conceivable literary figure—mainly of the nine-teenth century—every idea or literary custom, especially those that have be-come fads in the twentieth century. Existentialism seems to be his main tar-get. The roots of that lie in Nietzsche, though his particular target is Dostoyevsky. But others are not spared: Tolstoy is of course also a main source of allusion (*War and Peace*) and from twentieth-century authors, so is T. S. Eliot, whose lines from "The Love Song of J. Alfred Prufrock" Boris quotes. The degradation of character matches the degradation of the epic form. As the hero becomes a coward, the epic becomes a caricature of itself, lacking length, epic sweep, hard-fought battles, or anything that uplifts or energizes the human spirit. But here the epic is also exposed as an empty, grandiose composition that exaggerates human activity, making it sound pompous, un-real, and impossibly superhuman. It also gives the coward his human dimen-sion. Why would one fight a war when one is small, physically weak (though oversexed), and unwilling to sacrifice his life for vague purposes? Convenient sex, a pleasant life, intellectual sparring with females, hatred of marriage as an institution that degrades love—these are common Allenesque themes, found here and in his other movies; in fact, it can be inferred that most of his comedies are mock epics, in one way or another. Most deal with failed ambi-tion, or, more specifically, with the failure of the modern individual to adapt to overwhelming demands, both social and personal. Allen never made it to the mainstream as a filmmaker, although admittedly he is brilliant and has a circle of fans. He is a small fry in the Hollywood milieu, unable, or unwill-ing, to adjust to a system of escapist exploitation, and thence eager to tear it down. There have been plenty of overblown epics in the Hollywood produc-tion lines, but few movies with length and spectacle that also qualify as true productions of the human condition. Woody Allen is willing to take a stab at exposing the big epic for the empty bubble that he thinks it is.

Don Juan DeMarco (1995); Director: Jeremy Leven

Don Juan DeMarco qualifies as a mock epic mainly because of its literary connections, though there are other reasons: It is a variation of the roman-tic comedy, the type of movie that has abounded in modern times, though in this film both the terms "romantic" and "comedy" must be enlarged upon to fit the definitions of the mock epic. At first sight, *Don Juan DeMarco* is an enjoyable yarn/fantasy, lighthearted, and light from all points of view. The movie features some fine performances—all on the lighter side—on the part of Marlon Brando, Faye Dunaway, and especially Johnny Depp, per-fectly cast here. The music with its Spanish rhythms is somewhat obtrusive, but on the whole it is appropriate to the subject. Seen only as escapist fare by some, the movie actually addresses itself to a sophisticated audience, appealing to those familiar with Byron's comic masterpiece, *Don Juan*. Indeed, the movie may be considered a direct take-off of *Don Juan*, for whole scenes are taken directly from Byron's poem—Juan's adulterous affairs with Donna Julia, for instance.

Clearly, *Don Juan DeMarco* has its literary roots in Byron's *Don Juan*—the epitome of the mock epic in the nineteenth century. Always in a funny way, it mimics a literary genre—the epic itself—which is precisely what Byron's long poem aims at. *Don Juan* is based on the fictional Spanish conqueror of women immortalized in Mozart's *Don Giovanni*. (Brando's character is seen playing the opera on his stereo at a certain point, like a genuine Mozart aficionado.) In contrast to both Byron and Mozart, however, this movie's modern Don Juan is presented positively, as a rather innocent youth who fantasizes about love, and not as the notorious rake of the eighteenth century, who (in Mozart) is dragged down to hell, or as the amoral Juan of Byron, a complex individual who is the victim of circumstances (his mother's upbringing), rather than a victimizer of women. Leven's movie calls for a "return" to romanticism, if you will, a state of mind that has been suppressed by Western civilization (and its psychiatrists) as a dangerous delusion.

The fact that the story does not take itself too seriously argues in its favor. Marlon Brando plays a psychiatrist, Don Mickler, whose career had been brilliant in the past thirty years, but whose time has come to quit. When the movie opens, he is ten days from his retirement. But just then, a delusional case comes to his attention. An emergency crew is trying to dissuade a young man dressed in an eighteenth-century costume from jumping to his death, and Mickler is called to help. The young man (DeMarco) takes Mickler to be one of his relatives who lived in the eighteenth century, calling him Don Ottavio De Flores. Mickler goes along with his young patient's fantasies, intrigued by the story he hears during the ensuing sessions. DeMarco vividly—and cinematically through imagined flashbacks—tells how from his earliest childhood years he felt an irresistible urge to love women. His father had come to Mexico, where the imagined action he relates took place, on a business trip and met his mother, fought another man for her, and was killed in a duel. DeMarco was brought up by his mother, and during his adolescence, he falls in love with Donna Julia, a young woman of twenty-three, married to a middle-aged man whose name is Don Alfonzo; the latter catches the two lovers in bed, forcing Juan to flee and Julia to retreat to a monastery. The story here of course follows almost verbatim the Byronic poem—and the viewer realizes that the young man's madness has its roots in the reading of that poem. Many other adventures follow, including DeMarco's shipwreck and his capture and enslavement by a beautiful sultana, who forces him to her bed everyday and to provide his libidinal services to her entire harem consisting of fifteen hundred young women. That is all before DeMarco meets his true love, Donna Anna, in a desert island, Eros. These are substitutes for the Heidi of Byron, whose hero meets her on a Greek island. With some variations in name and theme, this part of the story/fantasy follows Byron's tale fairly literally.

Thus, the plot unfolds on both levels. The delusional youth tells his fantasy in such a passionate manner that even the jaded psychiatrist is impressed—to the point that he begins not only to admire the young man's inventiveness but also to renew his courtship of his own aging spouse (Dunaway). Mickler, of course, knows that the young man must be cured, and that the most practical and efficient way of doing this is by administering prescription medication to his patient. But by doing that he would lose the original character that the illness itself had created. He is so deeply affected by the youth's story that he begins lifting weights and taking his wife to candlelight dinners—also playing Mozart. Nevertheless, administer the medicine he must, having run out of time and facing his boss's intransigence. So DeMarco takes the pill, and a day or two later, during a hearing, now without his fanciful costume and in his normal Queens accent, he tells the tale of a youth who lost his father in a car accident, who lost his mother to a Mexican monastery, and who lived a shiftless life trying to court a magazine model. The judge pronounces him sane ("we all have fantasies now and then") and releases him, over the protests of the hospital staff. The three (Mickler, his wife, and DeMarco) take off for the island of Eros, where DeMarco again meets Donna Anna, with whom he reconciles. Brando and Dunaway dance on the beach. The psychiatrist is cured of his modern neurosis, a result of forgetting romanticism or relegating it to a disease.

The movie's appeal is partly due to its lack of pretension. Had it been a serious, overblown effort, as so many movies have been, its message would have been diluted. Its lightheartedness is what makes Don Juan DeMarco a bona fide minor delight. It is also a movie that recognizes its sources; the writers know both Byron and Mozart and succeed in reviving the message, renewing it while avoiding the darker and more sinister traits of its hero. The modern Don Juan is not headed for hell but for the island of Eros—the place where feelings flourish instead of being suppressed by psychoanalysis and razed by medicine. Modern man is sick, precisely because he has lost the capacity to imagine himself larger than what he really is. He (and she, presumably) is afraid of feelings. Hampered by the political correctness of the times, he cannot be rid of his fear that he might offend the other sex. Here DeMarco's modern innocence and loss serve him well in that crisis of nomenclature. Romanticism itself seems out of kilter, for it is weighed down by its excesses of the past, which promoted sexism, among other things; whereas a fantasy, a hyperbolic dimension of the male, which gnaws at his self-esteem, is considered an illness and is treated until it is eradicated. The female suffers as much, for the male persona, which today has been reduced by woman's struggle for sexual liberation, deprives her of this exaggerated worship. Exactly the opposite effect is achieved though, for both male and female are deprived of the ability to imagine themselves in any other way but the most pedestrian. The joys of the capacity of fantasizing gone, both man and woman remain captives of the psychiatrist, who strives to put excessively active imaginations back to the small cosmos of mundane reality.

O Brother, Where Art Thou? (2000);
Directors/Writers: Joel Coen and Ethan Coen

This episodic tale is told with elaborate symbolism and allegorical imagery, and entertains ambitions of being a literary work, resembling and reestablishing the form of the mock epic. Three members of a chain gang, played by George Clooney, John Turturro, and Tim Blake Nelson, escape and embark on a series of adventures that the directors want us to believe resemble the adventures of Odysseus in Homer's *The Odyssey*. In fact, the opening credits tell us that the story is based on that great classic, but the characters have, of course, been changed to resonate with a modern audience, and the added satirical elements point to modern-day ills. Clooney plays Ulysses, and Penelope (Holly Hunter) appears at the end of his adventures, waiting—or rather not waiting, for she has a suitor in the wings—with several female children, whose father has of course been in jail and is now a wanderer. The three men are a nondescript group of no great intellectual or moral compass, except of course for Ulysses, who possesses cunning that equals that of his famous literary predecessor, but also a few degrading qualities, such as a tendency to escape danger rather than confront it, and a sort of obtuseness that keeps him in the dumps. He and Pete (Turturro) vie for leadership, asking Delmar (Nelson) to break the tie in voting, but the latter answers that he likes them equally.

With no brains to speak of, no luck, hardly able to avoid the snags they constantly stumble into, they lead a deprived existence accelerated by the blighted conditions prevailing in the country at that time. This is the height of the Great Depression, and the southern region, Mississippi in particular, is the worst place to be. Once they free themselves from their chains, they don't know exactly what to do except for vaguely desiring to find a "treasure" hidden someplace the film never tells us. They encounter a young black, an aspiring musician, give him a lift, and end up at some "recording studio" run by a blind man, and, pretending they are singers, they cut a record that has the potential of becoming a hit. After many adventures, which include a bank heist and an attempted lynching of the black musician by a KKK mob in a masked ceremony, their success in singing surfaces and they become an overnight sensation during a country-singing contest. The ending is not as happy as in *The Odyssey*, for the Penelope in the movie is not as loyal as she is in the poem, and, despite a reunion, friction is in the works for Ulysses—but home is home, and having a wife and children is better than aimless wanderlust.

The film also features John Goodman as a brutally large, one-eyed Cyclops, who is in actuality a Bible-toting fraud, much like one of the characters in Mark Twain's *Huckleberry Finn* (the King comes to mind). Goodman robs the three vagrants of the fortune they ran into after the bank heist, beats them up, and escapes with the money. Of course, he is also totally corrupt and, as a member of the Klan, participates in the lynching. Charles Durning is a corrupt governor (like King Aeolos in *The Odyssey*), but favorably disposed to the three fugitives, after their success at in the singing contest. Holly Hunter as Penelope brings her female counterpart into modernity by suggesting she won't wait for even one year for a derelict, down-on-his-luck convict, let alone twenty, as Homer's Penelope did. She even has agreed to marry one of the suitors, a conceited and ungainly wretch but who defeats Ulysses in a pugilistic contest.

The film is more in line with Rabelais's *Pantagruel*[16] (1532), rather than with Homer's epic, but in a pinch it will do as a mock epic. The movie, a vintage Coen Brothers product, combines farcical low-life elements (like the antics of the Three Stooges), a sharply edged social satire, never quite serious though occasionally poignant, but unmistakably revelatory of its real intentions: to show the American South as an odd mixture of bigotry, compassion, apathy, ignorance, innocence (as in the black musician), and eccentricity, with even a streak of reason making its appearance now and then. The South is a blighted hellhole, punished for its sins, separate from the rest of the universe, existing on its own terms, abandoned by man but never quite by the gods, finding solace in expressing its extemporaneously composed songs, possessed by and possessing a bubbling, irrepressible will to survive (as that exhibited in Homer's Odyseus), and to be humane despite centuries of poisonous racism. There is a catharsis at the end (or near it), when the three companions are finally caught by the area's greatest bigot and are about to be hanged. A prayer uttered by Ulysses saves them, in the form of a flood—local authorities are flooding the valley to create new lakes—and that episode not only saves the three but also adds a biblical tone to the story. Perhaps the American South portrayed by this film in general needs a flood to wash away its misdeeds, and a flood is what the filmmakers choose as the means of Ulysses' final release from his bondage. The movie, somewhat handicapped by its own subject matter (bigotry and hatred), chooses not to take a cynical angle, avoiding violence (a modern staple in "hatred" films) for its own sake, and espouses a rather good-natured resolution.

The similarities with *The Odyssey*, somewhat submerged by the modern settings, characters, and concerns, do exist: in *The Odyssey*, too, the gods intervene in human affairs, after everything else is lost and humans stumble into self-inflicted falls. In *The Odyssey*, the greatest evils come from man's own stupidity. Odysseus, cagey when confronting the Cyclops, blinding him and escaping, is vain enough—and foolish enough—to reveal his identity to him, thus provoking the wrath of Poseidon and delaying his own return. Odysseus is vain, overconfident, arrogant, and too self-reliant. Ulysses (of the Coens) is by contrast a study in ineptitude. He lacks foresight and lacks cageyness, allowing a con man to beat him and steal his money. The story hurls barbs at the ethos of the Depression era, the time in which it is set. Classical erudition gives it an aura of literacy, a cleverness that the stereotypical Hollywood comedies do not manage to garner.

Spoofs

The Producers (1968); Director/Writer: Mel Brooks

The Producers, featuring Zero Mostel as Max Bialystock, Gene Wilder as Leo Bloom, and Dick Shawn as Lorenzo St. DuBois, is one of the most astonishing spoofs of the American ethos of "success at all costs," here savagely reversed as "fail at all costs." Portraits of con men abound in American literature and film, but none obtained the gusto and nihilism of those of Mel Brooks, especially as he lines up three of the funniest men in American screen—Mostel, Wilder, Shawn—all frantic clowns with an aptness for reducing an acceptable premise to absolute absurdity. The ethos of overriding success is mocked, destroyed, and torn to pieces. How does one succeed, meaning cheating on one's taxes, not to mention conning old ladies? Raise money, put on the worst show ever on Broadway, fail the same night, then take, not the proceeds, but the capital itself and flee the country. It does not work, because the show—with Shawn as Hitler—is hilarious, to say the least. The audience, initially offended by the idea, is leaving the theater, but turn back as soon as Hitler appears. Hitler had not been spoofed so savagely since the days of Chaplin's Hynkel. But Dick Shawn has an added advantage; as his character is nicknamed L. S. D., he assumes the identity of a nearly apoplectic (or epileptic) hallucinatory persona, known in those days when taking acid was much in vogue. Remade in 2005, the later *Producers* does not have the same zest or comic drive.

Blazing Saddles (1974); Director/Coauthor: Mel Brooks

Blazing Saddles is a spoof of the American western and its assortment of gun-slinger heroes, already well into its demise in the late seventies. Generations of westerns made in Hollywood brought about a stereotypical view of history of the nineteenth-century American West, and thus a false, but highly bank-able, view of what the country was at that time. The western epics promoted an exaggerated image of the hero, most of which was the invention of Holly-wood, but, as the age of realism approached at the end of the 1960s, the west-ern underwent the same transformation as other epics did and the result was the genesis of the western spoof. In *Blazing Saddles*, Mel Brooks, who is the coauthor of the script with comedian Richard Pryor, attempts to abolish the myth of the hero, the John Wayne/Gary Cooper persona in particular, men remembered as defenders of the townsfolk in *High Noon* (1952), *Rio Bravo* (1958), *The Man Who Shot Liberty Valance* (1962), and in numerous other westerns. These men appeared as brave, noble minded, selfless, and larger than life. Instead, Brooks surreptitiously inserts an unorthodox persona as the leader of the group, someone whom the group first rejects, for he is a black man who has barely escaped lynching. But he leads the town bravely—al-though comically—as well as any white man, though his deputy is an non-descript type, a formerly fast gun, now an inept drunk, known as the "Waco Kid," played by Gene Wilder, whose deconstruction of film personas (as in *Young Frankenstein*, for instance) is only second to Woody Allen's.

A spoof, as noted, is another name for a mock epic, but this movie is also a satire, and, of course, all these nomenclatures signify the same genre—one satirizes, mocks, or spoofs a past genre, celebrating its death, decon-structs it, and blows up its reputation. But the mock epic/spoof is not just about genre killing; it has a function, which is built into its contemporary mindset, to mock and satirize and cut down not only the past but also, and perhaps mainly, the present. The term "mock epic" signifies a literary de-rivative; that is, one genre overlaps, repeats, or attacks—or all three—the other. A "spoof," the other term applied to this film, is the same repetition, but it relies on gags to carry its day. Satire is a more serious genre, for un-derneath its malicious exterior the author, or screenwriter, intends to un-cover some social ill, expose it to wide public scrutiny, with the covert aim to correct such a social ill. The mock epic has practically the same aims, except that it has a target—the epic and its overblown concept of the reality it purports to present. In several generations of the filmmaking of westerns, sheriffs and U.S. marshals were the good guys, cattle barons and their hired army of gunslingers were the bad guys. Indians attacked the good guys—those family-oriented folks that drove west in their wagon trains—and they most often were cast as villains. The early westerns showed a bigoted America, though some of the greatest icons of Hollywood—John Wayne, Gary Cooper, Jimmy Stewart—were undoubtedly cast as good guys. The western epics—and many qualify for that title because of their length and action-packed sequences—set up this exaggerated image of the hero, most of which was the invention of Hollywood. The spoof undermined those noble personas and perhaps aided in the demise of the western, which had held sway for decades in the minds of mainstream audiences. What the covert aim of a spoof might be is not known, but cutting down or pulverizing an idol might be fun enough.

Pirates of the Caribbean: The Curse of the Black Pearl (2003); Director: Gore Verbinski

Produced by Jerry Bruckheimer, *Pirates* is a modern comic epic, or spoof, of the Disney World extravaganzas at their theme parks in Florida and California. It nonetheless contains all the elements of the blockbuster epic movie one is accustomed to seeing from Jerry Bruckheimer. Sets, costumes, action sequences—and the acting of the principals—all fit the category of entertainment for large mainstream audiences, especially those in pursuit of pure escapism, with not an ounce of thought-provoking material around—and none is needed. *Pirates* features Johnny Depp as Jack Sparrow, Orlando Bloom as Will Turner, Keira Knightley as Elizabeth Swann, and the latter's lover, and Geoffrey Rush as Captain Barbossa, a grotesque villain. This is also a spoof of the "pirate epic," frequent in the golden days of Hollywood studios—with Errol Flynn, Gene Kelly, and Burt Lancaster as the usual heroes. The genre pirate/costume epic, or swashbuckler, was given up around the end of the 1950s, because it was too expensive to produce. Today, thanks to digital photography, animation, and special effects movies are not only much cheaper to produce but also almost believable—to the extent that one has to "suspend disbelief" altogether. However, this being a project undertaken by Bruckheimer, the modern master of disaster epics, *Pirates* is made on a grand scale, with massive construction projects, meticulous research into seventeenth-century weapons and costumes, and shooting on location in the Caribbean. To the surprise of everyone, perhaps because of its star-studded cast, it became a blockbuster at both levels—a swashbuckling adventure and also its own spoof.

Casanova (2005); Director: Lasse Hallström

Casanova is a spoof of manners and mores of an earlier era as well as our own. It dwells on a sensitive subject—sexism—perhaps not the greatest of crimes but one that can sink an insensitive movie, one in which the story-teller must offer rebuttals, deconstruct characters, while in need of balancing antithetical viewpoints that the political correctness climate of our own time requires. Today, the Casanova persona is damned on all sides, for history has already pronounced its verdict on him and his like, remembering him as an unscrupulous rake that made the rounds of European capitals with no other goal in mind than the satisfaction of his sexual drives. Of course, none of that is that simple.

Giacomo Casanova (1725–1798), a low-class, Venetian-born adventurer, had considerable talents, managing to become an abbé, a soldier, a diplomat, a violinist, a free mason, a magician, an inventor (he invented the lottery), a spy, and a writer of several voluminous books, including his famous auto-biography, *Histoire de ma vie* (*Story of My Life*), which, among other things, describes his uncanny capacity for survival (he boasts of a spectacular escape from a Venetian prison—à la Count of Monte Cristo), and his daring spirit of adventure. Had he not been branded as a devil for his sexual exploits, he would have been called a hero by virtue of his not insignificant accomplishments in so many spheres. He was an adventurer, neither better nor worse than countless others who roamed throughout Europe reaping whatever rewards their reckless nature could win. But history simply cannot blunder by giving him good points, and, although he is not quite Hitler or Attila the Hun, he is seen as a bad guy who deserves no historical clemency.

Director Lasse Hallström is of course not the first filmmaker to broach the subject. Several versions of Casanova's life have been brought to the screen, including a farce with Bob Hope, *Casanova's Big Night* (1954), amusing and harmless, and *Casanova & Co.* (1976), with Tony Curtis. The only serious treatment on the subject, *Fellini's Casanova* (1976), with Donald Sutherland, is an attempt to make Casanova an existential hero, despairing and devoid of all human feeling, whose hell is his inner emptiness. Hallström's hero (Heath Ledger) is nothing more than a fluffy rake, unscrupulous, dashing, and amoral, but one who learns a lesson—from a female—and changes his tactics if not his ethos, and flees peril with the girl he loves at his side. The girl, of course, provides the movie's counterpoint: Francesca (Sienna Miller), an impecunious Venetian young lady whose mother (Lena Olin) has set her sights on a rich suitor, displays an independent spirit and a ferocious dedication to the cause of liberating women. She has a talent for writing that has brought distinction, and controversy, for she writes under the masculine nom de plume Bernardo Guardi. Often, in disguise, she lectures at the university, showing her considerable intellect, castigating the universal bias of her day—that a woman's place is in the home and that women cannot match men in intellect. The amazed Casanova, being pursued by the Inquisition for having seduced a nun, happens to witness one of her speeches, and he is instantly impressed by the realization that not all women are hapless objects of pleasure. He is even more impressed when he finds her a staunch opponent in a sword fight, taking the part of her brother who had foolishly challenged him. Casanova is in dire straits, as the doge, who has saved him from execution, has set limits to his activities forcing him to choose a respectable bride, Victoria (Natalie Dormer), who happens to be the object of attention of young Giovanni (Charlie Fox), Francesca's brother. Meanwhile, an inquisitor, Bishop Pucci (Jeremy Irons), a wicked, degenerate buffoon, arrives from Rome to apprehend heretics. Casanova is caught and is about to be put to death, when his mother arrives with her husband, a sideshow comedian, who pretends to be a cardinal dispatched by the Pope to pardon all those about to be executed on his birthday. Meanwhile, Francesca's mother, desperate for her daughter's match with a wealthy suitor, a lard merchant, Paprizzio (Oliver Platt), who arrived from Genoa, is about to marry him herself, and Francesca, discovering Casanova's identity but also his metamorphosis into a true lover, chooses to leave with him, and they all manage to escape in Paprizzio's boat. Her brother, Giovanni, however, remains behind, and, since nobody has truly identified Casanova, he marries Victoria, but assumes Casanova's identity, continuing his sexual exploits—just as Victoria, a predator herself, will continue to go after males of her choice. This switch is a convenient device, for the actual identity of the rake remains in doubt, and the older person who is shown writing his memoirs at the end is not clearly identified.

Casanova has won our sympathies, switches to a loyal husband, and Francesca of Venice remains loyal to her true principles, that a man and a woman should unite in love—not lust, which she delegates to beasts. Words float around in this farcical tale, amusing barbs as much thrust against lard merchants as degenerate bishops, corrupt inquisitors, and the like, while our hero escapes with the girl. The movie can be considered a light satire, aiming at those in high places, who can be seen as far worse and much more unscrupulous than a mere rake/lover who regenerates, as his inamorata is a paragon of intellect and beauty, a woman ahead of her times, but also a woman in love. She despises what he represents but loves the actual man, whom she finds not only physically attractive but superior to the corrupt environment of bishops, inquisitors, mayors (the doge was that), or other officials and servants, not to say the denizens of nunneries—to whom she proves superior not only in intellect but in morals. She falls for the rake, not because she reforms him, but because, like her, he is a philosopher, and, if need be, a monogamist. Checks and balances—the pith of this tale—work not only in government, but also in marriage. Modernizing Casanova is like an athletic feat of historical proportions, an act of reminiscence with a twist, but why not? Others have done that before when convenient, or amusing. It does not matter that the film has to mock the Catholic Church and the administrators of Venice to restore Casanova to respectability. It might be hubris in reverse.

Comic Strip Epics

The Raiders of the Lost Ark (1981); Director: Steven Spielberg

With *The Raiders of the Lost Ark*, Steven Spielberg, in collaboration with George Lucas, brings back the epic hero, this time in the form of a daredevil who goes out of his way to perform certain exploits in the service of his country, or to free humanity of some impending disaster. *Raiders* was so popular that it was followed by two sequels, all featuring the same hero, Indiana Jones (Harrison Ford), a seemingly innocuous archaeology professor who embarks on fantasy adventures that involve rescuing some valuable relic, such as the Holy Grail or the tabernacle, or other sacred item, from villains intent on acquiring these items as means of dominating the world. Jones shows his toughness, craftiness, and daredevil nature by venturing into snake pits and rat-infested sewers, dodging bullets, shooting bullies, and, if he has to, driving an armored car onto a precipice while battling vicious Nazis and glamorous but treacherous women. Audiences in the early 1980s, when the country was still in the middle of the throes of the Cold War, could appreciate a cartoonlike hero who single-handedly defeated an assortment of villains in quick succession. This hero, however, is a conscious transfer to older times—the fight against the Nazis—and not the Soviets or other conspirators of the Cold War era, a space already preempted by the Bond heroics.

Though simplistic in the concept of its hero, the movie is complex in its mythological associations, some derived from the Bible, others from medieval literature, though, on the surface, the action takes place in the contemporary world, when the Nazis had gained power and threatened humanity with domination. In a sense, *The Raiders of the Lost Ark* can stand on the allegorical level alone—for it is a battle of good against evil—but its solid historical and geographical basis gives it a sense of reality, almost believability; thus the movie works simultaneously on several levels.

Just like other comic-strip heroes already mentioned, the protagonist of *Raiders* has a double nature. Outwardly, he is a mild-mannered university professor, a doctor of archaeology, who seems less than enchanted—and almost torpid—as an everyday college teacher, bored with the tedium of lecturing archaeology to apathetic students. Underneath, though, he is simmering with a desire for exploration, and, when the opportunity arises, he embarks on various expeditions to collect ancient artifacts, some of which turn into harrowing adventures. Undaunted, he goes on a search for the tabernacle, the "ark," that in the Old Testament is described as containing the tablets that Moses obtained directly from God on Mt. Sinai. Though Jones's initial interest in the ark is at first purely archaeological, as soon as he is told by the U.S. government of the Nazis' interest in the West's most valuable traditional religious symbol, he agrees to find the ark first.

Jones's heroic archetypal dimensions are rooted in Hercules (physical prowess), Odysseus (mental agility), and a movie actor, Humphrey Bogart—whose tough persona he emulates admirably and precisely down to the fedora hat, adding a bullwhip and leather jacket for good measure. Jones is capable of dealing as many blows as he takes, outlasting, though often barely, his nastiest foes. Harrison Ford as Jones outshines most previous screen heroes, repeatedly eluding unimaginable perils, like climbing out of a snake pit and defeating a giant pugilist as he barely escapes decapitation by a moving plane propeller; and he survives being dragged behind a truck, like Hector behind the chariot of Achilles (in a reversal of roles). He is forced to kill a dozen foes in his righteous brawls, doing so without the overtly sarcastic asides of Bond, but on occasion, not less humorously. When a local swordsman—most of the action happens in Cairo, Egypt,—attempts to intimidate him by twirling his saber like a baton in the hands of an expert cheerleader, Jones coolly shoots him right on the spot—and all the swordsman's rehearsal tricks are in vain. In terms of sheer heroic daring-do, John Wayne, James Bond, and Clint Eastwood combined could not have done better. Jones is an amalgam of these personas—a summing up of an action hero's qualities that make him a potent and dynamic image for postmodern audiences. The fact that he remains a comic-strip creation is significant, for the audience can get its thrills and laughs without having to think seriously (or think at all). Daring and foolhardy, physically rugged, mentally nimble, lucky to the point of absurdity, and, most importantly, assisted by an equally hard-nosed female partner (Karen Allen, as Marion), Indiana Jones combines qualities that make him one of the most exciting screen heroes of the past several decades. Incidentally, the first name of the Jones character is actually Henry; he was nick-named "Indiana" after George Lucas's dog.

Indiana Jones and the Temple of Doom (1984);
Director: Steven Spielberg

Though *Indiana Jones and the Temple of Doom* retains most of the comic-strip qualities of *Raiders*, it has its own distinct characteristics. For one, it develops a darker, more edgy theme, pitting its hero against a horde of villains who command black magic with powers to exterminate Western civilization in its totality (if of course the hero does not intervene). *The Temple of Doom* shifts locales, from the Middle East to India, where Professor Indiana Jones helps an endangered tribe regain its most valuable totem—a magic stone dedicated to the god Shiva—which was stolen by a rival tribe that had conquered it and enslaved its children. As with *Raiders*, where the tribal totem was the ark, representing not only Jews, but Christians and Western cultures in general (including America), here the totem is an Eastern mystical symbol that empowers the tribe that owns it against its rivals, who in turn can dominate and crush every other culture in the world if they acquire all five of the stones. As the villain Mola Ram (Indian actor Amrish Puri) says, Muslims, Jews, and Christians will be exterminated by the Thuggees, who live at the Pankot Palace, ruled by a corrupt Maharaja, Chattar Lal (Roshan Seth), and already possess three of the Shiva stones. The West versus the East, incidentally, is a theme that has intrigued Western audiences since the era of colonialism. The Thuggees have now embarked on a search for the other two stones, deep in the cavities of the Temple of Doom, employing the children of Mayapore, the defeated tribe, whom they keep in chains. Jones (again played by Harrison Ford), who fled Shanghai after a brawl at a nightclub, arrives at Pankot Palace accompanied by a singer, Willie Scott (Kate Capshaw), and Short Round (Ke Huy Quan), a young boy who is his sidekick. With the aid of those two, and after incredible perils, Jones gets hold of one of the three stolen totem stones, brings it back to the Mayapore tribe, restoring their power and liberating the slave children.

Still retaining many the qualities of a "Saturday matinee serial," *Temple of Doom* is a darker story than *Raiders*, having the trio of saviors tested to the limit of human endurance, though Capshaw seems to be playing a decorative role and going along for the ride. But she, too, like the two others, must ride an elephant, cross a lagoon infested with alligators and snakes, and survive the torments of the palace, which includes having a meal where soup dishes of boiled sheep eyes, stuffed monkey heads, bug-filled custard pies, and snake bellies bursting with slithering tiny reptiles are served. Their descent to the palace's cavities resembles a trip to Hades, where Jones embarks on his quest of the stones, but he and his two companions are caught, tortured, and escape riding in a runaway mining car on rails through a tunnel. They cross a rope bridge, hang on to a vertical wall when it snaps, and are saved by the cavalry after Jones defeats Mola Ram, who plunges into the lagoon and is eaten by alligators. Thus, the redemption of the Mayapore tribe is achieved, thanks to a hero's intervention, though this was certainly not his tribe. We like to give a helping hand, the movie implies, when just people are oppressed and we the mighty can afford to do so.

Indiana Jones and the Last Crusade (1989); Director: Steven Spielberg
With the third Indiana Jones film Spielberg and Lucas once more turn to the theme of fighting the Nazis—something Spielberg will do again on a more serious note with _Schindler's List_. The totemic symbol this time is from the West as well, the West's most potent symbol, the Holy Grail (the cup of Christ), which the Nazis wish to obtain, for it is said that anyone who drinks from the Holy Grail will live for eternity. Three forces actually embark on a quest for the Holy Grail, which was passed on to Joseph of Arimathea by Jesus, was lost and found again during the time of King Arthur in the twelfth century (according to Arthurian legends), and has been since sought by a secret brotherhood centered in Venice; by Professor Henry Jones Sr., who happens to be Jones's father; and by the Nazis and their cohorts, Professor Walter Donovan (Julian Glover) and Dr. Elsa Schneider (Alison Doody).

Dr. Jones Sr., the father, played by Sean Connery with a Scottish accent ("It is better to be shafe than shorry!"), is ill matched to his not-much-younger, virile son, Indiana (who speaks a blatantly American accent), but the relationship is comic so these minor discrepancies don't seem to matter. Dr. Jones is an authority on the Grail and his quest is based on authentic documents; he has devised a diary with a map and instructions, and for that reason he is abducted by the Nazis. Indiana embarks on a pursuit, not of the Grail but of his father. He ends up in Venice, allies himself with Dr. Schneider, not knowing she is involved with the Nazis, and some comic mishaps occur in rat-infested tunnels and an obligatory boat chase in the Venice canals (scenes endlessly repeated in the James Bond movies). Soon, Indiana takes off for Castle Brunwald in Austria, where he finds his father and the two escape in a motorcycle chase; they end up in Hatay and proceed to the Canyon of the Crescent Moon, where the Grail is hidden. Indiana single-handedly defeats the Nazis who ride in the desert in a monstrous tank, which finally drops and smashes into a canyon; the Nazis are practically exterminated, but not Donovan, who, accompanied by Schneider, has followed a daring Indiana into the crevices of the Crescent Moon. Here we learn that Donovan pursues the chalice for himself—to attain personal immortality. To force Indiana to attempt to pass the three challenges needed to reach the Grail, Donovan shoots Dr. Jones, who can only be healed by drinking from the chalice. Through clever guesswork, Indiana solves the riddles, crosses a chasm, and finds himself in the chamber, where a knight-hermit has been waiting for him for seven hundred years! There are many cups there, and Indiana must choose the correct one. But Donovan, who has followed him with Schneider, picks the wrong one, drinks from it, and horribly disintegrates, turning to ashes in front of a terrified Schneider. Indiana picks the right one—a wooden cup, made by a carpenter—brings it back and heals his dying father; Schneider takes the cup and tries to leave, but the earth begins to shake and a great chasm opens in the floor. Schneider accidently drops the cup in the chasm and then she falls in while trying to reach for the cup. Indiana too tries to reach the cup, which landed on a ledge in the wall of the chasm, but is warned by his father that the cup is not to be had by humans. When asked what he has gained from the experience—the adventures, the quest—Jones Sr. utters, "illumination."

Suggested Films for Study

The Great Dictator (1941); director: Charlie Chaplin
Sullivan's Travels (1941); director: Preston Sturges
Casanova's Big Night (1954); director: Norman McLeod
One, Two, Three (1961); director: Billy Wilder
Dr. Strangelove (1963); director: Stanley Kubrick
Catch-22 (1970); director: Mike Nichols
MASH (1970); director: Robert Altman
Monty Python's Life of Brian (1979); director: Terry Jones
The Princess Bride (1987); director: Rob Reiner
Barton Fink (1991); director: Joel Coen
Deconstructing Harry (1997); director: Woody Allen
Spider-Man (2002); director: Sam Raimi
Superman Returns (2006); director: Bryan Singer
Epic Movie (2007); director: Jason Friedberg

Notes

1. *The Golden Ass* by Apuleius, a Roman author of the second century AD, is an example.

2. Witness the comedies of Aristophanes.

3. In his preface to his play *Pygmalion*, Shaw states, "it [*Pygmalion*] is so intensely and deliberately didactic, and its subject is esteemed so dry, that I delight in throwing at the heads of the wiseacres who repeat the parrot cry that art should never be didactic. It goes to prove my contention that art should never be anything else." George Bernard Shaw, *Pygmalion and Other Plays* (New York: Dodd, Mead, 1967), 6.

4. Aristotle, *The Poetics*, in Charles Kaplan and William Anderson, eds. *Criticism: Major Statements*, 3rd ed. (New York: St. Martin's, 1991), 25.

5. Aristotle, *The Poetics*, in Kaplan and Anderson, *Criticism: Major Statements*, 24.

6. "Aristodemus was only half awake, and he did not hear the beginning of the discourse; the chief thing which he remembered was Socrates compelling the other two to acknowledge that the genius of comedy was the same as that of tragedy, and that the true artist in tragedy was an artist in comedy also." Plato, *Symposium*, in *Dialogues of Plato*, edited with introductory notes by Justin D. Kaplan (New York: Washington Square Press, 1973), 234.

7. Aubrey Williams, ed., *Poetry and Prose of Alexander Pope* (Boston: Houghton Mifflin, 1969), 397.

8. Derived from the Greek word $\beta\alpha\theta o\varsigma$ (depth).

9. Here reference could be made to a first century AD, author Longinus, whose essay "Peri Ypsous" ("On the Sublime") influenced "exalted" language and thence had some effect on the pomposity of the eighteenth century that Pope ridicules.

10. In today's film world, the comedies (or parodies) of Joel and Ethan Coen are considered the modern version of a screwball comedy. See "The Mock Epic" section below.

11. A phrase attributed to the late Rodney Dangerfield, who achieved stardom playing middle-aged failures.

12. Discussed below.

13. T. S. Eliot, "The Love Song of J. Alfred Prufrock," in *The Complete Poems and Plays, 1909–1950* (New York: Harcourt, Brace & World, 1971), 5.

14. Not that Spencer was a stranger to comedy but screwball comedy, mostly with Katharine Hepburn, was his forte in that genre in the 1940s and 1950s.

15. Today, $350,000 would be worth approximately ten times more.

16. Son of Gargantua, a giant, and a man busy mocking Parisian aristocrats.

CHAPTER SEVEN

The Anti-Epic

The anti-epic film is a natural descendant of the classic epic and shares with it some of the usual characteristics—length, plot complications, spectacle—but it differs noticeably in the concept of its hero as well as in its narrative structure, which is more concerned with the inner thoughts of its characters and is more fragmented. In the modern and postmodern eras, which began in the early part of the twentieth century, the epic hero has often been transformed from the noble savior of his tribe and his cause (Moses, Ulysses, Spartacus) to a person who is alienated and often in conflict with communal interests. To use the common term, the hero has become the antihero, a term fraught with ambiguities, for the image of the antihero has crept into the literary form imperceptibly throughout the centuries and can even be traced back to antiquity. Just as the novel has become the antinovel, so the traditional hero has become the antihero.[1] And as the epic film has followed in the footsteps of the novel, the antihero crept into film almost imperceptibly, retaining, both in the formal sense and substantially, some of the characteristics of the hero. He or she, too, will undergo the rituals of initiation, as a distorted idea may take hold of him or her, maturation in the form of a plan to execute, and an assault against a community and its values he may have repudiated. In the frenzied moments of the attack, a holocaust may ensue and he or she may be engulfed in its flames. His or her most characteristic trait is alienation, from the smaller to the larger social unit (or vice versa)—from family, friends, workplace, local or larger community, or the world. Just as the hero defends the community, the antihero attacks it.

The antihero came into existence by a game of hide-and-seek. He has appeared during the classical era (in the plays of Euripides, for instance), during early modernity (during the Renaissance where traces of him are seen in Hamlet and Dr. Faustus), and during the nineteenth and early twentieth centuries when he took on a more distinct character in the works of Byron, Dostoyevsky, James Joyce, Thomas Mann, Andre Gide, and Albert Camus, and was developed even further in the works of later novelists, Saul Bellow, Gabriel Marquez Garcia, Michael Ondaatje, Milan Kundera, Salman Rushdie, and many others. As the reverse of the hero, the antihero has suffered iconic transformations, his persona has changed to the opposite of what it once was: Odysseus, the noble hero of Homer, becomes a villain in Euripides, Virgil, and Dante; and Satan, once one of the angels, is an archetypal destructive force in the Old Testament (the book of Job), a frozen demon in the pit of hell in Dante's *Inferno*, and a scheming fallen angel in Milton's *Paradise Lost*. In later literary works, he is the amoral Don Juan and Manfred of Byron, the deceiver Mephistopheles in Goethe, and the casuistic devil in Dostoyevsky. He could be an intellectual rebel, as is Stephen Daedalus in James Joyce, a weak pederast (though a noble man otherwise) in Gustav Aschenbach of Thomas Mann, and a depraved hedonist recanting his vileness, as in Humbert Humbert of Nabokov's *Lolita*, or an alienated persona in the novels of Kafka and Camus. The antihero has his female impersonation in the "anima" of Carl Jung, which can be traced in such literary figures as Shakespeare's Lady Macbeth, Keats's "La Belle Dame Sans Merci," Flaubert's Emma Bovary, and in D. H. Lawrence's Lady Chatterley, among others. Thus, the antihero, in male or female form, firmly established as a literary figure present throughout Western literature and continuing into the beginning of the twenty-first century, is now recognized broadly as an archetype but is also known in real life and in film. Epic antiheroes, male or female, could appear as cops, spies, revolutionaries, undercover agents, terrorists, mafia dons, drug kingpins, psychopaths, pedophiles, and an assortment of other deviant and antisocial types—excluding none, as long as some of the basic ingredients of the epic form are present and as long as their persona is placed within those contexts.

The Origins of the Modern Antihero

The antihero persona first finds its full expression in the underground man in Fyodor Dostoyevsky's novella, *Notes from Underground* (1864). Since then, the term "underground man" has reappeared in a variety of archetypal patterns, in the works of major novelists and filmmakers of the twentieth century—authors such as Andre Gide, Franz Kafka, T. S. Eliot, Thomas Mann, Ignazio Silone, Nikos Kazantzakis, Albert Camus, Alexandr Solzhenitsyn, Ralph Ellison, Saul Bellow, Gabriel Garcia Marquez, and in many other major and minor fiction writers of modern and contemporary times. Filmmakers, following the lead of novelists and theater of the absurd playwrights, soon came up with depictions of personas that conformed to the image of the underground person in its many transformations. A few examples will suffice, though one could cite many more: Fritz Lang's M (1931) portrays a pedophile murderer of children that has left a chilly imprint in cinematic history. American directors populated the screen with gangsters played by actors of star quality, Paul Muni in *Scarface* (1932), Edward G. Robinson in *Little Caesar* (1930), James Cagney in *The Public Enemy* (1931), and Humphrey Bogart in a series of roles as a gangster in the late 1930s and as cynical private eye Sam Spade in *The Maltese Falcon* (1941). Many directors picked up these patterns portraying villains or dark characters: Charlie Chaplin in *Monsieur Verdoux* (1947), Billy Wilder in *Double Indemnity* (1944), Carol Reed in *The Third Man* (1946), John Frankenheimer in *The Manchurian Candidate* (1962), Arthur Penn in *Bonnie and Clyde* (1969), Francis Ford Coppola in *Apocalypse Now* (1979), and in more recent times Woody Allen in *Crimes and Misdemeanors* (1989), Stanley Kubrick in *Full Metal Jacket* (1987), Martin Scorsese in *Taxi Driver* (1976), *Raging Bull* (1980), *The Last Temptation of Christ* (1988), and *Gangs of New York* (2002), Ridley Scott in *Thelma and Louise* (1991), and Ron Howard in *A Beautiful Mind* (2001)—and the list of films with antiheroes (or underground types, male or female) goes on.

Dostoyevsky himself said that the underground man is not merely a character in fiction but that he exists in society among us.[2] In real life the underground person has made his/her appearance in the form of a terrorist, provocateur, religious fanatic, an underground resistance fighter during the Nazi occupation of Europe (in this case having a positive image), in underground organizations such as the Weathermen during the Vietnam War, as a serial killer such as Ted Bundy,[3] a mass killer such as the Oklahoma City bomber Timothy McVeigh, a distance bomber such as Theodore Kaczynski (the Unabomber), a persecuted author such as Salman Rushdie, or a leader of an underground organization such as Osama Bin Laden, and even a former leader of a country literally hiding "underground," as in the case of Saddam Hussein, captured on December 13, 2003, while hiding in a hole. Many real-life underground men and women have become the objects of fiction or films. An alienated boxer (prizefighter), like Jake

LaMotta, became the object of the film *Raging Bull*, by Martin Scorsese. The defeat of Mike Tyson (June 8, 2002) by Lennox Louis prompted some sports commentators to brand him the "antihero of boxing"—Tyson's life and career having been perceived as self-destructive and his temperament as vindictive of his opponents.

The lines of demarcation between hero and antihero (or underground man) have not always been clear. Some real life persons who have become subjects of epic movies (George Patton, T. E. Lawrence) are men with true heroic qualities (bravery, for instance) together with fatal flaws that lead to their demotion in rank, public renunciation, obscurity, or self-flagellation. The inference is that the underground person is not always vicious but may share the benign qualities of the normal person, though through a single negative quality he may be removed from the masses; or to put it conversely, the normal everyday person sometimes shares some of the underground man's or woman's underground characteristics. By and large, however, and within the compass of slightly divergent lines, the story of the underground man is the story of alienation in the twentieth century, starting out with the premises that Dostoyevsky (and those who followed his path, Gide, Camus, Sartre, and from filmmakers, Kurosawa, Jean-Luc Godard, Scorsese) laid out in his famous novella, which guides us in the understanding of a character in fiction and film (as in life) whose drama is still unfolding.

Characteristics of the Underground Man

If one follows Dostoyevsky's *Notes from Underground* as a starting point in a discussion, one recognizes the main characteristics of the underground man as follows: self-hatred, vanity, conceit (a put-on), fear of insignificance, strong tendency to fantasize, striking back (being spiteful), possessing acute consciousness (a modern disease), hysteria, irrationality, fear of rationality, fear of science, fear of utopias (the Crystal Palace), refusal to be an object (an organ stop), refusal to be happy (prefers to suffer), freedom of choice, and wearing a mask (hiding underground). Underground does not always imply shackles, imprisonment, captivity, or physical separation and violence; being underground can be an entirely psychological condition (as in Kafka's Gregor Samsa in "Metamorphosis"). Someone suffering internal woes in isolation, resentful and vindictive, will harbor evil designs and plans to strike back, something that may not always be expressed as a physical act. Striking back can be entirely a verbal assault, and a negative piece of writing such as the "book" published by the Unabomber[4] can be an attack on real or imagined foes.

The most prominent characteristics of the underground man are his desire for freedom, his tendency to hide behind a mask, and his vindictive desire to strike back. The first is philosophical; the last two are psychological and responsible for his methods and motivations. The mask ("persona" in Jungian terms) is his most identifiable characteristic. The mask is a most elusive concept, for one can be entirely bare faced and still wear a mask. Every underground person wears a mask behind which the real person hides. Psychologically, the mask serves as a protective shield, behind which the underground person feels safer, and as a means of disguise, through which the underground man or woman achieves some of his or her objectives. A mask can conceal fear, anxiety, paranoia, and frustration; it can also conceal a design to harm. A mask can deceive and disguise guilt or a sense of inferiority; a mask can be a means to entrap. It is useful to study the use of a mask by characters in films that belong to this category and see the various metamorphoses the person behind the mask (and the mask itself) undergoes.

As for freedom (a much-used existential term), Dostoyevsky's underground man prefers freedom to conformity, even if freedom means cause for suffering. The Russian existentialist Nikolai Berdyaev examines this idea in Dostoyevsky, borrowing St. Augustine's terms, *libertas major* and *libertas minor*, freedom to seek God and to do good, and freedom in any other sense, including the freedom to do evil.[5] In a democratic society both freedoms should be allowed, leaving it to the individual to be an evildoer or virtuous. It is a characteristic of the underground man's descendant in the twentieth and twenty-first centuries—the antihero—that he has chosen *libertas minor* in that definition; generally he acts alone, rejects authority, prefers isolation to company or the group, or joins a group that is more or less allied to his own ideology. Paranoia germinates from that distorted concept of freedom.

The tendency to wear a mask has also been accelerated by the accessibility of modern technology that allows, for instance, a terrorist to elude the pursuing authority agents (FBI, CIA). False documents, plastic surgery (*Fight Club*, 1999), networking secretly inside a country (Al Qaeda), the Internet and its infinite disguises (e-mail, blogs, insidious viruses, for instance)—all these, and others—are means to escape or attract attention and to achieve difficult to achieve underground missions under normal circumstances. The mask conceals the desire to harm, especially in societies that are perceived as normal, progressive, democratic, wealthy, and on the path of peace. The same is true on an individual basis: if a modern underground man feels resentful and embittered because of his failure to be loved, he designs evil plans to destroy his opponents through assassination—though his motives are usually too complex to be pinned down exactly.

Characteristics of the Anti-Epic

The anti-epic film is recognized by various characteristics of form and content. The form of a film, influenced by the modernist and postmodernist movements, may be more fragmented and episodic than a traditional narrative; it may even call attention to itself through various techniques, such as characters speaking directly to the camera. The themes will likely be mundane, pessimistic, or even violent, the language common, and the endings often unhappy or even cruel. Cult classics (*Rosemary's Baby*, 1968), or "cult epics" (*The Beast*, 1975) can often be included in this category. Most of these films lack an optimistic outlook, as well as a likeable epic hero who is the leader—rather than the antagonist—of the tribe. Sci-fi thrillers (*Alphaville*, 1965; *Blade Runner*, 1982; *Dark City*, 1998), and futuristic or episodic films (*Matrix*, 1999; *Minority Report*, 2002) may be included in this (and also another) category,[6] for they all share in their conception of the antihero, or hero hunted down by evil aliens or other agents originating from a number of "darker" formats, although it might be far-fetched to characterize all the species spawned by the underground theme as epics. In the most formal sense, the anti-epic plot contains recognition and reversal scenes, as does the tragic genre. Plotwise, both epic and tragedy are moving along the same lines, allowing for the essential differences of length and the preponderance of spectacle in the classic epic. Cinematically speaking, the anti-epic uses plot techniques similar to those used by other epics or dramas, except for the endings. It also prefers such techniques as montage for quick editing, fish lenses to achieve special effects, rapid pacing, and is photographed in chiaroscuro and other color variations matching darkness of theme, as in *The Godfather* and with occasional black-and-white shooting, as in *Schindler's List*. Sets are always innovative and draw from sci-fi adventures such as in *Sin City* (2005).[7]

Modern Epics with Antiheroes or Underground Personas

The Day of the Jackal (1973); Director: Fred Zinnemann
The Day of the Jackal (*TDOTJ*) is as timely today as it was at the time it was made, for one could easily rename it "The Day of the Terrorist." In the aftermath of 9/11, which is engraved in the national consciousness as perhaps the most important event of the new century, the terrorist in film must be seen as one of the variant types of the underground man. Of paramount importance is the understanding of the workings of the mind of such a person as described in literature and film, and if the underground man definition pro-

vides a point of departure, it could be useful to follow this line of thinking. Generally, terrorists have a goal, make plans, and set out to execute the plans with meticulous preparation. Even though some of them may be thought of as psychopaths, mad, criminal, or devoid of conscience or morals, many of them still operate within a perfectly rational framework, behaving normally (though hidden under a mask), and they possess cunning, the ability to plot, and in many cases extraordinary skills, such as martial arts, that enable them to face any opponent—single-handedly and as a group.

Such is the case with the hero (or antihero in our context) in *TDOTJ*, a movie made over thirty years ago that still resonates and perhaps sheds light on the question we ask here: What is the mindset of a criminal person such as a terrorist who sets out to do harm to a community and whose methods and motives are concealed in such a way that it is almost impossible to trace them? Do the methods of terrorists resemble each other, and is it possible to understand them in general terms through the example of one and thus deduce the possible methods of others like him? These questions—and any answers derived from any fiction—are entirely hypothetical, but it is worth exploring them, especially in a film such as *TDOTJ*, which is as compelling and worth viewing today as it was then. Directed by Fred Zinnemann, an Austria-born American director, whose credits include *High Noon* (1952), *From Here to Eternity* (1953), *Oklahoma!* (1955), and *A Man for All Seasons* (1966), the movie is an adaptation of the best-selling novel of the same title by Frederick Forsyth, which was based on an actual event, the attempted assassination of President Charles de Gaulle in 1963, an attempt that preceded the assassination of President Kennedy by only a few months. What is worth noticing in this film is its technique—the double point of view that allows the viewer to follow the terrorist's meticulous preparations, while on the other hand, crosscutting (and superb editing) allow the viewer to follow the equally compelling attempts of the English and French authorities to uncover and foil the plot.

There is some historical background to the story: When French president Charles De Gaulle granted independence to Algeria in 1963, extremists, mostly from the army, calling themselves the OAS, swore to kill him in revenge. A first attempt was made and 140 shots were fired in the space of seven seconds, but De Gaulle was saved as if by a miracle. Six months later, the conspirators were caught, tried, and their leader executed. Demoralized, the OAS retreated to Austria, where they sought the services of a contract killer to carry out the mission for them. After examining several "dossiers" of professional assassins, they finally opted for an Englishman who had done several jobs abroad, among which was the assassination of a

Caribbean dictator (Trujillo), just a few years before. The Englishman, nicknaming himself "the Jackal," agrees to do the job for them for a million dollars. Soon, however, the French Secret Service is on their heels, and it assigns to one of its best detectives, assistant commissioner of the French police, Claude LeBelle (Michel Lonsdale), the job of tracking down the Jackal. LeBelle and the Jackal (played by Edward Fox) engage in what seems a cat-and-mouse game, with the Jackal always a step ahead of his pursuer. The entire action is packed within a few weeks, from the end of July to the middle of August 1963, when the Jackal, eluding all the precautions taken by LeBelle, does actually succeed in taking a shot at De Gaulle during a ceremony, but again the president is saved, his head leaning forward as he pins a decoration on the chest of a war veteran, the bullet hitting the pavement harmlessly. But as the Jackal is preparing to take a second shot, LeBelle arrives just in time and kills him.

If the story illustrates anything, it shows how easy it is for a terrorist to hit his target, despite security measures that, in this case, amount to an all-out national emergency. The word "easy" is relative here and can be applied only to a terrorist/agent who has a clear goal, plans carefully, has alternative plans in place, anticipates methodically, acts unemotionally, and stays on course despite unforeseen drawbacks. The movie achieved precisely this effect. It shows that the terrorist does not need to be a fanatic himself but can be a hired instrument of those who wish to destroy a high-value target, in this case the president of a country. The fact that the members of OAS claim that they are "not terrorists" but "patriots" does not change the configuration, but makes the term "terrorist" relative, depending on one's point of view. In our day, the term is used to signify a killer who targets civilians, unable to hit the high-value target, although those are not excluded. A suicide bomber is the most common phenomenon, although terrorists who plan to get away, whether fanatics or professionals, are also common (Lee Harvey Oswald, John Wilkes Booth). Again, by following carefully and lucidly the killer's point of view, his step-by-step preparations, his detachment, his ability to kill with his hands only, *The Day of the Jackal* is a movie that pinpoints his mental process, the physical and psychological makeup of a person determined to kill in a methodical way regardless of motive. Speaking of motives, the Jackal's are only partly clear; for though he states he does the job for money, his actions show a certain vanity, and even pride in achieving something that a whole underground organization had failed to do, and which is practically a superhuman feat. This is not an ordinary man, as LeBelle grudgingly admits, not one "who makes many mistakes." This portrait is frighteningly negative, but Edward Fox, dapper and looking more like an English aristocrat than a terrorist, invests it with a certain aura of mystery and charm that leaves the viewer befuddled as to whether to root for the Jackal or hate his cold-hearted murderous spree. The objectivity and style (docudrama) of the movie leaves this question open, as in a morality play where the moral of the story is not stated. The Jackal's assured step, ability to foresee and forestall even the remotest obstacle in his path, and his "cool" under pressure leave the viewer unable to avoid a gasp of admiration, but also illustrates that a man both charming and ruthless is the most dangerous. In anticipation of identity changes, the Jackal prepares by obtaining four different IDs: Already having used and discarded a London man's passport (Charles Calthrop's—which ironically becomes Scotland Yard's first clue), he also obtains the name and identity of a dead man (Duggan), steals the passport of a Danish schoolteacher (Pere Lindquist), and has a forgery specialist (whom he murders) obtain the driver's license and ID of a French war veteran. He will use all of these at different phases of his "mission," but he will also need his ready wit and endless resourcefulness to cope with the various snags in his way. When he learns that his secret is blown, and still has a choice to turn back, he forges on, undeterred, thus gaining credit with the viewer for his courage. If anything, he is no coward. He kills, not as a psychopath does, but out of absolute necessity, yet without hesitation or scruple. In the end, he remains a mystery, both metaphorically and literally. For though an Englishman, he is denounced by his own countrymen ("He is not from these islands," declares one official who helped to uncover him), and he is buried in an unidentified grave, with LeBelle, his foe and admirer, as the lone attendant.

As stated, the movie is a morality play, one that fits our modern temper, told objectively, even clinically, without the usual accompaniment of patriotic hyperbole. The movie states that that is what a terrorist is—or can be: an emotionless machine, operating out of totally selfish motives—profit or pride, no matter. As the underground man, he is the image of complete and total alienation. He has no family, no ties, no friends, no identity (all he carries on him are false documents), no country (that will accept him), and no ideals. Ironically, he is not so far removed from Camus's Sisyphus, in *The Myth of Sisyphus*, for he is like a man who performs a singularly laborious task, only to repeat it, taking his satisfaction from just doing it, nothing else. Still, a morality play illustrates other themes, playing on other variables. One of them is the power game. Both the Jackal and LeBelle are involved in it. LeBelle says at the outset to his assistant (Derek Jacobi) that from this point on, "we can start by recognizing that outside of De Gaulle we are the two most powerful people in France." Though quietly, he manipulates the council of ministers, telling them he would appreciate it if they did things "his way," and he even wiretaps all their telephones. When he is dismissed, thus losing his power temporarily, he is hastily called back when the police fail to locate the Jackal, and then he regains his power until he has practically stopped the Jackal and saved De Gaulle. It can be guessed the Jackal plays his role for the same reason. A man whose assignment—even a professional one, and for money—is to assassinate the head of a country gains enormous power, and if that president is the head of the most powerful country in the world (as with the Kennedy assassination), the terrorist, insofar as he succeeds, becomes, temporarily, the most powerful agent on the planet. If an underground man's motive is vanity—as per the Dostoyevsky premise—then murder is his means of satisfying it.

Taxi Driver (1976); Director: Martin Scorsese

Martin Scorsese did for film what Dostoyevsky did for the novel: he defined the alienated character—his own version of the underground man. He was not the first to do so in film—but he has been the most consistent filmmaker to take on the dark subject of the antihero for decades (something that might have cost him an Oscar win, that is, until 2007 when he finally won for the first time for *The Departed*, for Americans love optimistic heroes). As mentioned, Fritz Lang's M portrays perhaps the first true underground hero in the movies, a hunted pedophile, but it was Scorsese's *Taxi Driver* that sketched the antihero's persona in full regalia for the first time, establishing the model of alienation as an indelible entity in American and world cinema. A string of such heroes in the Scorsese canon followed, real and fictional—Jake LeMotta, Jesus Christ, Tommy DeVito, Max Cady, Frank Pierce, Bill the Butcher, and Howard Hughes, all bearing underground characteristics, and most of them framed within the epic mode. Of course, *Taxi Driver* is not an epic in the classic sense, but it is arguably the truest specimen of the "underground epic" whose hero displays most of the characteristics of the underground man. Travis Bickle lives at the margin, harboring a huge resentment that soon becomes the catalyst for his actions, prompting him to retaliate against the social milieu he finds himself in. Seething with hatred and unable to adjust to his environment, he makes a crucial decision to strike back, arming himself to pursue his goal, wearing a mask that both serves as a disguise and reveals his psychological transformation. Pauline Kael describes Martin Scorsese as "the director to define the American underground man's resentment," and *Taxi Driver* as "a movie in heat, a tabloid version of *Notes from Underground*,"[8] remarks not far removed from the main philosophical premises laid out in the Dostoyevsky novella. Travis Bickle (Robert De Niro), tormented by insomnia, takes up a nighttime taxi-driver's job as a means of escape, but, ironically, this means of escape imprisons him even further. His cab becomes his own trap, for he is compelled to practically live in it, cleaning up the "blood and semen" every morning, tormented by witnessing scenes of the hell around him. His revolt is an attempt to regain his freedom, the *libertas minor* of Berdayev, for he is incapable of understanding the other kind of freedom, *libertas major*, which would involve him in community action (surprisingly, an ironic reversal brings him back to the societal mold at the end of the film). His is an idiosyncratic, willful, self-defined, and self-sustaining freedom—like the freedom of thieves to steal, or of sexual predators to abduct children, or of criminals to kill. In his delirium of paranoia, which blinds him to a full understanding of freedom, he pursues the freedom of an alienated man, regardless of the boundaries of commonly perceived social behavior. As a Vietnam War veteran, he has some idea of discipline and work ethic, and he conforms to regulations as far as his practical duties in the taxi driving business are concerned. He works hard, saves his money for a "purpose," and gives vent to his fantasies by keeping a diary, which we hear in a voice-over, a practice that may be his liberating mechanism—the monologue of Dostoyevsky's *Notes from Underground*.

His disturbed inner world becomes apparent, however, as his resentment increases when he fails to win the girl he likes, though his desire for her is not the result of a normal sexual drive but of his fantasy, to "save" her from the corrupt environment she lives in. This is part of his idea of freedom, which he imagines as his right to "liberate" and dominate those around him who are captive to the same corrupt system. The chance arrives when he meets a girl, Betsy (Cybil Sheppard), working at the election headquarters of a presidential candidate, Palantine (Leonard Harris), and her beauty entrances him immediately. Dressed in white, walking the streets with an ethereal step, she seems an angel to him just descended from heaven. His immediate reaction is not to cross over to her world, but to draw her to his, as a means of her "salvation." His deceptive charm and seeming forthrightness impress her, and she consents to go with him on a date, for to her he seems unusual, sincere, and alive. But when he takes her to a porno movie, she walks away in revulsion and refuses to have anything to do with him from that point on. Rejected, Bickle becomes bitter, retreats to his inner world, and prepares to strike back. At this point he makes a crucial decision, which defines him as both an underground man and an epic anti-hero. When he tries to confess his problem to a fellow cabbie, nicknamed the "Wizard" (Peter Boyle), the latter, seeing him troubled, advises him to relax, take it easy, find a girl, and, most importantly, become what his job is. Wizard has done that, like every working person that usually merges with his environment and takes on the identity that his profession/occupation requires of him. Bickle rebels at this premise, and that refusal to conform defines him as a hero who takes on a cause, and in the context of this discussion as an antihero. He had tried to save Betsy from her sterile electoral office environment, telling her that she and Tom (Albert Brooks), an assistant working there and courting her, do not connect, and attempted to attract her to his world, to him more alive and real. Up to this point he has tried to change the system with peaceful means (for up until now he has been entirely harmless), but now he resolves to do it by resorting to the use of violence: he buys an armory of guns, trains in his apartment to regain his physical shape, changes his appearance, and begins to plan the assassination of Palantine, the presidential candidate. His meticulously kept diary allows the viewer to hear his reflections in voice-over.

Meanwhile, he has met twelve-year-old prostitute Iris (Jodie Foster) and her pimp (Harvey Keitel), and his self-righteous idea of rescuing her from her plight takes root. Bickle is not aroused by sexual desire for the young prostitute but by a sanctimonious wish to "drive sense" into her. He declines to make love to her, as is expected of a paying customer, and he becomes a surrogate father figure. His intense hatred of Sport (Keitel) combined with his rejection by Betsy and Palantine's effusions in public speeches about "saving the common man," feed on his resentment and hatred of the system. He arms himself with guns and knives and dons a cowboy outfit with an Indian chief's hairstyle, and approaches Palantine, who is delivering a campaign speech at a public gathering. But Bickle fails to hit his target, as alert secret service men spot him. The movie ends in a holocaust: Bickle kills Sport, the apartment owner, and a man visiting Iris where she works. He is wounded and attempts to kill himself, but is saved and remains in a coma for some time. Ironically, he is perceived as a national hero by the press for having fought the "mafia" and for saving Iris, who is now back with her parents, who write him expressing their gratitude for saving their daughter. Travis drives his cab again, where one of his passengers is Betsy, now looking at him with admiring eyes. She too had underestimated him. Smiling, he takes her to her destination, leaving her standing at the curb, only saying that newspapers "exaggerate these things," and that he only suffers from "a little stiffness, that's all." He knows she is his for the asking, but the rest is left to the viewer's imagination.

The antihero became a hero, but it is doubtful that his change in social standing is anything like a real metamorphosis that would restore him to normalcy—for his now enhanced vanity will not allow this. He has "won," but is still hiding under the everlasting underground man's mask. He could go on "converting" people to his "cause." Dostoyevsky prophesied that the underground man would inherit the earth; he could not have imagined that his mission would include getting rid of pimps and assassinating presidential candidates. Ironies reverberate as Scorsese's work might suggest that the mask is the hero's means of his dominance.

Fight Club (1999); Director: David Fincher

Fight Club seems at first glance to be another bloodbath of the nineties, such as *Pulp Fiction* (1995) and *Seven* (1998). However, in *Fight Club*, based on the novel by Chuck Palahniuk, one finds many of the characteristics of the anti-epic: a gloomy tone, montages connected with hallucinatory scenes, violence coming in brief spurts but ghastly enough and, above all, a negative hero—or antihero—a person with a lost identity embarking on a nightmarish adventure for self-discovery, both on an inner level and a metalevel, that ends with a greater nightmare than that with which it began. A common man (Ed Norton) who remains anonymous (just called "Jack") throughout the movie discovers, in the progress of the action, that he also carries with him, subconsciously, the identity of another person, Tyler Durden (Brad Pitt)—a demon who pulls him toward irrational freedom to destroy the world around him.

Thus, the movie runs on two planes: on a basic level, it is the story of one person, with all of his external actions shown. Meanwhile, his voice-over narrative explores his inner world, a step-by-step horrific discovery of his double identity. As the action progresses, his voice will, in the tone of a detached observer, gradually inform us of the doubleness of his character, which is as much a revelation to us as it is to him.

Jack has a monotonous desk job at an automobile company, and can't sleep at night. He is a classic insomniac who runs for help and joins several support groups made up of various hapless individuals—a woman who is dying of cancer and wants her last chance at having sex; an emasculated man with oversized woman's breasts; and Marla (Helena Bonham Carter)—pretty, homeless, oversexed, and who eventually becomes sexually involved with Tyler Durden.

Jack "meets" Tyler during a plane flight, and Tyler becomes his friend and mentor. He expects to be guided and illuminated in his distress by Tyler, despite the fact that he perceives his oddness and sexual excesses with Marla, things he regards as part of the "support" he is to have from him; and thus his unshakable confidence in Tyler develops, in a nightmarish sort of way.

The two establish a "fight club" in the basement of a dilapidated building, where boxing bouts between nondescript members are conducted—although at first it seems hard to tell what purpose the activity serves. Unbeknownst to Jack, the group gradually develops into an underground organization dedicated to vandalistic activities, headed by Tyler, who appears as a notorious (but well-hidden) terrorist preparing to blow up several credit card companies, in the name of creating financial chaos and the destruction of consumerist materialism and corporate power. The secret of his success is that he has a facial makeover every two years or so, so nobody can actually recognize him. Tyler's aim in befriending Jack is, for one, to prepare him to take over as leader once Tyler's present face is recognized; and two, to groom him for this mission. Far from suspecting that Tyler is actually his very own second identity, Jack is appalled by both Tyler's goals and actions, but he nonetheless goes along with Tyler's plan to establish the fight club, for Tyler's personality has had a magnetic effect on him. If Tyler's plan succeeds, Jack will not change physically; he will fully assume Tyler's personality and mission—to destroy present society as it is.

Though Jack is the rational part of his split personality, Tyler, the demonic and irrational side, is an underground man in his own right. His mindset is revealed in occasional passionate outbursts rather than in logical discourse. He is a prophet of doom, disdainful of desk jobs, the corporate ladder, and television sitcoms as a medium of entertainment (or an opiate) for the masses. Society is sick at the roots, he thinks, and he must demolish it. He is a superior physical specimen—as Brad Pitt's sculpted physique renders him perfectly so—making him an athlete, mentor, and superman, a lover of staggering prowess (ask Marla), and a man for all (underground) seasons. He can take punishment in the ring with the best of them, and he does not mind having his face bashed in by the Mafioso who owns the building, "rising" from his prostrate position to choke the latter's face with his vomited blood. He displays other such oddities, but these seem mere pranks to the innocent Jack, who is a bit too unaware—and catches on only too slowly—to the true nature of Tyler's twisted psyche.

Jack does gradually become cognizant of the latter's lunacy and his aberrant plans, but also has to come to terms with the realization that Tyler is ultimately the other side of himself. When people start calling him "Tyler," his new name after his "transformation," Jack pleads with Tyler to stop his plan to blow up several buildings. But the plan is already underway, and Jack's pleadings are in vain. Jack then knows that to kill Tyler he must kill himself, and, in a desperate final moment, he puts a gun in his mouth and pulls the trigger. Though he is miraculously (and unexplainably) saved by Marla, he has succeeded in killing Tyler. However, the doomsday mechanism Tyler has set in motion goes off, and all around them skyscrapers collapse in an apocalyptic explosion.

The movie has its literary (or filmic) predecessors. Thematically it is linked to Kubrick's *Dr. Strangelove*, and Scorsese's *Taxi Driver*, and even to Hitchcock's *Psycho*, since the Norman Bates mansion is shown briefly in one of the montages. Like *Dr. Strangelove*, *Fight Club* features a lunatic/maverick—albeit a double persona played by two actors—who fears that the nation (and society) will be destroyed by external forces. In the case of *Fight Club*, corporate

America and the television sitcom replace the Communists who polluted our "vital fluids," as in *Dr. Strangelove*. The maverick, as often is the case, takes matters into his own hands. In both films, the maverick/lunatic is a neofascist, though Tyler's intentions are subject to interpretation.

In *Taxi Driver*, Travis Bickle has no particular political leanings (and generally neither does the underground man), though his attempt to assassinate a presidential candidate who has a left-leaning message and, as his outfit and tomahawk hairstyle suggest, at least in appearance, the neo-Nazi mindset. The underground man's main characteristic, though, is his tendency to be antisocial—and this spurs his paranoid passion to destroy structure in society, as, of course, it is seen by him. Politics, as such, with its fragmentation into political parties, does not concern him. He will not blow up a Republican or Democratic Party building; but he will blow up federal or financially-based buildings, as in the Oklahoma City bombing, which *Fight Club* seems to somewhat draw a comparison with in its final scene.

Perhaps the most interesting feature of this movie is the protagonist's split personality. Jack, whose voice-over makes him the dominant figure, remains the protagonist, and thus has the basic characteristics of the underground man. He could be conceived as an epic hero because he has embarked on a quest for meaning—his life is sterile, aberrant, and purposeless. He needs to be healed from the ailments that his static life has afflicted him with, and to that effect he finds his alliances in the support groups. This is a mid-America cure-all, especially the group confessional type of activity—perhaps the twin of the new-age tendency to find healing in group activities, physical therapy, inane music, yoga, calmness, relaxation techniques, and the like. Sex is an avenue too, but Jack chooses not to use it, though the film reveals that he is ignorant of the fact that he is the actual lover of Marla. On the whole, his intentions are honorable, and the last thing that would cross his sane mind is to blow anybody or anything up.

The fight club he organizes, however, seems to revitalize him. Boxing is a form of physical therapy, as, cinematically speaking, Scorsese has shown us in *Raging Bull*, which this film mimics to a certain extent, in the scene where Jake LaMotta takes punishment in the ring, a form of crucifixion from Sugar Ray Robinson that is without retaliation from Jake. Similarly, Jack takes several beatings in the film, and even metes out one in an extremely brutal scene. But his rational mind has not abandoned him. Alone, he probably would have found his issues cured and returned to his desk and married Marla. But Tyler won't let him, having drawn him to his side and made him part of his scheme. Jack's persona has become captive to Tyler's, but willingly so on the part of Jack, and this symbiosis has certain identifiable characteristics. As the movie progresses, we see Jack's side become conscious of the abnormality, attempting to free itself from its bondage. Jack implores Tyler not only to let him go, but also not to go ahead with his catastrophic plans. The two fight and wrestle—metaphorically, of course, as they are two sides of the same coin. One can figure out this relationship in a number of ways. Jack represents the "rational" element of the psyche, while Tyler represents the irrational side. Throughout his exploration (or quest), Jack has retained his rationality, and, though he is willing to explore new possibilities for living life, he is not prepared to destroy the world—he says he is not "mad." On the other hand, Tyler exhibits characteristics of the devil, known to literature for centuries. For instance, the Satan of Milton's *Paradise Lost*, for one, is bent on destroying God's creations; Goethe's Mephistopheles in *Faust* is likewise determined; and in *The Brothers Karamazov*, we see Dostoyevsky's "devil" visit Ivan Karamazov in a dream sequence and plant the seeds of agnosticism in his mind. But the paranoia expressed in the postmodern film is unprecedented in actual history (meaning *written* history). For one thing, here, the director, Fincher, has assembled all the means at a director's disposal—sound, montage, lighting, action, voice-over—into a combination of cinematic narratives that show physical torment and mental disintegration of staggering proportions. This is an expression of an apocalypse that surpasses all its precedents in film and literature, a film to fit the moldings of the age of terror we live in.

Fight Club is an aftermath of the Oklahoma City bombing and a precursor to the horrors of September 11. It shows us the mindset of the "villain," who can be both a normal person and a terrorist at the same time—in this case revealing in-depth the mind of the underground man. The one serious drawback of this movie is that it is told from the point of view of the "weaker" side of the man, the rational side; the hero is feeble, and the antihero inspires. Yet the horrors suggest no catharsis of pity and fear—only fear itself. Neither side of this split personality elicits any sympathy. The film is a dissection, brilliantly done, of a sick mind—a mind infected and trying not to die—the evil spirit fighting with the half-good, or the conscious fighting the unconscious. In the postmodern world, the fight in *Fight Club* is uneven. It is the apocalypse without the lamb.

Suggested Films for Study

The Third Man (1949); Director: Carol Reed

In tone, photography, music, and evocative imagery, *The Third Man* offers perhaps the quintessential underground hero of all time. Orson Welles as Harry Lime has the slick persona of an immoralist who steals penicillin from hospitals in postwar Vienna hospitals without the slightest scruple, eluding the combined occupying forces who hunt for him by hiding in the elaborate sewer system underneath the city—thus being underground both literally and metaphorically. What defines him, though, is the speech he delivers to Holly Martins, an American writer/drifter, in the Ferris wheel scene, where he cynically deplores peaceful nations like Switzerland, which has given civilization the "cuckoo clock," while crime-ridden Renaissance Italy gave us immortal art. He is not above eliminating the dots of humanity below him if that will enrich him.

Breathless (1959); Director: Jean-Luc Godard

Jean-Luc Godard's Michael Poiccard (Jean-Paul Belmondo) is perhaps one of the most crucial antiheroes in film from one of the principal directors of the French new wave. Poiccard projects a picture of total isolation, living in an alien cosmos. After he shoots a cop, he lives briefly with his American girlfriend, but he has no other connections, no permanent residence, no job, no family, no friends, and he accepts the betrayal of his girlfriend with a mocking smirk as he dies. Breathless became a noteworthy American remake (with director Jim McBride) in 1983, with Richard Gere, who adjusts the antihero image to fit contemporary alienation and amorality.

Dr. Strangelove or: How I Learned to Stop Worrying and Love the Bomb (1964); Director: Stanley Kubrick

Though the "honor" of being an underground figure here belongs to a mad general, Jack D. Ripper (Sterling Hayden), who orders a nuclear attack on the Soviet Union, all the major characters (most played by Peter Sellers—including the president of the United States) in this small epic movie (and "dark" comedy) are afflicted by some kind of madness, either sheer idiocy, or lack of capacity to comprehend what is going on, or afflicted by the paranoid hysteria of the times—the height of the Cold War—that nothing short of nuclear attack will save the Western world from perdition. The "superpatriotic" pilot of the plane that will drop the bomb is Major T. J. "King" Kong (Slim Pickens), a figure who exceeds the parameters of any conceivable underground man by being a mere caricature of what in the popular imagination could be seen as a self-sacrificing hero. His mission is to drop a hydrogen bomb on Laputa, in Russian territory, and his "epic" flight in the B-52 bomber is successful, despite the plane being hit by a missile and partly incapacitated en route. This action, brave as it may seem and smacking of high-level patriotic sentiment, can also be interpreted as paranoid mania that ignores the dreadful outcome, the triggering of the "Doomsday Machine," which brings about the apocalyptic end of the world.

Raging Bull (1980); Director: Martin Scorsese

Scorsese's epic-length, black-and-white masterpiece presents an even bleaker picture of alienation than *Taxi Driver*. In *Taxi Driver*, Travis Bickle is an isolated man fighting a system, pitting himself against the world while under the illusion that he can win. In *Raging Bull*, Jake LaMotta (Robert De Niro), a real-life boxer, is portrayed as a self-destructive individual, whose insane jealously prevents him from having normal relations with his closest family members, his wife and brother, both of whom he suspects of infidelity. His "rage," however, is fully expressed in the ring, where he suffers blows at the hands of a superior opponent (Sugar Ray Robinson) as a means of cleansing his inner turbulence. Masterful montage captures the intensity of the brutal beatings he takes at the hands of his opponent.

Schindler's List (1993); Director: Steven Spielberg

Filmed in black and white, Steven Spielberg's movie has the distinction of qualifying as both an epic proper due to its formal qualities—length, spectacle (such as it is), and a heroic figure that saves a particular group from extermination—and as a anti-epic due to its dark subject and the antihero figure in it who serves as a thematic counterpoint. In fact, both main characters here—Amon Goeth (Ralph Fiennes) and Oskar Schindler (Liam Neeson)—possess underground characteristics: Goeth, "the Butcher of Plaszow," is perhaps too monstrous to be counted as hero in any sense, but he does appear to have a double persona, often hiding his monstrous nature under a mask of civility and disguising his lustful passion for one of the female captives, Helen Hirsch, which shows him in an occasionally tormenting fit of conscience. As for Schindler, the film portrays him in the process of metamorphosis from bad to good (not unusual in epics), for he starts out as a war profiteer, meaning only to acquire riches by exploiting slave labor, but ends up as a philanthropist and a hero who saves the lives of eleven hundred Jews during the Holocaust. His mission requires that he hide his true identity, thence his mask becomes a means of deception, enabling him to function as an underground man who fights for the preservation of the community. Both impersonations are acceptable in the Dostoyevskian sense, for the underground man is seen as having interchangeable goals—he can be a person intent on destroying a social group, or one who endeavors to save it. It is a rare occasion when the antihero casts off his masks and reveals his good self.

The English Patient (1996); Director: Anthony Minghella

Based on the novel by Michael Ondaatje, this epic-length movie reveals the latter-day underground persona perhaps in its fullest dimension. A lover, a traitor, and a man lying sick and burned beyond recognition confesses his unlucky love to a third person while war is still raging around him. Count Laszlo Almasy (Ralph Fiennes), a cartographer in Africa before the war, turned over documents to the Germans in order to return to the cave where he had left the dying Katherine (Kristin Scott Thomas), after her jealous husband attempted to murder both of them. The amoral Almasy slowly disintegrates physically and mentally, suffering from pangs of conscience, recollections of love lost, and vague but torturous apprehensions of his crimes as an adulterer and a traitor. His alienation is total—and tragic—as he is visited by images of ghostly beauty, memories of horrid crimes, and tormented by a vengeful Caravaggio (Willem Dafoe) who has vowed to eradicate any peace of mind left a dying man. This is a form of alienation known only to those visited by both guilt and physical decay.

A Beautiful Mind (2001); Director: Ron Howard

A Beautiful Mind features Russell Crowe as John Nash, a mathematical genius afflicted with schizophrenia and thus taken advantage of by an imaginary secret agent (played by Ed Harris) who asks Nash to break a code from the Soviets regarding an atomic threat. Nash accepts and gets heavily involved in situations that present extreme danger—the chase and shooting scene is very real. He is also haunted by an old friend and his little daughter, both of whom follow him judging his actions. The movie is about distinguishing reality from the hallucinations of a schizophrenic. Survival depends on being cured, and Nash contends that his rational mind can overcome an illusion, though he is the victim of a psychiatrist (Christopher Plummer) by turns a demon and a savior. Nash is a hero in many senses: not just as a genius who influenced modern science—biology—but also as a human being who learns to overcome his shortcomings and his ill luck. Nash finally triumphs and his is a victory for humanity, not just this man. Nash is an antihero, at first alienated by a lethal mental disease, but finally liberated by his own determination to fight the odds—an example for humanity, not just those who know mathematics.

Ted Bundy (2002); Director: Matthew Bright

This minor (by epic standards) film shows clearly the distinction between an antihero who may commit crimes out of distorted ideology and a full-grown psychopath, such as Bundy, who deserves none of the pity that a sick person may be entitled to. Though he does share some of the characteristics of the underground man—the mask, for instance—he is more or less different in the sense that the underground man can be basically sane, quite knowledgeable as to what he is doing, though deliberately engaging in deceptions, and he is guided in his actions by a thread of philosophy, no matter how tenuous. A film like Ted Bundy is a painful experience, either to re-create or to view. It is an honest try, but perhaps an incomplete one. But it is made in the spirit of understanding the vilest side of human nature, and it does caution innocence against the diabolical conniving of such killers. There is no attempt to offer any extenuating circumstances, and the execution of Bundy is given as realistically as possible, including his head shaving and castration. "Execution is obscene," director Matthew Bright remarks in his commentary, "but that does not mean it is wrong."[9] The executioner was revealed to be a woman.

Collateral (2004); Director: Michael Mann

Collateral is a thriller/action movie involving a contract killer (Tom Cruise) whose intent is to eliminate six targets in one night. For that, he hires a cabbie (Jamie Foxx) and forces him to take him to each victim until his mission is completed. One critic[10] compares Cruise's character, Vincent, to Carol Reed's portrait of Orson Welles's Harry Lime in The Third Man (1949), an immoralist holding condescending views on the countless victims that die as a consequence of his actions. Collateral can also be seen as a character study of two people thrown together by chance—an assassin, into whose twisted psyche we are invited to delve and who talks of his motivations at intervals, and an ordinary cab driver, into whose path the assassin inadvertently stumbles. Psychological portraits are drawn as the action in the movie progresses, but it is doubtful that an action movie whose tempo is regulated by its violent scenes can successfully hold these elements together seamlessly. Thrillers possess a certain rhythm, unknown or unnecessary in other movies, and adding psychobabble (passing for wisdom) may have brought the whole structure to a different level—for better or worse. In The Third Man intellectual exchange became possible through a careful control of a tragic tone, which was evident from the outset, as the voice of the naive American writer arriving at a war-torn city is combined with montages of the surroundings ruins. Collateral, on the other hand, offers an idea far from original to twenty-first century audiences already saturated not only by an excess of violence and gore on the screen but also by the worn path of watching hired villains targeting their victims. Since the days of The Godfather series, these routines have been explored with unremitting frequency and do not carry the weight they used to. But Collateral is still a movie that aspires to something beyond the ordinary thriller genre, and director Michael Mann, whose list of credits includes films of thought and adventure,[11] here attempts to combine action with insight into the mind of a killer, a combination that has not always worked to the advantage of an action movie.

Notes

1. For a more extensive definition of postmodern literary forms as well as the postmodernist period, see William Harmon and C. Hugh Homan, *A Handbook to Literature*, 8th ed. (Upper Saddle River, N.J.: Prentice-Hall, 1999), 403–405.

2. "I have great hopes for it," Dostoyevsky wrote in one of his letters. "It will be a powerful and candid piece; it will be the truth." Fyodor Dostoyevsky, *Notes from Underground*, trans. and ed. Michael R. Katz, A Norton Critical Edition, 2nd ed. (New York: Norton, 2001), 97.

3. Discussed below.

4. The so-called manifesto by the Unabomber, who was later identified as Theodore Kaczynski, appeared in the *New York Times* in June 1995, and subsequently in the *Washington Post*, in September of the same year. The FBI had identified the Unabomber as the person responsible for three murders and sixteen bombings, and more violence had been threatened if the manifesto was not published. It was a virulent attack on Western industrial society and its practices. Kaczynski was on trial from November 1997 to January 1998, and after lengthy legal proceedings which involved psychiatric examinations for mental competence, Kaczynski asked to defend himself, pleaded guilty, and was sentenced to life in prison.

5. Nikolai Berdyaev, *Dostoevsky*, trans. Donald Attwater (London: Sheed and Ward, 1934), 24–47.

6. See chapter 8, "The Information Age Epic."

7. For more examples, see the "Suggested Films for Study" section below.

8. Pauline Kael, *For Keeps: 30 Years at the Movies* (New York: Plume, 1994), 681–82.

9. Quoted in the running commentary of *Ted Bundy*, DVD (First Look Pictures, 2005).

10. David Denby, "Thrilled to Death," *New Yorker*, August 9, 2004.

11. *Manhunter* (1986), *The Last of the Mohicans* (1992), and *Insider* (1999) are some of his most noted movies.

CHAPTER EIGHT

The Information Age Epic

Information age epics might be defined as those that appeared with the advent of digital technology, the Internet, and the video game in the 1980s, 1990s, and continuing into the 2000s. Digital photography, in particular, has influenced just about all action movies, thrillers, mysteries, fantasy epics, war epics, historical epics, and, of course, animated features. This technological advancement has undoubtedly become one of the most dominant popular features of the epic film, though not necessarily the most momentous. The epic needs to remain a popular vehicle, and the sci-fi epics of George Lucas, *Star Wars* (including the more recent ones), and fantasy films such as *The Lord of Rings*, the Harry Potter epics, the Batman and Spider-Man epics, and *The Matrix* sequences have come into prominence and captured the popular imagination as perhaps no other entertainment medium has. Whether the digital epics are the greatest epics yet remains a question, but the modern formats and the technologies responsible for their success are, of course, due some space in this book.

Despite a shift in aesthetic approach in the information age epics, one can also see in them the preservation of the core values of the traditional epic, with its mythological dimensions—a phenomenon that the epic shares with literature—which pitted heroes against assorted villains who tried to destroy normal societies by any means possible. The question is, has the aesthetic of the digital world affected the epic format, and, if so, to what extent? Has the epic of digital form suffered a diminution as a popular vehicle of expressing and projecting communal wishes—something that might be looked upon as the main attribute of the epic form in general?

One other point that may be considered relevant to the above questions is the impact that digital technology has had on the economic status of the epic form. The epic is and has always been a very expensive film to make, increasingly so with passing decades, and digital, computer-generated images have brought about a reduction in costs, specifically in the number of extras, the cost of sets and art direction in general, and filming on location in many parts of the world. The epic always relied on spectacle—special effects—and digital technology can produce visual images of huge structures, whole cities, and background landscapes, or dovetail digitized people to real ones in battle scenes, for instance, or reproduce multitudes in battles that look immense on the screen—as in *The Lord of the Rings* or *Alexander the Great*—and a great fleet can appear on the screen sailing the seas as if by magic (as in *Troy*). In *Ben-Hur* (both the 1925 and 1959 versions) a sea battle had to feature real ships, built to actually simulate[1] a sea-fighting episode, and when the viewer sees one ship ramming into another, such action actually happened. In *Troy*,[2] a modern epic which makes full use of digital effects, an entire fleet of "one thousand" ships was reproduced by computerized imagery that digitally multiplied two actual model ships built for that purpose into many hundreds dotting a screen to create the impression of a vast fleet. There can also be a blending of photography of actual structures and digital enhancement, as in the case of *Gladiator* (2000), in which the Roman Coliseum was photographed on location but completed and enhanced digitally for the movie action.

No doubt, digital imagery significantly reduced the cost of making today's epic. In *The Birds*, Hitchcock had to have actual birds trained to fill his screen (though some fake ones went into the mix); in *Batman Begins* (discussed below), a swarm of countless bats unleashed from the caverns of Batman's residence were entirely the result of digital imagery. Fleets, cities, exotic structures on mountainsides, blue stretches of ocean beyond real beaches—such things, and an infinite number of others—can be easily presented on the screen, all visual (and auditory at times) tricks created by modern technology.

Again, the question is, do these work, or do they stretch believability? The inevitable "suspension of disbelief" question intrudes upon the sensibilities of an audience, and the results can be mixed—as they were in earlier times, when such things were painstakingly constructed on studio sets, for cinema always relied on some degree of deception. Total realism, as in the "neorealistic" Italian school of the post–Second World War period in Europe, came into existence partly out of necessity, and many directors prefer that approach. But cinema in general relies on illusion, making things believable, eliciting an audience response by simulation of reality—with the full consent of patrons who bought tickets. In the grand age of the epic—the 1950s—Charlton Heston as Moses parts the Red Sea with a motion of his hands. Waters retreated to let the pursued race of Israel pass, and then roared back to drown their pursuers. Perhaps Cecil B. DeMille could have done better with today's digital wizardry. Some fake things have to be presented as real, though a chariot race in the memorable scene in *Ben-Hur* really did take place, albeit after weeks of photographing the event and using stunt work that looked as real as possible. Perhaps that may be the aesthetic principle an audience looks for. No matter how reality is simulated, it must look convincing. Digital photography has shown that such effects can be achieved, especially with pictures that are clearly announced as fantasies. Digital photography is still a new technology in its early stages, serving a rather aging art, which has no alternative but to hone its methods as it goes.

Believability of what one sees on the screen is always an issue, something that came along as film came along. What one sees on the screen is the result of photography, which reproduces reality exactly as one sees it. This point has induced many discussions among theorists, but suffice it to say, that it is on the basis of this illusion of reality that cinema owes its success—to a large measure. The result is better if photographic images are also creating illusion. The films of Sergei Eisenstein, Jean Cocteau, or Orson Welles (not to mention of Michael Powell and Carol Reed)—all of whom created epics (or movies with epic elements in them)—are subtle, balanced blending of illusion and reality. They project worlds that seem real enough but have elements of the fantastic, or reality which is ingeniously manipulated to be accepted. Stories—adventures, romances, comedies—were told that seemed real enough, in full knowledge that disbelief was suspended. The epics undertook to add and to stress one other element to cinematic story-telling that placed an additional burden on that delicate balance between believability and suspension of it: spectacle. That was fine in swashbuckling adventures, sea battles, chariot races, sea partings, and treks along deserts or in isolated regions of the world. Spectacle was accepted as long as it was reasonably presented. Digital photography came along in the 1970s and entertained audiences, but the tricks produced were neither entirely convincing as actual human deeds nor ever taken seriously. Fantasy was, of course, known to the cinematic universe since its inception—*A Trip to the Moon* (1902), *The Wizard of Oz* (1939), *Pinocchio* (1940), and animated features in general—these were highly successful cinematic ventures, but they had their limited domain. From its outset, the epic always relied on extravagance, whether such spectacle was offered in the athletic feats of Douglas Fairbanks Sr. or Errol Flynn, or in the depiction of menacing monsters—Frankenstein, King Kong—or given as cataclysmic events, earthquakes, typhoons, or falling asteroids, not to mention extraterrestrial visits. One can say that the digital epic is the natural descendant of the traditional film epic in an exaggerated form, given the constantly developing technology, which makes such things possible. But these were almost always done at the expense of depth of character and meanings in a story. Few directors managed to avoid such pitfalls—W. D. Griffith, Sergei Eisenstein, Akira Kurosawa, David Lean, Steven Spielberg—though such directors endowed their epics with a dimension that transcended mere spectacle.

Star Wars Episode IV: A New Hope (1977); Director/Writer: George Lucas

In creating his famous trilogy of the 1970s, George Lucas claims that seeing *The Hidden Fortress* by Akira Kurosawa inspired him (in part) to write the script for his popular *Star Wars Episode IV* (as it is now named[3] in view of the numerous sequels and prequels[4]), and that statement must not go unnoticed. For one thing, both movies involve groups of people cast out of their previous authority positions and hiding in remote locations until they can regroup, counterattack, and reclaim their previous authority. In order to do so they must traverse vast distances (expressed in relative terms), elude or confront numerous natural obstacles or hostile hordes, and in the process show bravery, courage, cunning, ability to conceal their real identity, and readiness of wit needed to face and elude adversity that often comes their way. Theirs is a difficult, arduous, and exhausting task that more often than not goes beyond the pale of human endurance. And the tasks are performed, and the people on the right side (those winning our sympathies) are victorious and achieve their ends. It is a story in which known archetypal formulas have been repeated since the beginning of time, from Gilgamesh to Odysseus, King Arthur, Robin Hood, Hamlet, Hercules (in movies), and Harry Potter. Audiences delight to see heroes win in the end, especially if their ends coincide with those of the community at large.

Star Wars is clearly a fantasy (Lucas calls it "space opera" rather than science fiction—a name that Lucas does not favor), a story that takes place in the galaxy, and involves fantastic shapes of planets, asteroids, intergalactic vehicles, robots, weapons (laser beams), and other such paraphernalia, most of which Lucas introduced to the screen in grand manner (though Kubrick's *2001: A Space Odyssey* preceded him). Only a certain amount of realism is achievable in such a context and narrative format—the main heroes are human, for instance, and some of the locations in this particular movie were filmed on actual locations, rather than being composed digitally, as happened with the later series.

Star Wars begins the saga of interplanetary wars between two great powers in the galaxy, the Empire, which stands for a dark force of evil, and the tribe of the Jedi, previously defeated by the Empire, now living on an isolated planet, practically bereft of its previous powers. But they undertake a mission to save Princess Leia (Carrie Fisher), who has been living in the Empire and has dispatched a message with the plans of the Death Star craft, which is the main weapon of the Empire, and using it the Empire is able to strike and destroy whole planets. The message is carried by two androids (or "droids"), R2-D2 and C-3P0, in a pod that lands on the planet where Luke Skywalker (Mark Hamill) lives on a farm with his uncle and aunt. He is a restless youth who yearns for adventure rather than school or farming. When the pod carrying the androids lands on his uncle's place, Luke soon discovers that old Obi-Wan Kenobi (Alec Guinness) lives not far from there, and from him Luke learns the secrets of the Force, though not his own actual identity, for he is the son Darth Vader (nor does he know that Princess Leia is his twin sister). To undertake the expedition to rescue Princess Leia, Luke and Obi-Wan Kenobi enlist the services of Han Solo (Harrison Ford), a mercenary, who owns the fastest ship in the galaxy, capable of traveling at the speed of light and maneuvering through asteroids to reach its destination. Their mission is to get to the Death Star, and escape from it with Leia. They make it to the Death Star and find Leia, but during a battle with Darth Vader (played by David Prowse, his voice dubbed by James Earl Jones), Obi-Wan Kenobi is killed, while the rest escape and return to their planet safely. The Empire launches a counterattack, led by Grand Moff Tarkin (Peter Cushing) and Darth Vader, but the valiant fighters of the planet manage to destroy the Death Star. However, Darth Vader, though defeated, manages to escape and flee back to the Empire, from where he will await his opportunity to counterattack, something that happens in the next episode, *The Empire Strikes Back*. The victors celebrate their victory and receive medallions of honor. Of course, with two sequels (in the seventies) and the later prequels, the story becomes much more complicated, for in the process of all the rest of the episodes, we learn the origin of the evil Darth Vader, that he is the father of Luke and Leia, and the transformational power of the Force, which can turn a human being toward either good or evil.

George Lucas explains[5] that, in addition to being inspired by Kurosawa's work, he got his initial idea from Saturday matinee serials of earlier decades, which had a band of evil guys doing numerous battles with a group of good fellows; the battles went on for weeks on end, always ending each episode with a cliffhanger, so audiences would be eager to come back the next week and see what happened. This method of episodic storytelling was adopted by television and dominated daytime soap operas (on a different note—intrigue rather than physical adventure), and in the late seventies and eighties, when television was still undeterred by the entrance of the video and VCR, the formula transferred to nighttime serial dramas, such as *Dallas*, *Dynasty*, and several spin-offs, which went on to dominate nighttime television for years. *Star Wars*, however, put a bit of a spin on chronological storytelling. The movies made in the later years (1999, 2002, 2005) were conceived as "prequels" to the story already told in the first three movies (1977, 1980, 1983).

Lucas, again, acknowledges his debts to Kurosawa, whose epics (among them *Seven Samurai*) showed him the way to depict warring tribes where not the most vicious or malignant prevail, but the most valiant. Though simplified to suit his own tastes and predispositions, this dramaturgical approach to moviemaking (in the epic genre) won Lucas millions of fans and fame throughout the world. The *Star Wars* episodes, counting all the sequels and prequels, delve deeply into psychological tribal roots and resonate with audiences who wish their heroes (and villains) straight, uncomplicated humans or robots, androids (droids) or apes with feelings, simplified but not entirely cartoonish, nor devoid of emotion or other human elements (jealousy, hatred, generational gaps, etc.). The first three movies, which according to Lucas were conceived as one whole story with three chapters, are the most ingenious, storywise, the most inventive, and by far the most popular, although the last three, made in modern times, have benefited from advances in technology and sparkle with computer-generated, digitally superior spectacle. But the first movie (now titled *Episode IV: A New Hope*) ushered in the digital age (though most scenes were composed in traditional animation) and the vast consequences, commercially and artistically, of the virtual-reality image now generated for the big screen. It is a brave new world, now at its peak, and still evolving, with no end in sight. Despite this technological progress, the last three movies, though prequels, have not achieved the wide popularity of the first three, just as the later James Bond sagas, despite their technological/special effects innovations, have lost the gloss and heroic glitter of the first four or five made in the sixties. Lucas states that the first *Star Wars* was filmed in actual locations, in Tunisia, for the desert shooting, and in Death Valley (California) for the scenes in the canyons, although of course the galactic battles and interiors were of computerized/digital design. This gives the early episodes some air of reality, however remote, for the emphasis is on galactic wars, and the entire thing had to be seen as science-fiction fantasy.

But the battle between good and evil is the crux of the matter, and viewers thought they recognized a sort of American western transferred to the skies. Lucas explored a myth, the eternal battle of good (the Force), envied by evil—strangely also motivated by the Force—which is an unrecognizable entity in the universe, and only sages like Obi-Wan Kenobi can recognize and master it to some degree, or transmit it to others through judicious advice. The Force rules the galaxy, and whoever masters its admonitions will become the eventual ruler—for eternal good and peace.

The Matrix (1999); Directors/Writers: Andy Wachowski and Larry Wachowski

This movie is typed sci-fi/action/epic thriller, but it may contain much more than any genre name could describe. It could be called an allegory, and, though it has pretensions of originality, it harkens back to past creations, either in literature or film. *The Matrix* illustrates the downward spiral of civilization that humans have brought upon themselves by being creative and ingenious—and more evil than good. Despite its dazzling and innovative techniques, and the debate it has generated, *The Matrix*[6] belongs to the epic genre, as, in modern terms, it redefines the hero who sets out to suppress overt threats to humanity, even if those threats have sprung out of our own imaginations. Its ostensibly complicated symbolism—names like Morpheus, Trinity, Neo, for instance—and robotlike precision of movement suggests innovation beyond compare, and yet its theme is common enough.

The premise here is that a machine created by a human takes over its creator's life and enslaves him, this time in cyberspace, a reality man himself has created, explored, put to use, and seen become a threat. Humans become the victim—in some way or other—of their own creations; one could even go as far back as the Tower of Babel, when humans, reaching for the skies, instead receive confusion of tongues—which breaks up innocent unity. Another example, from another mythology, is Prometheus, who invents fire, gives it to humans, and is punished by the gods for this daring innovation. Fire is the beginning of technology, and with that begins the story of humanity's self-destruction. Atlas is condemned to carry the globe on his shoulders—a task that some could see as mechanical—as punishment by Zeus for fighting against the Titans. Hercules is dying of a poisoned arrow, after numerous labors, some of which demanded wit more than strength, like cleaning the stables of Aegeus by diverting a stream from its course. And Odysseus is tossed about after inventing a war machine that could take an enemy by guile. In the Middle Ages, Dante has a great general, Guido da Montefeltro, in hell, for helping the pope take a city using one of his mechanized inventions. Folks that have invented mechanical contraptions are either heroes, or victims of their inventions and ingenuity—or both.

With advancing centuries, fear of machines grew. Humans, somewhat paradoxically, kept inventing machines and fearing them at the same time. There came the damascene sword, used in the Crusades to sever humans in half, and gunpowder from the East soon followed; later came cannons, battleships with big guns, iron ships in the nineteenth century, and all kinds of weaponry advancing with astonishing rapidity after a certain point in history (the Middle Ages), enabling armies to eliminate large numbers of humans in battles very different from the pitched battles of antiquity fought mainly with spears. Weaponry perfection and development culminated in the twentieth century, when bombs dropped from planes, machine guns razed dozens of people at once, and, finally, the atomic bomb destroyed thousands at a time. Of course, it wasn't just weapons that inspired fear. Machines of all kinds, invented for a number of practical purposes—printing, weaving, transportation, medicine—came along as well, but, whatever the purpose, fear of the machine grew, as the men who operated them could always turn them to evil ends.

Some literature of the past expressed this fear in mock-heroic fashion, as Jonathan Swift did in the eighteenth century, when he satirized the British Royal Academy in his "Voyage to Laputa" section in *Gulliver's Travels*. A flying island, moving about through the force of a magnetic lodestone, called Laputa (the "whore"), could float over a conquered land and drop large stones on those who threatened rebellion underneath. The nineteenth century accelerated this fear, as the Industrial Revolution gave birth to machinery that replaced human labor, as Thomas Carlyle describes in his essay "Characteristics," and during the twentieth century gadgets and devices were constantly invented to both help and inhibit the progress of civilized man. Fiction writers like H. G. Wells, and Aldous Huxley describe societies taken over by totalitarian systems of evil machines—the two now having become the same. Movies like *The Time Machine* (from Wells), *Metropolis*, and *Modern Times* brought this fear of the machine to the public, and this trend continued in horror movies, science fiction, and the modern epic/thriller, like *The Matrix*. But before *The Matrix* there came Stanley Kubrick's masterpiece, *2001: A Space Odyssey* and Ridley Scott's *Blade Runner*, not to mention the *Star Wars* franchise, already discussed.

All of these fantasies/myths have one thing in common: they express the takeover of humans by their own creations, often robots. Humans are finite and mortal, but robots can renew and live forever. Arthur C. Clarke actually expressed this idea in his book *2001: A Space Odyssey* (the basis for the film) when he said that the human body can have machinelike replaceable parts, and eventually will evolve into a machine, defying time and mortality. Clarke, of course, saw this as a benign development, which would free man of the wear and tear of the human body—as indeed scientific inventions have proven—kidney and heart transplants are now common and other human organs can be surgically repaired. Better fitting, better functioning, and more real-looking prosthetics are making life easier for those who have lost a limb.

The takeover of machines, however, retains its menace over society, for the machine can transform itself and take evil forms intent on enslaving humankind when utopias become dystopias. Robots, human-like machines, have been dreamed up by authors since Goethe. In his *Faust*, Wagner, an evil doctor, creates "homunculus," a human produced in an ovenlike contraption. Mary Shelley's Frankenstein brought about another manlike creature made of human parts. Today, robots resembling humans entirely, with all human characteristics in place, have been given to audiences through digital simulation, a so-called virtual reality, better suited for the cinema screen, which can imitate without violating verisimilitude. Being robots, they are of course practically indestructible, so their control over ordinary humans is nearly complete.

In *The Matrix* the battle between good and evil emerges from these myths. It has always been thus: from the first chapters of Genesis, to Homer's *The Odyssey*, through the great myths of mankind, good battles evil, or rather, good defends its existence against evil forces that refuse to die through the centuries and millennia. Teilhand de Chardin prophesied that the end of time may be marked by a paroxysm of evil forces over good. There is no certainty that good is ever going to prevail—nor are we told where the evil forces come from. Christianity and the Manicheans have the world split between good and evil, though the former predicts victory, while the latter leaves the matter unresolved.

The Matrix may be considered small potatoes compared to these grandiose theories, but it does stay on the plane of preconception of the evil battling good. It shows the eternal struggle, but with all the modern twists that human imaginations can produce. Here the robots are in cyberspace—something that, according to Jean Baudrillard,[7] a contemporary French theorist, indicates the practical enslavement of the ordinary human to a "vast simulated reality" created by the computer space. We think we are in control of ourselves when we make choices, but in effect choices are made for us. The computer itself is a menace, for it controls our basic functions of communications, but the hacker and the viruses create an even greater menace. Protecting ourselves from the myriad attacks launched against our systems is a heroic task, which involves time and energy taken from other endeavors. In a sense, that task makes a hero of the average man, who is forced into battle but knows little about defenses and has to be constantly on the alert. The Middle Ages had the plague and the constant attacks by tribal warriors—witness the invasion of Russia by the Mongols in the sixteenth century in Tarkosvski, *Andrei Rublev*—today we have the wars in cyberspace, which has now become universal.

The Matrix innovates this theme by suggesting that we are also assailed by a lack of consciousness of this reality. We are in a state of sleep—that is the meaning of the name Morpheus, given to the leader of the group who is aware of the menace of the matrix—the complex forces that have taken over and dictate our moves. In *The Odyssey*, Morpheus is one of the dwellers of the land of the dead, a ghost that has the power to come in human form to give instructions to humans. In *The Matrix*, Morpheus (Laurence Fishburne) creates the dream world in which humans live in the present. They are near Hades, the region of the dead, therefore they have already lost their sense of reality to a certain extent. Morpheus, however, possesses wisdom, for he can awaken slumbering humans from the torpid state they live in. He can see through the dream, so he invites a naive young executive to look beyond his placid existence and see through the dream deception to the menace that is enveloping him. In this sense, the young executive, Thomas Anderson, becomes Neo (Keanu Reeves), a Greek word meaning "new man," who will join forces with Morpheus and his group in order to do battle with the forces around them—in the film represented as three "agents," wearing dark glasses, featuring similar haircuts, and dressed in black, who come to arrest him. To this extent, the story takes a Kafkaesque turn—for Neo is interrogated, tortured, and almost destroyed. But through Morpheus's efforts, Neo is freed and begins his battle, aided by Trinity (Carrie-Anne Moss), a female who will eventually save him through the power of love. The movie at this point takes the character of the comic strip, for Neo battles with his martial arts skills as well as with bullets. He is rescued from death by Trinity, which has its obvious connotation of love, after he is defeated by agent Smith. The movie has an ending but it is unfinished, for the forces of evil are not totally defeated and will gather for a final confrontation. Two sequels[8] bring the epic to a victory of good over the diabolically contrived machines.

The Lord of the Rings (2001–2003); Director: Peter Jackson

Though *The Lord of the Rings* is an epic of the digital era, in essence it is a traditional tale of the battle between good and evil, a worn-out topic among epic makers, both in literary works and in film. But it is an information age film because digital technology, bursting onto the scene in the early 1990s, became a decisive tool in the hands of filmmakers, especially those whose work relied largely on special effects. Thus, the film's director, Peter Jackson, was able to give his masterwork the look and form that this type of spectacular film epic needed as the translation of an extremely descriptive, three-part fantasy novel that had appeared nearly half a century earlier. Jackson decided that one film, no matter how lengthy—in an age of shrinking screen length for epics—would not do and that three films would be required to translate the massive novels of J. R. R. Tolkien, published in the mid-1950s, into adequate screen time. The three films, which in their entirety approach nine hours, were filmed simultaneously in a nearly two-year period with main locations in New Zealand, and they were released for the screen in three sequential seasons, 2001, 2002, and 2003. The project of three combined stories became the longest epic[1] in the history of cinema, and it was rewarded with record-breaking worldwide attendance and numerous awards, especially the third film, *The Return of the King*, which garnered eleven Oscars, including Best Picture for 2003. Of course, trilogies were not unknown to literature and film, from Aeschylus to Francis Ford Coppola and George Lucas, but this was the first time that all three compositions were conceived as one work with all three parts filmed at the same time, while released (or performed) separately. The concept worked, and to this day, several years after the final release, *The Lord of the Rings* trilogy retains its cinematic power and even its relevance to our fast-changing times and mores.

With all its innovation in technique, the information age epic has not affected the basic appeal to communal and tribal interests that the traditional epic format has exhibited for centuries or even millennia. The epic, with its numerous archetypes and patterns of strife, has narrated communal battles during which a hero or heroes (sometimes joined by a heroine) try to defeat an evil enemy that threatens the tribe with submission, destruction of its life and culture, or total annihilation. Despite advances in technology that affect its various formats, the twentieth-century epic offers numerous examples of communal heroes leading the battle against evil opponents in basically similar ways.

The Lord of the Rings trilogy conforms to that pattern. Specifically, it is based on Nordic mythology, which is not particularly Christian. It does not draw its material from Greco-Roman history or mythology, as has been the case with epics for decades, nor is it directly derived from contemporary themes. Still, *The Lord of the Rings* story does contain some Christian symbolism and themes, just as Tolkien was undoubtedly affected by his experiences with World Wars I and II. Tolkien was an Oxford scholar and an expert in Nordic mythology, having authored critical works on that subject, in particular on the old English epic poem *Beowulf*. Since most film epics are derived from history, legend, or mythology from the Greco-Roman or Christian eras, including the medieval legends such as King Arthur, Tolkien's trilogy seems to have introduced a new concept—legends derived from pre-Christian Nordic folklore, up to then rarely used as source material by Hollywood. E. M. Forster[2] complained once that English mythology, with all its elves, folktales, and fairy tales, is truly impoverished and does not have the richness of Greek mythology, so admired by the British and the Western world in general. Tolkien's intent was to show that England had a "prehistory," found not in actual written annals (though *Beowulf* is proof that it existed) but in its legends of the Nordic tribes that fought in old England and the countries of northern Europe, including Denmark and Scandinavia. Of course, *The Lord of the Rings* does not claim historical authenticity; it is a fairy tale, but it has, and its makers wanted it to have, the pulse of history. If translated in allegorical terms, it can reflect the historical reality of the time during which it was created.

Right at the outset in the first part of the trilogy, *The Fellowship of the Ring*, we see a peaceful community known as the Shire, a green valley that looks like an earthly paradise. The Shire is in Middle-earth, a large region of, presumably, Europe during a bygone era where people lived in peace and prosperity. Tiny Hobbits, the inhabitants of the Shire, are an easygoing, pastoral people who love life, cultivating the earth, enjoying the benefits of peace and good fellowship, and living in harmony with nature. Gandalf (Ian McKellen), a wizard visiting this little corner of Middle-earth, has befriended a very old resident, Bilbo Baggins (Ian Holm), a Hobbit who is celebrating his 111th birthday and is about to leave the Shire forever. Bilbo, who possesses the Ring of Power, explains that he found it decades ago and that it has delayed the coming of his old age. Gandalf later reveals that it was actually forged by the Dark Lord Sauron in the fires of Mount Doom and that it was taken from Sauron by Isildur, the High King of Condor. The inscription on the ring reads, "One ring to rule them all." The ring, consequently, has the power to bring all the other powers of darkness under the one who possesses it.

Gandalf explains to Bilbo's nephew Frodo Baggins (Elijah Wood), a youth who leads an innocent life at the Shire and who inherits the ring, that the forces of darkness are already unleashed, that the search for the ring is on, and that it must be protected at all costs. Evil is stirring at Mordor, and the ring has "awakened," having heard its master Sauron's call. Sauron only needs the ring to enslave all the lands and cover them with darkness. As Gandalf cannot have the ring because he is afraid of its power, he asks Frodo to carry it. The latter is persuaded to undertake a journey with his gardener and friend Sam (Sean Astin) to help destroy the ring, the first step being a meeting with Gandalf at the Prancing Pony Inn to gather more information.

Meanwhile, Gandalf visits Saruman (Christopher Lee), his fellow wizard and his superior in wit and cunning, and tries to enlist his powers to fight Sauron, but when Saruman proposes that the two join forces with Sauron, Gandalf tells Saruman that he has abandoned reason for madness, causing mortal strife between the two. The simplicity of "white" versus "black" symbolism is turned on its head in this scene, as Saruman is a "white" wizard but is almost as corrupt and evil as Sauron. This reversal shows that no one is truly safe from the power of the ring's evil force. Sauron temporarily holds Gandalf in bonds, and Gandalf loses power.

The viewer has already felt the impact of digital technology in the Shire scenes and the early scenes with Saruman. Gandalf stands several feet higher than the Hobbits and must hunch over in Bilbo Baggins's tiny home, and during the fight between Gandalf and Saruman, digital photography works its own wizardry.

At the Prancing Pony Inn, Strider, a ranger who is truly the exiled Isildur heir Aragorn (Viggo Mortensen), warns the small group of four friends (Frodo, Sam, and Pippin and Merry, young Hobbits who joined the journey as their friends left the Shire) that the dark horsemen to whom Sauron has given the nine rings of power are arriving; they are ring wraiths, horrifying and powerful creatures, neither living nor dead. As we know, Gandalf cannot meet the Hobbits at the inn, but Strider agrees to lead them on their journey. If it weren't for Strider's advice, the Hobbits would have been murdered in their beds that night, as a quick shot of the would-be future or into the minds of the ring wraiths shows the viewer. Instead, they are safe in another room.

During their flight, Frodo is badly wounded, but Arwen (Liv Tyler), princess of the elves, finds the group and carries Frodo and the ring to Rivendelt, where her father, Lord Elrond (Hugo Weaving), heals him. The friends regroup there with several others who join them, eager to figure out what to do with the ring. Transformed into a bird, Gandalf escapes Saruman's stronghold and joins the council members, who decide to join forces to try to prevent the end of the world by destroying the ring at Mordor. One of the group, Boromir (Sean Bean), son of Lord Denethor of Minas Tirith, proposes the use of the ring for their own power—a view rejected by the council, and Boromir concedes to the majority. Frodo volunteers to take the ring to Mordor, and eight of the council lend their assistance—thus the fellowship of the ring is formed. Viewers get the sense that only a Hobbit would be humble enough, and perhaps pure-hearted enough, to carry the ring without succumbing to its evil power. Boromir joins the group, and so does Aragorn, reconciled to the idea that he is the son of Arathorn and the Isildur heir. The rest of the group consists of Legolas (Orlando Bloom), an elf and expert archer, and

Gimli (John Rhys-Davies), a brave and hard-fighting dwarf who provides much-needed comic relief. The group also includes the four Hobbits and Gandalf. Meanwhile, Aragorn has fallen in love with Arwen, who will lose her immortality if she marries him.

When Saruman causes an avalanche to block the newly banded group's path through the mountains, Gimli proposes an alternative route by way of the dreaded mines of Moria. There they fight a Cyclops-like giant, whom they eventually kill with arrows. When goblins and more Orcs surround the group, viewers experience one of those movie moments where it seems there is no hope, but then Balrog, a monster demon from the ancient world, storms the scene, and all foes disperse. In a fight with Balrog, Gandalf falls into a chasm and disappears, thereby allowing the rest of the group to escape the mines alive. Disheartened, they go through the Realm of the Lady of the Wood, where a female prophet, Galadriel (Cate Blanchett), reveals to Frodo the horrors he will encounter in his mission. Continuing the trek, the group must battle the fast-approaching dark horsemen. A complication arises when Boromir desperately and shamefully covets the power of the ring that tempts those who approach it, especially the prideful. When he tries to regain his dignity, he is mortally wounded and falls. After Boromir's betrayal, Frodo decides to continue the journey alone, crossing a lake by himself, but the loyal Sam follows him and almost drowns as he swims to join his friend. Despite the disconnected nature of the story, which prevents audiences from being fully tied to the characters, the bond between the two Hobbits, mostly shown by Sam's defiance of death, is moving. The two will continue on their perilous path, and that is where the first film of the trilogy ends, leaving the viewer with the expectation of more to follow. Unlike the next two films, *The Fellowship of the Ring* does not stand on its own but merely serves as bait.

The Two Towers, the second part of the trilogy, is darker and scarier, and it concentrates on the human part of the longer story. A few crucial incidents advance the plot beyond its initial stages, and new characters and locales are introduced, while the earlier theme—the impending destruction of the world by the evil forces of the Dark Lord Sauron—remains the same. The team of the nine has broken into three groups. Frodo and Sam continue their trek toward Mordor, soon joined by Gollum, or Smeagol, a half-human creature (presented in animated form) who becomes their guide after being subdued by them. The second group consists of Merry and Pippin, who after being captured by Orcs manage to run away into a magical forest, where the Ents, shepherds of the trees, rescue them. The last group consists of the three loyal companions—Legolas, Aragorn, and Gimli—who attempt to rescue Merry and Pippin. The three fighters are soon stopped by Eomer (Karl Urban), nephew of King Theoden (Bernard Hill) of Rohan, who tells them that his warriors killed a troupe of Orcs and all who traveled with them. But Gandalf, now restored to life and transformed from a "grey" to a "white" wizard with increased powers after escaping from the clutches of the monster Balrog, saves Merry and Pippin and rejoins the group. His metamorphosis makes him a stronger and more determined leader. They all travel together to the Kingdom of Rohan, where a peaceful people, the Edores, are being threatened by Saruman and Sauron.

King Theoden has been reduced to a zombie, thanks to the evil spell of a traitor amidst his court, Wormtongue (Brad Dourif), who is the secret agent and emissary of Saruman. Gandalf's renewed powers allow him to reverse the spell of Saruman and restore Theoden to youth and authority in a scene showcasing the film's impressive special effects. Meanwhile, a second love story develops, for Theoden's beautiful daughter Eowyn (Miranda Otto) cannot conceal her admiration for Aragorn, who, however, cannot forget his emotional tie with Arwen. Another development, a subtler one in the context of the mythical tale, is the change in Frodo, who begins to feel the corrupting power of the ring eroding his will. This shows that no matter how innocent and good a hero is, an evil power such as the ring is capable of attacking him. Although a humble Hobbit, Frodo is susceptible to such power, capable of making him feel a sense of entitlement and even pride.

A weakened and fearful Theoden commands his people to escape to Helm's Deep, a strong fortress that has protected them in the past. The reluctant heroes accompany them there. Saruman has been creating an army of Orcs seemingly out of mud, something that recalls the biblical story of the mud people, a tale twisted in the modern day by white supremacist groups to justify racism. This lends a disturbing undercurrent to the film, even if it was an unintentional connection. To add to this somber tone, African chants underscore many of the war scenes in this section. Soon, the combined forces of Sauron and Saruman attack the last remaining stronghold of the human race in a vast siege, using battering rams to break open the gate of Helm's Deep. After an all-night battle, despite stout resistance by Rohan's remaining forces and the elves, it seems the battle is lost until aid arrives from Eomer, Theoden's nephew, who dashes into battle with his long-speared horsemen from the side of a hill; unexpected help also comes from the Ents carrying Merry and Pippin with them. Despite the destruction of the Kingdom of Rohan, the joint forces of Eomer and the semihuman trees defeat Sauron and Saruman's plan to wipe out the human race.

The Return of the King, the third film in the trilogy, begins with a retrospect showing how Gollum obtained the ring. It appears that he was originally a

Hobbit-like creature called Smeagol, and he and his friend Deagol were fishing when his hook caught a fish that led him to the ring. Smeagol, in his struggle to possess it, kills Deagol, and from then on he is a divided being, for the ring transforms him physically into a hideous creature with a treacherous mind. He, too, craves absolute power. Meanwhile, despite the defeat of Saruman, Sauron still has overwhelming might, and he soon will attack the king's last bastion, Minas Tirith, in the kingdom of Gondor where Lord Denethor reigns. He is the father of Faramir and of Boromir, who has already died valiantly. Denethor is a half-mad, dissolute, and decadent king who does not believe danger exists and continues with his gluttonous ways and later even tries to burn his own son alive. Gandalf arrives with Pippin and appeals to him to fight, but Denethor remains in his mordant state. But the others know that if this last bastion of freedom falls, Sauron will win.

Upon the attack on Gondor, Theoden nonetheless sends forces to aid, accompanied by a band that includes Aragorn, their natural leader; Legolas, brave and expert with his arrows; and Gimli, the valorous dwarf, wielding his ax. Theoden's daughter Eowyn, a valiant fighter, joins the mission and takes Merry along on her horse. The latter two represent a cry for the underdog, both in the form of a woman, who many have claimed cannot fight but who displays here the courage and strength of the men, and a Hobbit, who due to his size heard the same defeatist message but also proves himself in battle. Interestingly, Eowyn is badly hurt and—unlike Aragorn, for example, who is hurt and picks himself up to fight again and again—remains out of the battle scenes for the remainder of the film.

Strangely, the evil followers of Sauron look remarkably like a colonialist vision of Asians and North Africans with their dark skin, face paint, and giant elephants. Aragorn, knowing they cannot beat Sauron's troops without more fighters, arrives on the scene with an army of ghosts. He, Legolas, and Gimli have enlisted the aid of the "forgotten people," long-dead humans who abandoned their king and suffered a curse until they could help his heir. The ensuing battle scene is almost too amazing, wowing viewers to the point of fatigue.

Theoden's and Aragorn's troops defend the city, but Theoden dies fighting one of the monsters. They may have defeated Sauron's forces momentarily, but Mordor still stands, and Aragorn, now exhibiting his leadership qualities as strategist, suggests that they attack the stronghold as a diversion in order to give Frodo a chance to reach Mount Doom. The others soon join, and they approach the gates of Mordor, where Sauron views everything with his fiery eye. They are united and determined but soon are surrounded by vastly superior forces. When all seems lost, Frodo faints but is carried up Mount Doom by the loyal Sam. He is apparently ready to throw the ring into the fire when Gollum attacks him. At this point, it is not clear whether

Frodo will destroy the ring whose wickedness has infected him with a desire for power. Just as a "white" wizard is not necessarily a "good" wizard, a humble Hobbit may not have been pure enough to complete this mission. Finally Gollum falls into the molten lava beneath, and he perishes along with the ring, which boils and melts out of view and is gone forever. The battle is won. The tower collapses, the earth opens and devours the Orcs, and Aragorn, as the son of Arathorn, is crowned as the legitimate King of Condor. He marries Arwen, who decides to become mortal. The four Hobbits return home, but Frodo, unable to find peace because his experiences have forever divided his nature and made him a loner, departs with Gandalf for a long sea voyage, presumably to also become a wizard one day. Sam, however, remains home and marries his sweetheart, and we soon see him happily kissing her and hugging his two kids. Normalcy has returned to Middle-earth, now a free land.

A philosopher once said that he gave up playing chess because it was too serious to be a game and not serious enough to be an occupation. With some rearrangement of imagery and stretching the analogy a bit, one could say that the digital epic is too serious to be a video game and not serious enough to be an art. Peter Jackson, Oscar-laden and world-recognized, stated more than once that he did not wish the special effects to overwhelm the story.[3] This is honestly said, and much effort went into achieving that end. And yet, the story (and the acting and actors) seems at times overwhelmed, even dwarfed, by the awesome spectacle one witnesses in these three giant movies. They leave the audience gasping with wonder at the majesty of digital wizardry, the sound effects, the sheer motion and dynamism of action, and the incredible precision of arrangement of the structures, not to mention the photogenic landscapes of New Zealand ingeniously blending with the special effects.

Jackson also states that he wanted the story to be convincing and as true to life as possible, and to a large degree, he was successful. There is no doubt about the artistry and digital ingenuity used to reproduce a bygone imaginary world that supposedly was related, at least in part, to historical reality. Some commentators have indeed likened Aragorn's struggles to defend the inhabitants of Middle-earth to such historical battles as the Battle of Agincourt, where Henry V defeated the vastly superior forces of France in 1415, or to Winston Churchill's inspirational leadership in England's fight against Nazi Germany in World War II.[4] But the flying Lepidoptera, the giant Jurassic Park–type elephants, and the massive numbers of the deformed Orcs—all these are so impressive that they work, at least to some extent, against an audience's need to relate emotionally with the people in a story or to connect the various threads between the characters involved. And that becomes another problem for the trilogy: The aesthetic effects need to be organic to the rhythms of the story, but the story—one in three parts—seems so fragmented that the ties loosen, and thus the involvement of the viewer following these events is diluted. An example is the romance between Arwen and Aragorn. They are destined to be lovers, and indeed in the end they marry. But their romance simply limps along, given in small flashes here and there, and the emotional impact is missing when the two lovers unite in the end. Of course, epics are not necessarily love stories, for too much action is demanded of the heroes for one to really get involved in romance. Aragorn has things to attend to other than paying attention to the inactive Arwen, who just enters and exits again, having more scenes with her father than with the man she loves.

The numerous lords, kings, vassals, evil agents, monsters, and assorted villains also come and go far too frequently. Of course, this is supposed to be a remarkable collision between good and evil, but something beyond that, as Jackson also said.[5] He wanted to develop character, a task that is achieved sparingly, as, for instance, in the relationship between Frodo and Sam, two friends exposed to the same perils and sharing their fortunes until they achieve their goal. But even that relationship is submerged under the deluge of events that are simultaneously taking place. Christopher Lee's Saruman is also given with all the subtle touches of malevolence that this actor, who honed his skills with roles such as Dracula and a Bond villain,[6] is capable of exhibiting. But he is totally absent from the third movie (he had been defeated in the previous one), while Sauron, the main villain of the third movie, is invisible except as a flaming eye darting malignant glances into Middle-earth, which he wishes to subjugate. Gandalf is steadily involved in practically all main incidents, and Ian McKellen's performance renders this character impeccably. Gandalf, thus, is the only character besides Frodo and Aragorn who plays a decisive role in the emotional impact of the trilogy. Do any of them have enough "clout" to hold all the threads together—speaking in terms of the magnetic effects of an epic figure? Great epics of the past, like *Ben-Hur* and *Lawrence of Arabia*, had the good fortune to feature strong lead actors who held the threads of a narrative together for not inconsiderable lengths of time, for those epics were four-hour affairs in one sitting.

The large canvas (one should say canvases) of *The Lord of the Rings* trilogy, as insidious as the creatures it represents, manages to create sensation—fear, terror, revulsion, awe—but not a truly aesthetic effect. Some understatement—an alternative means of telling a big story effectively—could have left the audience less stunned by the constant bombardment of special effects but more pleased with the development of emotional ties of the numerous characters. A vast tale, vastly populated and told in the most exaggerated way possible, hits the audience right between the eyes—leaving the "heart" petrified and barely able to recover its own rhythms.

Having said all that, one also has to highlight the fact that the epic trilogy works well on the allegorical/archetypal level, which is possibly the cause for its popularity. As stated before, the battle between good and evil is the topic more explored by epics than any other. The epic has generated two basic methods, which have become its lifelines: it gives audiences unparalleled entertainment, and it appeals to the communal instincts, mainly to those of survival. Wizards of the medium, like Cecil B. DeMille, David Lean, Steven Spielberg, and, these days, Peter Jackson, understood this point, but they also knew, though perhaps less consciously, that heroic figures help wider audiences to overcome fears of annihilation. As in previous ages, ours has had its share of such fears. Plagues, such as the Asiatic flu pandemic early in the century; natural disasters, such as Hurricane Katrina in 2005 or earthquakes and tsunamis that overwhelm regions of the earth; and above all, human-generated conflicts—two major wars, countless minor ones, and the all-too-real fear of terrorism—and many others leave their imprint on public consciousness, often shattering its fragile sense of security. As other epics have done, *The Lord of the Rings* movies explore—and attempt to mollify—those fears. A single weapon can destroy humankind: the ring is an artifact that, despite its beauty, has a grip on those who possess it, corrupting them with dreams of power and eventually weakening and destroying them. Perhaps it is the fear of the "machine" itself, which we saw in *The Matrix* and which was so feared by some writers of the nineteenth and twentieth centuries, from Mary Shelley to Thomas Carlyle. In fact, Tolkien was perhaps a neo-romantic at heart, describing the idyllic existence of the Shire threatened by intrusions of the outside world; the world of the elves is also threatened with extinction—as was the all-peaceful existence of the human inhabitants of Middle-earth. And the revolt of the trees, which come to the rescue of the Kingdom of Rohan, shows nature's revolt against those who would destroy it. Contrarily, the army Saruman creates reflects mechanized war that came into existence during World War I. But the story may even go deeper than the romantic era or further back than *Beowulf*'s medieval Europe; it may go back to the Garden of Eden, where the serpent introduced "knowledge" as the beginning of all man's travails in the path of civilization. Finally, perhaps the underlying cynicism revealed in the fact that the world is saved almost by accident makes the story more relevant to a postmodern audience.

The trilogy provides food for thought, even at the simplistic level that it presents its action-packed story. It may not be the epic to end all epics, but it is one that has come to the rescue of the epic form, giving it new splendor, for the makers were all conscientious, unusually talented, and possibly a bit prophetic. The epic always thrived on its populism. One should not forget that Homer's poems were read at public festivals and that Dante read his *Divine Comedy* at popular feasts and gatherings. When you fall back on the couch—or chair—exhausted, feeling as if enough is enough, *The Lord of the Rings*, taking its cues from the burning eye of Sauron, lashes out its flaming tongue and says, "Nothing is enough!"

Batman Begins (2005); Director: Christopher Nolan

Like most modern action movies, *Batman Begins* is hyperkinetic, tense, murky, dark, and unpleasant for the most part, and features the usual action patterns: heroes chasing villains. Yet, viewing it had its rewards, mainly because of the change of direction—literally.

Director Christopher Nolan declared his intention to make (or remake) the latest feature film of the Batman franchise in a serious and realistic style, showing the human side of the batlike flying hero who has entertained America and the world for decades, first as a comic-strip hero in the daily papers, then as a TV-screen matinee idol, then in a series of motion pictures, some of which were mere flops. The first movie, *Batman* (1989), featuring Michael Keaton as Batman, was a huge popular success, for the audiences loved their superhero on the large screen, but Michael Keaton, a gifted actor, did not quite fit the persona of the man with wings—as Superman fits his cape—not having the physical charisma demanded by that role. The movies that followed, three in all,[16] did not fare better, and the last of them, *Batman and Robin* (1997), sank the franchise to inanity to such a degree that a resurrection seemed highly unlikely.

Nolan's movie, however, added both new luster and new life to the moribund series. Nolan, already known for his gritty and innovative *Memento* (2001), and his remake of the Norwegian murder story, *Insomnia* (2002), took the new project with intentions of giving it depth and believability, without sacrificing its fantasy aspects, for Batman remains a pop fantasy with all the gadgetry that that entails. Thus, a dimension would be added to the character of Batman—his childhood traumas that led him to choose his path, for chasing and battling villains and protecting a city from them is choosing a violent way of life. In a sense, Batman, a cartoon hero, is the equivalent of a western plains roamer, a Paladin[17] of sorts, but one whose persona is endowed with darker sides, for a bat, from which he borrows his stamina and ability to fly, is a dark, nocturnal creature, is not a bird, which has more innocent connotations attached to its name, but a mammal, capable of inflicting wounds on the flesh with bites, and, of course, an inspiration for sinister figures such as Dracula. It lives in holes and caverns, and flies in multitudes, emitting shrill dissonant yelps that frighten children and inspire nightmares. Thence, Batman's psychic makeup is more complex, showing a split between a man's rational personality and his subconscious drives, a split that has some of the underground traits of the antihero.[18] Nolan capitalizes on such traits, highlighting his hero's dark nature and giving him an extra dimension by allowing the viewer to know something of his past. As a child, Bruce Wayne, Batman's secular name, witnessed the murder of his parents by a casual mugger, and he is plagued with guilt, for it was for a whim of his—special effects had frightened him—that his parents left an opera performance they were attending. When the murderer is about to be paroled fourteen years later, Wayne, still nourishing his rage and guilt, kills him, and then he flees to the East, where he seeks guidance from a clannish martial arts school, called "League of Shadows," whose leaders include Ra's Al Ghul (Ken Watanabe) and Henri Ducard (Liam Neeson). The latter tries to instill in him the stern teachings of the league—which include defeat of fear and turning revenge feelings into a sense of implacable justice. But when Wayne is asked to practice this principle by decapitating a condemned man, he refuses to be "an executioner." He sets the school on fire, and flees after a battle, in which he thinks he has killed his mentors, including Ducard.

Wayne returns to Gotham city and his parents' home. The house is like a mausoleum, and the loyal butler Alfred (Michael Caine) is still there, having managed to preserve the family's immense fortune. Crime in the city is rampant and soon Wayne is embroiled in his pursuit of justice, donning his dark mask and floating cloak, and trying to foil the plans of Gotham's chief villain, mafia don Carmine Falcone (Tom Wilkinson), who is involved in drug trafficking and other crimes. Prosecutor Rachel Daws (Katie Holmes) and the cooperative detective Jim Gordon (Gary Oldman) are at the point of nailing Falcone, but the latter receives unexpected help from a pernicious villain, a young doctor, Jonathan Crane (Cillian Murphy), who is also disguised, wearing the straw mask of a scarecrow—he, in fact, calls himself the Scarecrow. Scarecrow attempts to murder Rachel (and almost succeeds) and spreads toxins that all creatures, even bats, fear. He has intentions of poisoning the city's water supply, when Batman's old instructors, Al Ghul and Ducard, whom Wayne had presumed dead, also appear on the scene, and Ducard, in particular, tries to foil and kill Batman. Fierce individual battles between Ducard and Batman ensue and there is destruction and mayhem throughout Gotham, but Batman prevails after several hard-fought battles as scores of villains attack him. Also in imitation of Bond, Batman uses the "Tumbler Car," a fantastic, futuristic automobile capable of soaring over obstacles and demolishing and outrunning any opposition. Batman and Ducard engage in a martial-arts duel on a moving monorail that is both breathtaking and decisive.

As with other information age epics, *Batman Begins* blends digital imagery with photography of actual places and animated figures with actual stunt work and does so with seeming ease, which is the result of a deliberate attempt to make images on the screen appear as close to real life as possible. The city of Gotham, for instance, is presented as "a heightened reality of contemporary New York," in the words of Nolan[19] himself. It also combines the looks of Hong Kong and Chicago, and countless photographs of those cities were used to establish a look-alike digital version. The same intent of making every aspect of the film look as real as possible extends to the choice of actors to play the various characters. Morgan Freeman's Lucius Fox, for instance, is a wizened older fellow, who equips Batman with various gadgets, playing a role equivalent to that of Q in the Bond movies. Caine's Alfred is the epitome of a polished English butler, a father figure who helps Batman navigate the underground caverns of his elegant ancestral manor, a place that serves as Batman's headquarters and hiding place. Gary Oldman, whose expert metamorphoses as a screen persona include Beethoven and Dracula, makes a brave, determined, and incorruptible cop, much needed in a city pervaded with sleazy corrupt deals and in danger of falling apart. The same goes for Katie Holmes, an actress first known for teen roles. Here she is mature, brave, and anything but passive, though barely escaping Scarecrow's clutches. The latter is a perfectly honed villain whose youthful looks deceive one at first. A brilliant doctor with a diabolical mind—a "mad scientist" with a modern twist—he is an antagonist to Batman, knowing where he is and guessing his psychic insecurities. He calls him "a cliché Jungian archetype ripped from a psych book," a remark that does not stray too widely off the mark. For, indeed, Bruce Wayne, as played by Christian Bale, is a troubled individual. Whether he admits it or not, he had been adversely influenced by the insidious words of Ducard and the mockery of Scarecrow and at times seems unable to face fear or to totally uproot his deeply planted desire for revenge. He does what he does—saves his city from doom—for humanity and for justice, but the term justice is already a perverse notion in his mind, for, had he followed Ducard's poisonous instruction, he would have ended up as an executioner, something he abhors. Indeed, what is the difference? Does not any authority that pursues justice also become an executioner in the end? Nolan, who cowrote the script, wanted this point to remain ambiguous, but he clearly delineates the difference between one who wants justice enforced and one who carries out the justice. Thus his Batman is divided—as, one might remember, is the hero of his previous movie, *Insomnia*, where Bill Dormer (Al Pacino) kills a colleague for reasons he cannot quite fathom. Batman, as played by Bale, is a man whose steely and dark stare sometimes shows a glint of his inner confusion. Bale's Batman is tortured. It is difficult to kill so many adversaries—even in the name of justice and even if they are villains, although it is a different matter when it is done in self-defense. But

Batman here cannot entirely free himself from the burden that Bruce Wayne carries. Having witnessed his parents' death, the man became not only vengeful but also confused, especially after the poisonous tutoring of his mentors. His desire to save Gotham city is perhaps what saves his morality, and his increasing love for Rachel may be an added factor in the urgency of his metamorphosis. One almost wishes that he give up his perilous tasks, settle down, and marry a girl and have a family. But evil is loose upon the world and heroes are needed to save it. Christian Bale plays Wayne as a martyr— a very slight hint is given of this—and Nolan makes a serious movie with a hero who actually embodies the image of the archetype that Scarecrow so jeeringly speaks of. There are of course the swarms of bats flying all over, announcing the end of the world—very Hitchcock—but bats are also ambiguous, for they are mammals with wings, useful because they devour masses of injurious nocturnal insects (mosquitoes), something that preserves the balance of nature. As archetypal images, they work at a deeper level, for they also swarm the human psyche with doubt, not a bad feeling to have occasionally. Doubt is what stops Wayne from becoming an executioner, and his inquiring mind balances his raw instinct for revenge. Batman here is more human than the two-dimensional persona that has been presented in comic strips, on television, or in any of the previous movies. This is a murky version of Batman, yes, but one truer to a human entity than to a cartoon likeness of him.

Suggested Films for Study

Brazil (1985); Director: Terry Gilliam
This futuristic fantasy/dark comedy epic describes a society living a subterranean existence, where computers regulate human actions, as the pernicious Ministry of Education keeps track of everybody and everything that happens. When the system goes haywire through a computer error, society loses track of a would-be terrorist threatening to destroy it. Celebrated for its art direction (for which it received an Academy Award nomination) and innovative script (by Tom Stoppard and Charles McKeown), Brazil invokes Kafkaesque tones (The Castle), in which a society falls victim to its overelaborate and menacing ingenuity. Many consider it an Orwellian type of allegory of what will happen to our society if it stays on its present course of technological surveillance.

The Terminator 2: Judgment Day (1991); Director: James Cameron
In terms of special effects, James Cameron's Terminator 2 is, perhaps, superior to The Terminator (1984), with Arnold Schwarzenegger, who played

cyborg T-800, sent from the future (2029) by machines to destroy an unborn John Connor, who is to lead humanity in a war of survival. In *Terminator 2*, Schwarzenegger plays a benign cyborg in order to foil a double, T-1000, who, in the form of a young policeman, is sent from the future to destroy the teenage John Connor (Kyle Resse). The protean, ever-changing T-1000 gives him a time before Schwarzenegger finally subdues him (it). Spectacular, but rather shallow, it nevertheless illustrates the perils that audiences of the 1980s faced, such as terrorism, assassinations, and nuclear war.

Spider-Man 2 (2004); Director: Sam Raimi

The sequel to the popular *Spider-Man* (2002) is said to be superior to its original, for this time the comic-strip superhero, Peter Parker (Tobey Maguire) faces some internal conflicts when donning his notorious costume to perform superhuman feats, which include facing a mad scientist, Dr. Octavius (Alfred Molina), now the deformed-by-an-accident Dr. Octopus, who threatens society with extinction. Spectacular, with good performances, this comic-strip epic offers a bonanza of digital effects but does not transcend the level of commonplace pop-culture epic. It does keep pace with its contemporaries in forwarding the cause of good versus evil routinely exploited by information age epics.

Superman Returns (2006); Director: Bryan Singer

This revival of the older franchise brings back the celebrated Man of Steel, Clark Kent/Superman, this time in the person of Brandon Routh, who, aided by Kate Bosworth as Lois Lane (this time married and with a child) resumes his battle with Lex Luthor (Kevin Spacey), who is intent on destroying California. Of course, the most popular hero in fantasy screen epics wins again, but only after considerable stumbles. Routh does a passable job but is no substitute for the late Christopher Reeve, who stole the popular imagination as humanity's savior several decades earlier.

Notes

1. In the 1925 version of *Ben-Hur*, one of the ships that was supposed to appear to be burning before sinking actually caught fire by accident, so the art directors let it burn and filmed the whole thing, including the escaping crew, as it occurred. See "Bonus Features,"*Ben-Hur*, Four-Disc Collector's Edition DVD, Disc four (Warner Brothers, 2005).

2. Discussed in chapter 1.

3. The original film of 1977 was simply called *Star Wars*.

4. The sequels are *Episode V: The Empire Strikes Back* (1980) and *Episode VI: Return of the Jedi* (1983). The prequels are *Episode I: The Phantom Menace* (1999), *Episode II: Attack of the Clones* (2002), and *Episode III: Revenge of the Sith* (2005).

5. "George Lucas Interview," *The Hidden Fortress*, DVD (The Criterion Collection, 2001).

6. For a broader discussion of the film, see Karen Haber, ed., *Exploring the Matrix: Visions of the Cyber Present* (New York: St. Martin's, 2003). This book contains articles by Stephen Baxter, David Brin, Pat Cadigan, and John Shirley, among others.

7. Larissa MacFarquhar, "Baudrillard on Tour," *New Yorker*, November 28, 2005, 62–64.

8. *The Matrix Reloaded* (2003) and *The Matrix Revolutions* (2003), both directed by Andy and Larry Wachowski.

9. Other famous lengthy epics are Erich von Stroheim's *Greed* (1925), which originally was intended to be an eight-hour epic and out of necessity was trimmed to 140 minutes. The Russian-made *War and Peace*, in excess of eight hours (507 minutes), was released theatrically in the United States in 1968.

10. The opinion was expressed in some of his novels—*A Room with a View* in particular.

11. The symbolism is too evident to ignore. Frodo resembles Samuel Taylor Coleridge's *The Rime of the Ancient Mariner*—though there is no evidence that the similarities are anything but coincidental.

12. Peter Jackson, "Special Effects," *The Lord of the Rings*, DVD Disc two (New Line Cinema, 2002). Jackson also mentions this idea in Brian Sibley, *The Lord of the Rings: The Making of the Movie Trilogy* (New York: HarperCollins, 2002), 78.

13. Peter Jackson, "A Filmmaker's Journey: Making *The Return of the King*," *The Return of the King*, DVD Disc two (New Line Cinema, 2003).

14. Jackson, "A Filmmaker's Journey."

15. Christopher Lee plays a man with a golden gun in the Bond movie, *The Man with the Golden Gun* (1974).

16. *Batman Returns* (1992), again with Michael Keaton; *Batman Forever* (1995), with Val Kilmer; and *Batman and Robin* (1997) with George Clooney.

17. The hero of the 1950s (and early 1960s) TV series, *Have Gun Will Travel*, with Richard Boone as Paladin, a vindicator of the weak and unprotected, and a menace to assorted villains.

18. Described in detail in chapter 7.

19. Christopher Nolan, "Special Features," *Batman Begins*, DVD Disc two (Warner Brothers, 2005).

CHAPTER NINE

The International
and Art House Epics

Epics were also the province of international cinema and were not confined to American production, though the epic thrived mostly under the Hollywood system, which took advantage both of its commercial character and the glitter and spectacle that appealed mostly to large audiences, both at home and outside the United States. International epics as a whole are not made with the lavish production values used by Hollywood in its heyday, and some international producers seek smaller, discriminating audiences, even making epics with pretensions of "art house" works, a term that does not stand well with the Hollywood screen products, which are ostensibly designed for the masses. But epics were not always popular works designed for mass consumption. Even some American epics—*Judgment at Nuremberg*, *Schindler's List*, *Flags of Our Fathers*—are works of serious intent, but in this sense, international epics may have an advantage and merit some attention. Works by Sergei Eisenstein, for instance, the Russian pioneer in montage and other innovative film techniques, can be characterized as epics, for they had the epic length and other epic traits. Another Russian, Andrei Tarkovksy, made at least one great epic, *Andrei Rublev* (1966). Sergei Bondarchuk's *War and Peace* (1968), the mammoth production based on Tolstoy's novel is certainly one of the most distinguished (and lengthiest) epics ever made. The works of Akira Kurosawa, especially those of the samurai period (1955–1965) are also epics in the fullest sense of the word, and so are some of the works of another distinguished Japanese auteur, Kenji Mizogushi, who composed war epics of the conflicts of sixteenth-century Japan, the period when most of the samurai epics were set. Many European directors, such as Fellini, Antonioni, Visconti, and even some of the French new wave auteurs, ventured into epic forms—though these were by no means epics that smacked of Hollywood tastes or methods. Other European and international directors made epics, either in imitation of Hollywood, or to satisfy their audiences or their own artistic predilections. Epics are not an exclusive American provenance, and continue in the international arena with the works of Emir Kusterica (*Underground*, 1995), Theo Angelopoulos (*The Gaze of Ulysses*, 1995), Jean-Pierre Jeunet (*A Very Long Engagement*, 2004), and many others, although one does not expect the international epic to command the large budgets, star-studded casts, and overall high production values of Hollywood.

La Dolce Vita (1959); Director/Writer: Federico Fellini

Federico Fellini's movie took Western audiences by storm in New York and other places in 1959, mostly because of its (for then) sexual explicitness. It is an epic by mere force of length (at 175 minutes), but also, and mainly, because of the concept of its hero. An underground man by rights, Marcello (played by Marcello Mastroianni) marches in the underworld—a hero of "no exit," who seems to dwell in a Catholic Hades in perpetuity. *La Dolce Vita* has been compared to Dante's *Inferno*, showing a Dante-like figure progressing through a dark forest, having lost the way. Marcello, the "gossip journalist" who wanders through a decadent Rome in search of the "true way," is a Dantean equivalent in that he too is lost in the modern world, caught between the paralysis of the vogue crowd and the religious mass hysteria of the populace, while he is haunted by a genuine inner-born (but unbeknownst to himself) desire to redeem himself spiritually. This movie's unstructured action reflects the depiction of Marcello's inner drive. Blind, though not entirely unenlightened, he connects with various groups that come his way, a Swedish/American sexpot, Sylvia (Anita Ekberg) and her escort Robert (Lex Barker), an ex-Tarzan Hollywood movie star; an eccentric, sex-driven heiress, Maddalena (Anouk Aime); and his down-to-earth fiancée, Emma (Yvonne Furneaux), who expects him to marry her and settle down in an everyday connubial existence. For spiritual nourishment, he pays an occasional visit to a mystic/philosopher, Steiner (Alain Cuny), who ostensibly leads a harmonious existence surrounded by a group of eccentric friends and is blessed with a beautiful wife and two children, but who, it appears, nourishes a cancerous self-doubt, which Marcello is unable to detect.

Marcello makes love to the amorous Maddalena, then takes Emma, his fiancée, to an emergency room after she attempts suicide; later he witnesses a "miracle" in which two children see the Madonna, a scene of maddening irreverence that only Fellini is capable of filming. Marcello attends several decadent parties with dissolute partners, aristocratic English ladies, unisex lovers, transvestites, pseudointellectuals, and hedonists of all sorts. After the sudden and unexpected death of Steiner, who kills his two children before committing suicide, Marcello spends the night at a party, an all-night orgy, culminating in a morning exodus to the beach, where the weary party participants witness the capture of a sea monster by the local fishermen. Squeezed in between these larger episodes is a smaller one, barely noticeable in the "larger-than-life" events that lace Marcello's wanderings, a tiny episode at a seaside café where a young waitress serves Marcello some refreshments and chats with him for a few moments while he is trying to write a report on his typewriter. Marcello is annoyed by her playing loud music on the radio and asks her to shut it off, which she does, urging him to eat something. She is not from Rome, but from Umbria, and misses her family; she is an adolescent and looks like a mere child. Marcello, with an eye for delicate beauty, notices the young girl's Madonna-like (in the painter's sense) features, and asks her to let him look at her in profile, which she does, always smiling. But of course he forgets this encounter in the avalanche of events that follow. In the movie's final scene, while he and the other partygoers are still amusingly and curiously looking at the hideous dead monster on the beach, Marcello's eye is caught by the same young girl, who is gesturing at him from across the dune, but in his debauched state, he can hardly remember her or understand what she tries to tell him. He can't hear her in the roar of the beach waves. She beckons, smiles, and talks to him as loudly as she can, but in vain, because he cannot hear her above the noise of the waves. He does not remember her, though a vague reminiscence of something pure lightens his face for a few seconds. Then all is oblivion. Marcello, unlike Dante, whose Beatrice ultimately guides him to Paradise, has forgone his last chance for salvation.

The Leopard (Il Gattopardo) (1963);
Director: Luchino Visconti

Based on the novel by Giuseppe de Lampedusa, Luchino Visconti's epic reflects the collapse of aristocracy in Sicily circa 1860 (coinciding with the American Civil War, as many have pointed out), a period known as Risorgimento, during which the rebel forces of Garibaldi, the "Redshirts," invaded Sicily to annex it to the then-forming kingdom of a united Italy. As the new regime gradually takes over, one lone aristocrat, Don Fabrizio Cobrera, Prince of Salina, known as the Leopard (Burt Lancaster), sees the decline of power of the aristocracy, a tradition of over two and a half thousand years, but he refuses to take part in the resistance, and, when the new regime is established, he quietly declines the rank of senator that he is offered in the new government. His realization of the collapse of an era, of the passage of nobility in favor of a vulgar nouveau-riche society, is profound and shattering, especially as he sees his nephew (Alain Delon) engaged to the daughter of Don Calogero (Paolo Stoppa), a wealthy tradesman of the now prevailing class. After dancing with Angelica (Claudia Cardinale), his future daughter-in-law, at a ball given to honor the new regime, he walks home, alone and totally alienated from his own kind, unable to bear the sight of crude generals mixing with compromised aristocrats, the betraying class whom he himself refused to betray. This is an art epic, one of the best photographed, but it is perhaps too slow for American tastes, probably because only a truncated version of it was offered to the American screens in 1963.

Alphaville (1965); Director/Cowriter: Jean-Luc Godard

Alphaville, a somewhat enigmatic film by new wave director Jean-Luc Godard, is science fiction, a detective story, a spy thriller, a poetic and philosophic reflection on totalitarianism, a holocaust simulacrum, a parable of galactic hypothesis, and a parody of all the above. It is also a sort of populist movie with Eddie Constantine, who was a cult figure throughout Europe, as private eye Lemmy Caution during the 1950s and early 1960s. Godard smoothly transfers his persona to that of a philosophic inquirer of space engaged in a search for meaning, thus transforming Constantine from a B-movie hack to a hero with mental dimensions unknown to Bond and his like. *Alphaville* features no spaceships, no *Star Wars* gadgetry, and no digital screen magic. Caution arrives in Alphaville by train, is driven through a perimeter highway, and checks into a hotel using the false name of Ivan Johnson. The hotel's logo reads, "Silence, Logic, Security, Prudence," the mottos of Alphaville, which is the capital of the Galaxy. As he is given his room number, Caution learns that he must register at Residents Control. But, of course, Caution has no intention of doing that. He is an agent from the Outlands, and his mission is to find Professor Vonbraun (Howard Verson), inventor of the death ray, and bring him back alive or liquidate him. He is escorted to his room by a robot-like blonde ("a third-rate seductress," he learns later) in suggestive dress, who asks him polite questions regarding his comfort and offers him a Bible, tranquilizers, and sex, as soon as he is in his room. The Bible is actually a dictionary, where words such as love and conscience are constantly disappearing.

After Caution dismisses the robotlike blonde, he is attacked by a mysterious onlooker, whom he dispatches easily with the bathroom stool. Gradually, Caution becomes more aware of the peculiarities of the environment at Alphaville. Everyone is programmed to think logically. To think "illogically" means death. A man is executed for weeping when his wife died. When Caution meets Natasha (Anna Karina), Vonbraun's daughter, she does not understand him when he says he wants to court her. Emotion is unknown in Alphaville. Caution gradually awakens a feeling in Natasha, since love cannot be suppressed. And Caution finally finds Vonbraun and kills him. He rescues Natasha, and the two head back to the Outlands.

War and Peace (1968);
Director/Cowriter/Actor: Sergei Bondarchuk

This epic, based on the celebrated novel by Leo Tolstoy, is said to be the longest movie ever shown in theaters worldwide. Made in the Soviet Union in the midsixties, it deserves special note, mostly because it is said to be a completely faithful rendition of the original Tolstoy novel. *War and Peace* offers spectacular action scenes, excellent cinematography, splendidly photographed battles of Borodino and Austerlitz, ballroom dance scenes, and the French retreat when Napoleon was defeated—scenes still worth watching, even by today's more technically advanced standards. The characters are accurately portrayed; the main focus is on Pierre Bezuhov (played by the film's director, Sergei Bondachuk) and on two lovers, Natasha Rostova (Lyudmila Savelyeva) and Prince Andrei Bolkonsky (Vyacheslav Tikhonov), though these two actors do not manage to connect emotionally and be convincing as lovers as Vivien Leigh and Clark Gable were in *Gone with the Wind*, where their embattled relationship is convincing and real. This is an epic of romance, as well as war, and the romance seems not to click. Of course, this is not true of the book, where the romantic interest remains vivid throughout and ends in a heart-breaking scene in which Natasha witnesses Andrei's death. As for the philosophy, Tolstoy's apotheg-matic sayings are sprinkled throughout the film, most spouted by Bezuhov, an awkward man and an idealist, supposedly representing Tolstoy's point of view. Voice-overs turn out tiresome simplicities and the film needs the voice-over to convey thought, and dialogue, which of necessity must be clipped and simple; otherwise, you have hard-to-follow banalities (the dubbed version is not any better) in subtitles that you sometimes hear in Fellini and Bergman, the least convincing of their techniques (but Fellini and Bergman have the stunning visuals to compensate).

Andrei Rublev: The Passion according to Andrei (1969); Director: Andrei Tarkovsky

In Russia, Tarkovsky has been called "the poet of the cinema," and *Andrei Rublev* is recognized as his masterpiece, an epic made explicitly for the sake of art only and not for any commercial purpose. Cinema, Tarkovsky claims, "Is an unhappy art because it depends on money and is marketed like cigarettes." Films for a large audience cannot be produced, "for it is now difficult to surprise the spectator," and "good films are not seen by the masses." But Tarkovsky feels, and hopes, that "cinema will see a brighter day."[1] *Andrei Rublev* is a stunning work, with breathtaking photography, deeply emblematic and emotionally charged images that provoke ideas about the relevance of art to life. The film unearths a corner of history when atrocities of such magnitude were committed that one begins to doubt that the evil hidden in the human heart can be uprooted. Above all, *Andrei Rublev* is a deeply religious movie, which manages, without a shade of irreverence or desire to seek thrills or audience approval, to equate the passion of an artist with the compassion of the West's greatest religious leader. Here the artist does not merely "imitate life," as a painter aloof and safe in his studio does, but mingles with his society's sufferers, undergoing their suffering himself, doubting dogmas he has cherished, witnessing unspeakable horrors, questioning faith and purpose, and even dreaming what kind of resurrection humanity can achieve after the inferno on earth it has created. These are not weak-kneed questions, and Tarkovsky interweaves them in this film with conviction and force. *Andrei Rublev* was filmed in black and white, it is episodic in nature, and portions of it are told from a subjective/oneiric point of view, as the protagonist, wandering through the vastness of Russia, early in the fifteenth century (from approximately 1402 to 1425), witnesses scenes of unbelievable cruelty, miserable living conditions, acts of faith, pagan rituals, a massacre of a Russian village by Tartars, and atrocities where the weak and innocent are crushed by the strong and ruthless. The wanderings of Rublev (Anatoly Solonitsin) are given in seven episodes, the first being the exodus of Andrei and his two companions, Kyrill and Danil, from the monastery and the start of their wanderings; the last episode shows the casting of a bell under the orders of the prince, undertaken by a boy, Boriska, son of a famous bell maker, now dead. Two episodes show an oneiric (dreamlike) state, where Rublev is engaged in discourses with Theophanes the Greek, Rublev's teacher, who appears to be debating the role of the artist in society. The middle episode is the longest, detailing the cruelties of the Tartar invasion. Tarkovsky's technique allows for lengthy takes and is said to be the opposite of Eisenstein's, whose montages and frequent crosscutting include only shortened versions—or glimpses—of photographed objects, and thus only a momentary emotional response. Later, when the invasion is accomplished, the camera witnesses the massacre in detail, but close-ups of the suffering victims are avoided, by and large. Tarkovsky's technique stresses the whole more than the part, and thus the viewer witnesses this period from a distance, never fully participating in the action as would happen in a modern action movie where dismemberments are seen in close-up. In the pagan ritual, Jesus is indeed seen being nailed to the cross. His sufferings are for our sins. Russians—and all suffering victims—will survive, while their tormentors will burn in hell. Rublev, for all his suffering as witness or participant, is painting the story of Russia, a country tormented by its enemies and nearly exterminated by cruel winters, passionate and ruthless invaders, and inner conflict. The canvas presents the mingling of the bestial and the spiritual, both parts of life, and the film implies that this is what the artist should attempt to represent. Rublev does not sit secluded in his cell and imagine what he will paint, for thus he would know life only remotely and without its harsh realism. Instead, he chooses to see it first-hand, and live it as intensely as possible, though his life becomes endangered in the process. Tarkovsky demonstrates this approach to an extreme, filming under the most harrowing conditions, on a snowy steppe, in a cold forest, in scenes that resemble real torture and suffering. No movie can succeed in recording, subjectively, what goes on in an artist's mind. Whatever is visually presented is an extraneous record. The artist must remain a recorder, even as a sculptor, working with stone, must. Here Tarkovsky has thrown out an idea and a challenge to all artists: stay close to experience as much as you can, be honest, and ruthless if you must; that is not a bad message for an art such as film that seems increasingly repetitive, and spurious.

Aguirre: The Wrath of God (1972); Director/Writer: Werner Herzog

This epic movie presents a fictional account of Francisco Pizarro's expedition to the Peruvian Andes in the sixteenth century. Though the story is largely fabricated, there is some historical evidence that Pizarro and the Spanish conquistadors pursued a dream of finding gold in the remote areas of the Amazon and the Peruvian jungles. The myth of El Dorado had attracted adventurers who penetrated tropical forests and mountain peaks in search of gold, riches, and power. Pizarro's expedition was presumably sponsored by the Royal House of Spain and the Catholic Church, and his retinue included both ranking clerics, royal representatives, and Aquirre's mistress Inez, who volunteers to escort the expedition. The movie focuses on one incident only, the breakaway of Don Lope de Aguirre (Klaus Kinsky) from the main body of the expedition led by Gonzalez Pizarro and his commander's group in order to penetrate the jungles further and search for El Dorado for himself. The Royal House of Spain is represented by Don Fernando de Guzman (Peter Berlin), and the word of God is to be brought to the pagans by Brother Gaspar de Carvajal (Nel Negro), who also is commissioned to keep a diary of the expedition. The group, consisting of forty men, starts out up the river using rafts, but soon one of the rafts is caught in a whirlpool and its seven passengers are killed with spears by invisible Indians. At this point Aguirre proposes an edict that will make the group an independent unit, and through a vote, Don Fernando de Guzman, a weak and compliant person, is elected "emperor," while Don Pedro de Ursua (Ray Guerra), the man in charge of the expedition, is deposed. In effect, Aguirre has appropriated power for himself. But attacks by invisible Indians using poisonous shafts deplete the force, food is scarce, and what food is left is eaten by the gluttonous Guzman. Aguirre, pressing on, ruthlessly (he calls himself "the Wrath of God") intimidates his subjects, a few soldiers, and several slaves, to follow him in what becomes a trip of fear, murder, and starvation. As the raft floats down the river (it is not clear whether it flows up, down, or in circles), the last few remaining rebels die of sickness, starvation, or Indian shafts, one of which kills Flores, Aguirre's daughter. Aguirre watches his child die slowly, and then, as the raft is being invaded by rat-sized monkeys, he dies, and the story ends. His dream of a new discovery, of empire and riches, dies with him. The grim tale, with practically no relieving moments, is told serially, chronologically, with no cuts or flashbacks, only with the diary voice-over to mark its progress in time and place. The rain forest jungle provides an eerie menace, and though the light is intense, one feels the progress toward the "heart of darkness," a phrase made known in the famous novella, *Heart of Darkness*, by Joseph Conrad—and indeed the two tales carry certain similarities. In both a heartless man and leader of a group is involved, and in both moral boundaries are crossed. This story is also a story of the rebellion of a diabolical figure with a twisted mind and body. Aguirre, handicapped by a bad leg, wearing a grotesquely and ill-fitting uniform, his head hidden by a helmet, his protruding eyes taking in everything around with insane ferocity, schemes, murders, and subverts the will of others with titanic malice. He is an unredeemed villain, leading renegades and weaklings to their death, feeding their greed with fantasies of riches, conquest, and absolute power. His insanity and his fantasies are on an equal level, for he totally believes that El Dorado is there and can be discovered and conquered—as Cortez persisted and discovered Mexico against everyone's predictions. His intensity, as he silently twists and trots on the raft, carries the day, for no one seems to be able to offer any resistance to him. Only Inez seems heroic in resolutely leaving the raft when she realizes the expedition is lost and Aguirre is mad. She walks into a treacherous forest to certain death. Flores dies uncomprehending, following her father blindly, for she is the only person he has affection for. He plans to reach El Dorado and there marry her (incestuously, of course, for that is part of his evil and insane nature) and reign among their descendants, in "the purest race the world has ever seen." Aguirre is a great villain, like Satan, Mephistopheles, and the very real Adolf Hitler. Herzog does not make any allusions to the German dictator or either of the above figures in his picture, or in his running commentary in the DVD version of the movie. Perhaps he does not need to, for in his brilliant collaboration with Klaus Kinsky, he has hammered the image of eternal evil into its most hideous human form.

Das Boot (The Boat) (1985); Director: Wolfgang Petersen

Das Boot, a celebrated World War II sea epic, describes the adventures of a German submarine that escapes numerous perils, mostly while submerged, only to be sunk by enemy bombs when it arrives back at its destination at a German port. Told entirely from the German point of view, rather than the double point of view used to tell war stories decades after they were made (as in *Tora! Tora! Tora!* and *Midway*), *Das Boot* elicits the sympathies of any audience that witnesses the incredible courage, fears, anxieties, and extremely suspenseful sequences during which the submarine nearly founders while trying to escape through the Strait of Gibraltar. In terms of characterizations, the suspense, and the heroic spirit impartially rendered, *Das Boot* is perhaps the greatest World War II sea adventure ever filmed outside Hollywood. Most Hollywood sagas filmed in the early decades after the war commonly presented such conflicts entirely from the winner's perspective. Deeply tragic and perfectly structured, it evokes feelings of pity and fear as do the great literary epics of the classical past.

Cinema Paradiso (1990); Director: Guiseppe Tornatore

Cinema Paradiso was recently restored in a DVD edition to its original length (173 minutes), allowing it to show three phases in the life of one man, but in a fuller sense, three epochs of Italian cinema. The movie starts with Salvatore (Jacques Perrin), in middle age, learning from a phone call that Alfredo has died. This sparks his memories, first of a young boy (himself), Toto (Salvatore Cascio), who likes to frequent the local movie theater, run by a grizzled, middle-aged projectionist, Alfredo (Phillipe Moiret), who grudgingly lets him into the local movie house. The movie house is a showy building in the middle of a little town somewhere in Italy, in which the local populace enjoy the fantasies of the day, mainly Hollywood fare with glamorous stars like Humphrey Bogart, Ingrid Bergman, Errol Flynn, John Wayne, and a host of others who caught the heartstrings of those provincial folk. Toto loves the movies, fantasizes about them, and becomes "big" in his own mind, and, like the simple folk around him, he is swept away by a world of glamour and success that is beyond the reach of most people who, like him, look fascinated at their idols on the screen. But when the flammable film stock catches fire and the movie theater is ablaze, it is Toto who goes into the burning building and saves Alfredo, who lives, but becomes blind. Salvatore's second memory is of Toto, now an adolescent Salvatore, running the theater, which a rich sponsor has rebuilt, with lush seats and boxes, and a large screen. The time is now postwar Italy, and Italian cinema is flooded with postwar melodramas of war widows weeping over dead husbands buried in cemeteries—and floods of tears are shed in the process. Not all postwar Italian cinema was neorealistic. Most of it was cheap melodrama—B or C movies—just like everywhere else. But the new Cinema Paradiso does not mind accommodating the tastes of locals, who by now are less starving and more middle class. Salvatore spots one of the local girls, Elena (Agnese Nano), a young student in his school, approaches her shyly, makes his point, and is promptly punched unconscious by her would-be suitor (the one who marries her later). She is wealthy, and her father forbids her to make the slightest movement in Salvatore's direction. Unfortunately, he is called to military service, and by the time he returns, she has disappeared with her family into the fantasyland of Tuscany, where he cannot visit her. The film returns to the present-day—in the film's third hour—and Salvatore, now a successful movie director in a big city, decides to go to Alfredo's funeral. It is a simple affair, but lots of people from the old town attend, for Alfredo's death marks the end of an era. Naturally, Salvatore, his memories revived, searches for Elena. He thinks he spots her looking at her daughter, and finally discovers where she lives, and they reconnect. She is now married to the wealthy suitor her parents wanted, and she is "happy" and a mother. But she does go with Salvatore to the beach where they used to meet, and they make love, for the first and last time.

Salvatore stays to witness the demolition of Cinema Paradiso and it goes down in an implosion. This is the honor paid to Alfredo, for with his death the magic of the movies—and of old times—is gone. The past has been replaced by modernity, and Salvatore is sentimental for a period of magic that has passed away.

Kandahar (2001); Director: Mohsen Makhmalbaf

Based on a true story, *Kandahar* describes the adventures of a woman, Niloufar Pazira, who travels to the place of her birth, Kabul, Afghanistan, to rescue her sister who is about to commit suicide during a solar eclipse. When she was sixteen, Niloufar and her family left the country because of the war with the Soviets and went to live in Canada but they had to leave her sister behind because the young girl had lost her legs in an explosion. In real life, Niloufar's sister was really her friend Danya, with whom Niloufar kept in touch after she and her family left Afghanistan. When the Soviets left and the Taliban took over, Danya wrote to Niloufar that she was depressed and that she might want to end her life. Niloufar, who by now had been educated in the West, decided to make a trip back to Afghanistan in 1998, to find her friend. But, for safety reasons, her trip was interrupted, and she never reached Kabul. During her return trip, she met the Iranian auteur, Mohsen Makhmalbaf (*The Cyclist*), to whom she related her story. Two years later, Mohsen contacted her in Canada and asked her to participate in his new film project, which was based on her story. Niloufar returned to Iran, where the film was being made, along the Iranian-Afghanistan border. The film shows Niloufar making her way from the Iranian border, but before reaching her destination, she is captured and taken to jail. The film was made in 2000, and its release coincided with the events of September 11, making Niloufar an instant celebrity. *Kandahar* gives a stark picture of the conditions the Afghan population lived in under the regime of the Taliban. The film's intent is to shock its Western audiences into realizing what this foreign culture, a hideaway of terrorists, is like. The people in it are the victims of conflicting factions, who make a pretense—and a mockery—of law and order. It is a film of compassion and humanity. Technically not an epic (the film is only 88 minutes), the film is nevertheless of epic sweep, for a women undertakes a mission of humanity and compassion; she is patient, tolerant, brave, determined but not stubborn, understanding, and her taping of the natives is intended to show their plight and aid in their defense. She is a true humanitarian, and the film sets an example of honesty and well-meant realism, which is to guide and inform apathetic viewers. It is done with a gentle hand, a true story of a modern woman set on a selfless humane mission.

Note

1. Quotes are from an interview with Tarkovsky by Harvard professor Vlada Petric. See "Rare Film Interviews with Andrei Tarkovsky," in *Andrei Rublev*, DVD (The Criterion Collection, 1999).

Significant DVD Editions

Andrei Rublev

The Criterion Collection offers a digitally transferred copy of the original aspect ratio of 2.35:1 of Andrei Tarkovsky's epic, including a 205-minute director's cut. The "Special Features" section contains an audio essay by Harvard specialist Vlada Petric, a film interview with Andrei Tarkovsky, and a brief historical overview of the events narrated in the film (1998).

The Battle of Algiers

The Criterion Collection of Gillo Pontecorvo's work of a crucial historical event is presented in a three-disc, high-definition, digital-transfer version. Disc two contains a documentary of the making of the film and interviews with directors Spike Lee, Mira Nair, Steven Soderbergh, and Oliver Stone. Disc three contains extensive historical background of the events in the film and commentaries by Richard A. Clarke and Michael A. Sheehan (2004).

Ben-Hur

This set includes a four-disc collector's edition by Warner Brothers that features a restored version of the sixty-five millimeter original in digital transfer, the 1925 version, various documentaries of the making of the epic, and a booklet that details the filming of the epic at Cinecitta Studios in Italy (2005).

Cleopatra

This three-disc set by Twentieth Century Fox features a digitally remastered version of the original 1934 film starring Claudette Colbert and commentaries by Chris and Tom Mankiewicz, Martin Landau, and Jack Brodsky (2001).

The Godfather

This four-disc Paramount edition of the classic gangster epic contains all three movies in their original wide-screen formats, with running commentary by Francis Ford Coppola. Disc four contains information about the making of the films, additional scenes, filming locations, and storyboards (2001).

Gone with the Wind

This four-disc Warner Brothers collector's edition includes a digitally remastered transfer of the epic and numerous commentaries, including one by historian Rudy Behlmer (2004).

The Greatest Story Ever Told

This two-disc MGM special edition of the epic includes interviews with director George Stevens, a photo gallery, and a collector's booklet (2001).

La Dolce Vita

This two-disc collector's edition by International Media Films contains an audio commentary by film historian Richard Schickel and an introduction by director Alexander Payne (2004).

Lawrence of Arabia

This two-disc exclusive limited edition by Columbia Pictures, in digitally remastered anamorphic video, contains a documentary on the making of the epic, an interview with Steven Spielberg, and a booklet with historical material about T. E. Lawrence (2002).

The Lord of the Rings

This six-disc edition of the three epics by New Line Home Entertainment features numerous commentaries on the making of the films by director Peter Jackson and many of the actors (2003).

Munich

This two-disc collector's edition by Universal Pictures features exclusive interviews with director Steven Spielberg, members of the cast, and a narrated retrospective on the real-life events as they occurred at the Munich Olympics (2006).

Patton

This digitally remastered edition of the epic features an audio essay on General George Patton and a documentary on the making of the film (1999).

Seven Samurai

This Criterion Collection edition features a remastered version of the Japanese epic, with a running commentary by film expert Michael Jack (1998).

The Ten Commandments

This three-disc fiftieth anniversary collection by Paramount Pictures features the 1923 silent epic film as well as its remake in 1956. Among its special features is an essay by Katherine Orrison, author of *Written in Stone: Making Cecil B. DeMille's Epic, The Ten Commandments* (2006).

Selected Bibliography

Allen, John Alexander. "The Hero." in *Hero's Way: Contemporary Poems in the Mythic Tradition*. Englewood Cliffs, N.J.: Prentice-Hall, 1971.

Ascher, Steven, and Edward Pincus. *The Filmmaker's Handbook: A Comprehensive Guide for the Digital Age*. New York: Plume, 1999.

Babington, Bruce, and Peter William Evans. *Biblical Epics*. Manchester: Manchester University Press, 1993.

Barra, Allen. "The Incredible Sinking Epic," *American Film* 14, no. 5 (1989): 40–45.

Beaver, Frank E. *Dictionary of Film Terms*. New York: McGraw-Hill, 1983.

Boyum, Joy Gould. *Double Exposure: Fiction into Film*. New York: New American Library, 1985.

Campbell, Joseph. *The Power of Myth: With Bill Moyers*. New York: Anchor Books, 1988.

Campbell, Richard H., and Michael R. Pitts. *The Bible on Film: A Checklist, 1897–1980*. Metuchen, N.J.: Scarecrow Press, 1981.

Carnes, Mark C., ed. *Past Imperfect: History according to the Movies*. New York: Holt, 1995.

Coates, Paul. *Film at the Intersection of High and Mass Culture*. New York: Cambridge University Press, 1994.

Durgnat, Raymond. "Epic, Epic, Epic, Epic, Epic," *Films and Filming* 10, no. 3 (December 1963).

Earley, Steven C. "The Epic/Spectacular." Chap. 13 in *An Introduction to American Movies*. New York: New American Library, 1978.

Eisenstein, Sergei. *Film Form*. New York: Harcourt Brace, 1949.

Elley, Derek. *The Epic Film: Myth and History*. Boston: Routledge and Kegan Paul, 1990.

Everson, William K. "Film Spectacles," *Films in Review* no. 5 (November 1954).

Ferry, Anne. *Milton's Epic Voice: The Narrator in Paradise Lost*. Chicago: University of Chicago Press, 1983.

Freud, Sigmund, "Creative Writers and Day-Dreaming." In *Criticism: Major Statements*, 3rd ed., edited by Charles Kaplan and William Davis Anderson, 420–28. New York: St. Martin's, 1991.

Grant, Barry Keith, ed. *Film Genre: Reader II*. Austin: University of Texas Press, 1995.

Griffin, Jasper. "Homer." In *Past Masters Series*, edited by Keith Thomas. New York: Hill and Wang, 1980.

Hirsch, Foster. *The Hollywood Epic*. New York: A.S. Barnes, 1978.

Iaccino, James F. *Jungian Reflections within the Cinema: A Psychological Analysis of Sci-Fi and Fantasy Archetypes*. London, WestPoint, Connecticut: Praeger, 1998.

Joyaux, Georges. "The Bridge on the River Kwai: From the Novel to the Movie." *Literature/Film Quarterly* (Spring 1974): 174–82.

Jung, Carl G. *Psychological Reflections*. New York: Harper & Row, 1961.

Kael, Pauline. *For Keeps: 30 Years at the Movies*. New York: Plume, 1996.

Kaplan, Charles, and William Davis Anderson, eds. *Criticism: Major Statements*. 3rd ed. New York: St. Martin's, 1991.

Keyser, Les. *Martin Scorsese*. New York: Twayne, 1992.

King, Katherine Callen, ed. *Homer*. New York and London: Garland, 1994.

Kirk, G. S. *Homer and the Oral Tradition*. Cambridge: Cambridge University Press, 1976.

Kracauer, Siegfried. *Theory of Film: The Redemption of Physical Reality*. London: Oxford University Press, 1971.

Luce, J. V. *Homer and the Heroic Age*. New York: Harper & Row, 1975.

Lyon, Christopher, ed. *International Dictionary of Films and Filmmakers*. New York: Putnam, 1984.

Mayo, Mike. *War Movies*. Farmington Hills, Mich.: Visible Ink Press, 1999.

Murray, Gilbert. *The Rise of the Greek Epic*. London and New York: Oxford University Press, 1934/1967.

Rank, Otto. *The Myth of the Birth of the Hero*. New York: Random House, 1959.

Robinson, David. "Spectacle." *Sight and Sound* 25, no. 1 (Summer 1955).

Santas, Constantine. *Responding to Film: A Text Guide for Students of Cinema Art*. Lanham, Md.: Rowman & Littlefield, 2002.

Sarris, Andrew, ed. *The St. James Film Directors Encyclopedia*. New York and London: Visible Ink, 1998.

———. *Interviews with Film Directors*. New York: Avon Books, 1967.

Scorsese, Martin, and Michael Henry Wilson. *A Personal Journey with Martin Scorsese through American Movies*. A documentary directed by Martin Scorsese and Michael Henry Wilson. A British Film Institute TV production in association with Miramax Films, 2003. www.miramax.com.

Seyffert, Oscar. *Dictionary of Classical Antiquities*. Revised and edited by Henry Nettleship and J. E. Sandys. New York: Meridian Books, 1964.

Siegel, Scott, and Barbara Siegel. *The Encyclopedia of Hollywood*. New York: Facts on File, 1990.

Silver, Alain, and James Ursini. *David Lean and His Films*. Los Angeles: Silman-James Press, 1991.

Smith, Gary A. *Epic Films: Casts, Credits, and Commentary on Over 250 Historical Spectacle Movies*. Jefferson, N.C.: McFarland, 1991.

Taylor, Philip M. *Steven Spielberg: The Man, His Movies and Their Meaning*. New York: Continuum, 1994.

Waltrous, A. George. *Three Narrative Poems*. New York: Allyn and Bacon, 1924.

Weston, Jesse. *From Ritual to Romance*. Cambridge: Cambridge University Press, 1920.

Wheelwright, Philip. *Metaphor and Reality*. Bloomington: Indiana University Press, 1962.

Whitman, Cedric H. *Homer and the Heroic Tradition*. New York: Norton, 1958.

Wolk, Martin. "James Bond as the Moneyraker." MSNBC website. www.msnbc.com/news/835307.asp?vts+=11210020440.

Index

2001: A Space Odyssey, 2, 51, 182, 186, 187

Abbott and Costello, 131
Achilles, 6, 9, 10, 38, 42, 45, 46, 47, 48, 88, 92, 152
Aeneas, 9, 10, 45
Aeneid, The, 7, 45
Aeschylus, 88, 106, 189
African Queen, The, 122
Agamemnon, 46, 47, 88
Age of Innocence, The, 3
Agiuerre: The Wrath of God, 211, 212
Alexander the Great, 16, 29, 90, 92, 107, 108, 180
Ali, Muhammad, 62, 63, 94
Alighieri, Dante, 7, 10, 101, 158, 186, 197, 206, 207
Allen, Woody, 132, 139, 140, 141, 147, 152, 159
All the King's Men, 4
Alphaville, 162, 208
Altman, Robert, 155
Alyosha, 10
Amistad, 3

anagnorisis, 28, 43
Andrei Rublev: The Passion According to Andrei, 188, 205, 210
Angelopoulos, Theo, 206
Animal Farm, 130
Antonioni, Michelangelo, 123, 206
Apocalypse Now, 3, 24
Apollo 13, 2, 4, 89
Apollonius, 6, 7
Ararat, 31, 108
Argonautica, The, 7
Ariosto, Ludivico, 9, 101
Aristophanes, 129, 156
Aristotle, 6, 7, 17, 25, 26, 27, 28, 30, 32, 33, 39, 40, 48, 121, 128
Armageddon, 2, 32, 69
Arnold, Matthew, 7, 121
Arthur, King, 9, 69, 70, 123, 133, 154, 159, 182, 187, 190
Attenborough, Richard, 106
Auden, W. H., 8
Aviator, The, 3

Bacall, Lauren, 59, 60
Bale, Christian, 200

Balzac, Henri de, 8
Baroso, Mariano, 125
Barrymore, John, 12
Batman, 4, 5, 132, 133, 179, 180, 197, 198, 199, 200, 201
Batman, 198
Batman Begins, 180, 197, 199
Battle of Algiers, The, 92, 94
Baudrillard, Jean, 187, 203
Bay, Michael, 107
Beast, The, 162
Beautiful Mind, A, 159, 174
Beauty and the Beast, 113
Ben-Hur, 2, 3, 15, 16, 19, 29, 30, 33, 74, 75, 71–82, 100, 111, 116, 180, 181, 196
Bening, Annette, 12, 111
Beowulf, 7, 190, 197
Berdyaev, Nikolai, 161
Bergman, Ingmar, 51, 140, 171, 209
Bergman, Ingrid, 12, 13, 111, 121, 122, 126, 214
Berle, Milton, 136, 137
Besson, Luc, 125
Billy Budd, 68
Birds, The, 180
Birth of a Nation, The, 14, 53
Black Hawk Down, 3, 16
Black Stallion, 66
Blade Runner, 162, 186
Blanchett, Cate, 12, 111, 125, 192
Blass, Gil, 10
Blazing Saddles, 132, 147
Bloom, Orlando, 101, 148, 191
Boccaccio, 7
Bogart, Humphrey, 12, 122, 152, 159, 214
Bond, James, 4, 5, 15, 54, 55, 59, 105, 109, 124, 133, 151, 152, 154, 184, 196, 199, 200, 208
Bondarchuk, Sergei, 205, 209
Bonham Carter, Helena, 169
Bonnie and Clyde, 123, 159

Boyd, Stephen, 80
Branagh, Kenneth, 30
Brando, Marlon, 141–43
Braveheart, 11
Brave New World, 130
Brazil, 201
Breathless, 172
Bridge on the River Kwai, The, 30, 31, 40–44
Bright, Matthew, 175
Bringing Out the Dead, 64
Bringing Up Baby, 131
Brooks, Mel, 146, 147
Bruckheimer, Jerry, 69, 70, 148
Buddha, 4
Burke, Kenneth, 25
Burroughs, Edgar Rice, 59
Burton, Richard, 74, 79, 80, 116
Butterfield 8, 114
Byron, Lord (George Gordon), 10, 57, 130, 142, 143, 158

Cabiria, 3
Cagney, James, 12, 159
Caine, Michael, 199, 200
Cameron, James, 106, 125, 201
Camus, Albert, 8, 88, 158, 159, 160, 165
Candide, 140
Cannes Film Festival, 84
Canterbury Tales, The, 7
Carlyle, Thomas, 186, 197
Casanova, Giacomo, 149–51
Casanova, 149–51
Casanova & Co., 149
Casanova's Big Night, 132, 149
Catch-22, 130
Catherine the Great, 112
Cervantes, Miguel, 10, 129
Chanson de Roland, 7, 9
Chaplin, Charlie, 54, 128, 131, 132, 135, 147, 155, 159
Chaucer, Geoffrey, 7, 128, 129

Chearau, Patrice, 124
Chisum, 61
Cinecitta Studios, 75, 77
Cinema Paradiso, 213–15
Clarke, Arthur C., 187
Cleo From 5 to 7, 123
Cleopatra, 13, 15, 29, 30, 33, 111, 114–17
Clooney, George, 144
Close, Glenn, 12
Cocteau, Jean, 113, 181
Coen brothers (Ethan and Joel), 132, 144, 145, 156
Colbert, Claudette, 11, 76, 122, 131
Cold Mountain, 3, 17
Coleridge, Samuel Taylor, 7, 130
Collateral, 17, 175, 176
Comedy of Errors, The, 129
Connery, Sean, 12, 154
Conrad, Joseph, 59, 212
Cooper, Gary, 12, 54, 59, 63, 126, 147, 148
Coppola, Francis Ford, 49, 91, 159, 189
Count of Monte Cristo, The, 3, 149
Crawford, Joan, 111
Crime and Punishment, 140
Crisp, Donald, 134
Crouching Tiger, Hidden Dragon, 4, 17, 33
Crowe, Russell, 11, 67, 101, 174
Cuchulainn, 10
Cyclist, The, 215

Dafoe, Willem, 174
Dances with Wolves, 2
Dark City, 162
Das Boot, 213
Daves, Delmer, 83
Da Vinci Code, The, 84
Davis, Bette, 12, 13, 111, 121
Day at the Races, A, 66
Day of the Jackal, The, 162, 164
Dearden, Basil, 106

Decameron, The, 7
De Carlo, Yvonne, 83
de Chardin, Teilhand, 187
Deconstructing Harry, 132
Defoe, Daniel, 8
Demetrius and the Gladiators, 79, 83, 84
De Mille, Cecil B., 14, 74, 76–77, 83, 114, 122, 181
Deneuve, Catherine, 120, 121
De Niro, Robert, 166, 173
Departed, The, 166
Depp, Johnny, 141, 148
DiCaprio, Leonardo, 65
Dickens, Charles, 8, 64
Dick Tracy, 132
Disney, Walt, 133, 148
Divine Comedy, The, 7
Dolce Vita, La, 206
Don Juan, 10, 142, 143, 158
Don Juan (Byron), 130, 141–42
Don Juan DeMarco, 141–43
Don Quixote, 129, 133
Don Quixote, 129
Dostoyevsky, Fyodor, 8, 140, 141, 158–61, 166–68, 171
Double Indemnity, 159
Douglas, Kirk, 11, 12
Douglas, Michael, 12
Dracula, 3, 196, 198, 200
Dreyer, Theodore, 192
Dr. Strangelove or: How I Learned to Stop Worrying and Love the Bomb, 132, 170, 173
Dunaway, Faye, 123, 141, 143
Durante, Jimmy, 136, 137

Earthquake, 32
Eastwood, Clint, 54, 108, 126
Eco, Umberto, 8
Egoyan, Atom, 31, 108
Eisenhower, General Dwight, 5, 91
Eisenstein, Sergei, 15, 181, 182, 205, 210

Electra, 88
Eliot, T. S., 8, 106, 136, 141, 159
Elizabeth, 125
Elizabeth I, 87, 89, 114, 125
Elizabeth I, 114
Elizabeth II, 87, 114, 126
Empire Strikes Back, The, 183
English Patient, The, 174
"Enoch Arden," 8
Enuma Elish, 6
Epic Movie, 155
Euripides, 158

Fairbanks Sr., Douglas, 54, 182
Fall of Babylon, The, 3
Farewell to Arms, A, 12
Faulkner, William, 8
Faust, 10, 158
Faust, 171, 187
Fellini, Federico, 140, 149, 206, 207, 209
Fellini's Casanova, 149
Fielding, Henry, 8, 10, 129
Fields, W. C., 131
Fiennes, Ralph, 174
Fight Club, 169, 170, 172
Fincher, David, 169, 172
Fishburne, Laurence, 188
Fisher, Carrie, 114, 183
Flags of Our Fathers, 29, 108, 205
Flaubert, Gustave, 124, 158
Fleischer, Richard, 96
Fleming, Victor, 48, 122
Flynn, Errol, 12, 54, 57, 59, 148, 182, 214
Fonda, Henry, 59
Fontaine, Joan, 121
Ford, Harrison, 12, 59, 91, 151–53, 183
Ford, John, 34, 60
Fort Apache, 60
Foster, Jodie, 168
Foxx, Jamie, 175
Frankenstein, 147, 182, 187
Frears, Stephen, 126

Freeman, Morgan, 200
Freud, Sigmund, 2, 20
Friedberg, Jason, 155
From Here to Eternity, 163
Fukasaku, Kinji, 96
Full Metal Jacket, 159
Fuqua, Antoine, 69

Gable, Clark, 11, 12, 54, 57, 59, 131, 209
Galbraith, Stewart, 96
Gandhi, 2, 3, 14, 18, 89, 106
Gandhi, Mahatma (Mohandas), 4, 5, 57, 87, 106
Gangs of New York, 29, 31, 33, 64, 66, 159
Garbo, Greta, 12, 13, 111, 121, 122
Gardner, Ava, 70
Gargantua, The, 129, 145
Gaze of Ulysses, The, 206
Gere, Richard, 172
Ghosts, 28
Giant, 2
Gibson, Mel, 11, 57, 75, 85
Gilbert, John, 54, 122
Gilgamesh, 4, 6, 9, 10, 88, 182
Gilliam, Terry, 201
Gish, Lillian, 111
Gladiator, 3, 11, 17, 29, 33, 77, 81, 101, 111, 180
Glen, John, 124
Godard, Jean-Luc, 160, 173, 208
Godfather, The, 3, 49, 162, 176
Godfather: Part II, The, 3, 31, 32, 49, 176
Godfather: Part III, The, 3, 176
von Goethe, Johann Wolfgang, 158, 171, 187
Goldfinger, 55
Gone with the Wind, 11, 19, 48, 77
Goodman, John, 145
Gospel According to Saint Matthew, The, 84
Grant, Cary, 12, 131

Great Dictator, The, 132
Great Escape, The, 30, 40
Greatest Show on Earth, The, 15
Greatest Story Ever Told, The, 75, 84
Greatest, The, 62
Great Train Robbery, The, 3
Greeley, Robert, 8
Griffith, D. W., 14, 27, 31, 53, 182
Guinness, Alec, 183
Gulliver's Travels, 128, 129, 133, 186

Hallström, Lasse, 149
Hamill, Mark, 183
Hamlet, 4, 5, 9, 10, 38, 50, 65, 158, 182
Hamlet, 30
Hanks, Tom, 11, 12, 54
Hardy, Oliver, 131, 135
Harris, Ed, 167, 174
Harrison, Rex, 116
Harry Potter, 4, 179, 182
Harvey, Anthony, 123
Hawkins, Jack, 80
Hawks, Howard, 33
Hayek, Salma, 125
Hayworth, Rita, 12
Heart of Darkness, 59, 212
Hector, 10, 46, 47, 48, 152
Helen of Troy, 45, 46, 88, 112, 116
Heller, Joseph, 130
Hemingway, Ernest, 12, 57, 126
Hepburn, Audrey, 13, 121
Hepburn, Katherine, 13, 121, 122, 123, 131, 156
Hercules, 4, 9, 133, 152, 182, 185
Herzog, Werner, 211, 213
Hesiod, 6
Heston, Charlton, 11, 12, 74, 80, 83, 84, 106, 181
Hidden Fortress, The, 182
High Noon, 147, 163
Hitchcock, Alfred, 170, 180, 201
Hitler, Adolf, 63, 78, 104, 146, 149, 213
Holden, William, 41

Homer, 1, 6, 7, 17, 25, 26, 28, 30, 40, 43, 44, 45, 46, 47, 48, 128, 144, 145, 158, 187, 197
Hope, Bob, 131, 149
Hopkins, Anthony, 108
Horace, 30, 48, 77, 129
Howard, Ron, 60, 159, 174
Huckleberry Finn, 129, 130, 145
Hudson, Rock, 12
Hugo, Victor, 10
Hunter, Holly, 144
Huston, John, 122
Huxley, Aldus, 130, 186

Ibsen, Henrick, 28
Icarus, 4
Ike: Countdown to D-Day, 89
Iliad, The, 6, 26, 30, 35, 38, 42, 44, 45, 46, 47, 48, 130
Independence Day, 2
Indiana Jones and the Last Crusade, 154
Indiana Jones and the Temple of Doom, 153
Indochine, 114, 120
Insomnia, 198, 200
Intolerance, 3, 14
Irons, Jeremy, 101, 150
It's a Mad, Mad, Mad, Mad World, 136
Ivanhoe, 114
Ivan Karamazov, 10, 171

Jackson, Peter, 188, 189, 190, 194, 195, 196, 197
Jacobi, Derek, 165
Jameson, Frederick, 24
Jaws, 32
Jesse James, 3
Jesus, 4, 5, 79, 81, 83, 84, 89, 166, 211
Jeunet, Jean-Pierre, 206
JFK, 18, 57
Joan of Arc, 93, 114, 1125
Joan of Arc, 13, 122
Jolie, Angelina, 12, 92
Jones, James Earl, 183

Jones, Terry, 155
Joyce, James, 8, 41, 42, 158
Judgment at Nuremberg, 2, 12, 205
Julia, 111, 124, 142
Jung, Carl, 10, 57, 158
Juvenal, 128

Kael, Pauline, 166
Kafka, Franz, 8, 158, 159, 160
Kagemusha, 34
Kandahar, 215
Kapur, Shekar, 125
Kaye, Danny, 131
Kazantzakis, Nikos, 8, 84, 159
Keaton, Buster, 131, 134–36
Keaton, Diane, 140
Keaton, Michael, 198
Keats, John, 158
Keitel, Harvey, 168
Kelly, Gene, 148
Kelly, Grace, 12
Kennedy, John F., 57, 87, 163, 166
Kerr, Deborah, 78
Khartoum, 106
King, Martin Luther, Jr., 5
King Arthur, 69–70
Kingdom of Heaven, The, 99, 100, 102
King Lear, 34
King of Kings, The, 15, 83
Knightley, Keira, 12, 70, 71, 148
Koster, Henry, 79
Kracauer, Siegfried, 28
Kramer, Stanley, 136, 138
Kubrick, Stanley, 27, 49, 113, 155, 170, 173, 182, 186
Kurosawa, Akira, 34–37, 39, 40, 182, 183, 184, 205
Kusterica, Emir, 206

La Dolce Vita, 216, 217, 218
Lady and the Duke, The, 125
Lake Poets, 130
Lamarr, Hedy, 11

Lancaster, Burt, 12, 54, 148, 208
Lancelot, 9
Landau, Martin, 116
Land of the Pharaohs, The, 33
Lang, Fritz, 159, 166
Lansbury, Angela, 84
Lardner, Ring, Jr., 63
Last Samurai, The, 3, 107
Last Temptation of Christ, The, 75, 84, 159
Laughton, Charles, 77, 78
Laurel, Stan, 131, 135
L'Avventura, 123
Lawrence of Arabia, 29, 30, 39, 40, 49, 88, 111, 114, 116, 196
Lawrence, D. H., 8, 158
Lawrence, T. E., 39, 49, 88, 160
Lean, David, 27, 30, 40, 49, 88, 124, 182, 197
Leigh, Vivian, 11, 111, 114, 209
Leopard, The, 207, 208
LeRoy, Melvin, 77
Letters from Iwo Jima, 3
Leven, Jeremy, 141
Lewis, Daniel Day, 65
Lewis, Jerry, 131
Lincoln, Abraham, 87
Lion in Winter, The, 123
Little Caesar, 159
Lloyd, Harold, 57, 74, 79, 131
Lolita, 113, 158
Lord of the Rings, The, 3, 16, 24, 33, 180, 188–97
Love and Death (Allen), 139, 140
Lucan, 129
Lucas, George, 16, 151, 153, 154, 179, 182–85, 189
Lyndon, Barry, 10, 15, 49, 50

M, 159, 166
Macbeth, 28, 158
Maguire, Tobey, 202
Mahler, Gustav, 3

Makhmalbaf, Mohsen, 215
Malcolm X, 87
Malden, Karl, 91
Maltese Falcon, The, 159
Mamoulian, Rouben, 122
Manchurian Candidate, The, 159
Man for All Seasons, A, 163
Mankiewicz, Joseph L., 114, 116
Mann, Michael, 175–76
Mann, Thomas, 8, 158, 159
Man Who Shot Liberty Valance, The, 60, 61, 147
March, Fredric, 11, 76
Martin, Dean, 131
Martin, Steve, 131
Marx Brothers, The, 66, 131
Master and Commander: The Far Side of the World, 3, 29, 67
Mastroianni, Marcello, 206
Masuda, Toshio, 96
Matrix, The, 16, 33, 162, 179, 185–88, 197
Mature, Victor, 11, 74, 79, 83, 84
McArthur, General Douglas, 5
McCarthy, Joseph (Sen.), 2, 63, 73, 75, 91
McKeown, Charles, 201
McLeod, Norman, 155
McQueen, Steve, 12, 54
Mean Streets, 64
Melville, Herman, 59, 137
Memento, 198
Menander, 129
Mephistopheles, 10, 158, 171, 213
Merman, Ethel, 137
Messenger, The, 125
Metropolis, 186
Mickey Mouse, 133
Mid-summer Night's Sex Comedy, A, 132
Midway, 109, 213
Million Dollar Baby, 126
Milton, John, 7, 10, 136, 137, 171
Minghella, Anthony, 174

Minority Report, 33, 162
Mirren, Helen, 111, 126
Mitchum, Robert, 124
Mizogushi, Kenji, 205
Moby Dick, 68
Modern Times, 186
Monsieur Verdoux, 159
Morgan, Harry, 61
Moses, 4, 5, 9, 10, 12, 75, 83, 89, 152, 157, 181
Moss, Carrie Ann, 188
Mostel, Zero, 146
Mozart, Wolfgang Amadeus, 3, 119, 142, 143
Muni, Paul, 12, 159
Munich, 102, 103, 104, 105, 219
Mutiny on the Bounty, 67

Nabokov, Vladimir, 8, 158
Napoleon, 3, 69, 87, 140, 209
National Velvet, 66
Navarro, Ramon, 11
Navigator, The, 134, 135
Neeson, Liam, 65, 174, 199
Nietzsche, Friedrich, 10, 141
Nolan, Christopher, 198, 200, 201
Norton, Ed, 169, 170
Nosferatu, 3
Notes from Underground, 158, 160, 167, 170, 176

O Brother, Where Art Thou? 144
Octopussy, 124
Odysseus, 4, 9, 31, 38, 47, 88, 123, 144, 145, 146, 152, 158, 182, 185
Odyssey, a Modern Sequel, The, 8
Odyssey, The, 2, 6, 26, 28, 31, 38, 40, 45, 134, 144, 145, 146, 182, 186, 187, 188
Oedipus, 4, 5, 28, 31, 88
Oklahoma!, 163
Oldman, Gary, 199, 200
Olivier, Laurence, 77, 106

232 ～ Index

Omeros, 8
One, Two, Three, 132
Orestes, 4, 88
Orlando Furioso, 9
Orwell, George, 8, 130
O'Toole, Peter, 48, 123
Out of Africa, 13, 114, 117, 121

Pacino, Al, 200
Pantagruel, 145
Paradise Lost, 7, 158
Pasolini, Pier Paolo, 84
Passage to India, A, 3
Passion of St. Joan, The, 122
Passion of the Christ, The, 3, 31, 75, 85
Patriot, The, 3
Patton, 5, 18, 89, 91, 106, 160
Patton, General George S., 5, 18, 89, 91, 106, 160
Pearl Harbor, 2, 3, 16, 24, 30, 31, 32, 69, 91, 107
Penn, Arthur, 123
peripeteia (reversal), 28
Persona, 171
Petersen, Wolfgang, 44, 213
Pfeiffer, Michelle, 12
Philadelphia Story, The, 131
Pinocchio, 181
Pirates of the Caribbean: Curse of the Black Pearl, 69, 71, 148
Pitt, Brad, 45, 48, 57, 169, 170
Plato, 129, 156
Platoon, 24
Plautus, 129
Plummer, Christopher, 175
Poetics, The, 6, 25, 27, 48, 128
Poitier, Sydney, 84
Pollack, Sydney, 117, 119
Pontecorvo, Gillo, 92, 217
Pope, Alexander, 50, 99, 128, 130, 150, 186
Powell, Michael, 181
Preminger, Otto, 123

Presley, Elvis, 57
Pretty Woman, 113
Pride of the Yankees, 63
Prince and the Showgirl, The, 113
Princess Bride, 155
Producers, The, 146
Proust, Marcel, 8
Psycho, 170
Public Enemy, The, 159
Pulp Fiction, 69, 169
Pygmalion, 113, 156

Queen, The, 126
Queen Christina, 13, 111, 112, 122
Queen Margot, 124
Quo Vadis, 77, 78

Rabelais, Francois, 129, 145
Raging Bull, 39, 64, 159, 160, 173
Raiders of the Lost Ark, The, 15, 151
Raimi, Sam, 155, 202
Rains, Claude, 84
Ramses, 10, 83
Ran, 34, 37
Rank, Otto, 4, 75, 113, 126
Rape of the Lock, 128, 130
Rashomon, 34
Redford, Robert, 57, 117
Reed, Carol, 159, 172, 181
Reeve, Christopher, 134, 202
Reeves, Keanu, 188
Reiner, Rob, 155
Reservoir Dogs, 69
Richardson, Samuel, 8
"Rime of the Ancient Mariner, The," 7, 203
Rio Bravo, 147
Rio Grande, 60
Robe, The, 74, 79, 80, 83, 84, 111
Roberts, Julia, 111
Robin Hood, 182
Robinson, Edward G., 83, 159

Rock, The, 69
Rocky, 114, 126
Rohmer, Eric, 125, 126
Romulus/Remus, 5
Rooney, Mickey, 136, 137
Rosemary's Baby, 162
Ross, Gary, 66
Rousseau, Jean Jaques, 24, 59
Rush, Geoffrey, 103, 148
Ryan's Daughter, 124

Saint Joan, 123
Samson and Delilah, 11, 74, 84
Sartre, Jean Paul, 88, 160
Satan, 10, 158, 171, 213
Savalas, Telly, 84
Saving Private Ryan, 2, 24
Scarface, 159
Schaffner, Franklin J., 91, 106
Schiller, Friedrich, 28
Schindler's List, 2, 3, 12, 14, 30, 31, 32,
    89, 102, 104, 154, 162, 173, 174,
    205
Schwarzenegger, Arnold, 121, 201, 202
Scorsese, Martin, 39, 64, 71, 75, 84, 85,
    159, 160, 166, 169, 170, 171, 173
Scott, George C., 91
Scott, Ridley, 99, 101, 102, 159, 186
Scott, Walter, 37, 99, 130
Seabiscuit, 66
Searchers, The, 60
Sellers, Peter, 173
Sennett, Mack, 53, 54
Seven, 169
Seven Pillars of Wisdom, The, 88
Seven Samurai, 15, 34–40, 51, 184
Shakespeare, William, 9, 27, 28, 34, 81,
    114, 129, 158
Shaw, George Bernard, 114, 123, 128,
    156
Shawn, Dick, 137, 146, 147
Sheik, The, 55, 56, 57
Shelley, Mary, 187, 197

Shelley, Percy Bysshe, 10, 57
Sheppard, Cybil, 167
She Wore a Yellow Ribbon, 60
Shootist, The, 59, 60, 61
Sign of the Cross, The, 15, 74, 76, 78
Simmons, Jean, 80
Sin City, 162
Singer, Bryan, 202
Sink the Bismark, 2
Sir Gawain and the Green Knight, 7, 9
Smollett, Tobias, 10
"Sohrad and Rustrum," 7
Son of the Sheik, The, 56, 57
Sophocles, 88
Southey, Robert, 130
Spacey, Kevin, 202
Spartacus, 11, 16, 40, 77, 111, 116
Spider-Man, 179, 202
Spider-Man 2, 202
Spielberg, Steven, 102, 154, 157, 174,
    197
Stagecoach, 60
Stalin, Josef, 78
Stallone, Sylvester, 121
Stanwyck, Barbara, 12, 111
Star Wars, 2, 4, 11, 15, 16, 179, 182,
    183, 184, 186, 208
Stevens, George, 84
Stewart, Jimmy, 54, 131, 148
Stone, Oliver, 57, 107
Stoppard, Tom, 201
Streep, Meryl, 12, 111, 117, 119, 121
Sturges, Preston, 155
Sullivan's Travels, 58, 132
Superman, 4, 5, 132, 133, 134, 198,
    202
Superman, 11, 133
Superman Returns, 4, 202
Sutherland, Donald, 149
Swank, Hilary, 111, 126
Swift, Jonathan, 8, 128, 129, 186
von Sydow, Max, 84
Symposium, 129, 156

Taming of the Shrew, The, 113
Tarkovsky, Andrei, 210, 211
Tarzan, 57–59, 206
Tarzan and His Mate, 57
Taxi Driver, 64, 159, 166, 170, 173
Taylor, Elizabeth, 12, 13, 33, 66, 70, 78, 114–17
Taylor, Robert, 57, 74, 78
Ted Bundy, 159, 175
Ten Commandments, The, 2, 12, 15, 19, 40, 74, 75, 80, 83, 111
Tennyson, Alfred, 8
Terence, 129
Terminator, The, 114, 201
Terminator 2: Judgment Day, The, 201
Thackeray, William Makepeace, 10
Thelma and Louise, 159
Theogony, 6
Third Man, The, 172, 175, 176
Three Stooges, The, 145
Time Machine, The, 186
Time of the Butterflies, The, 125
Titanic, 3, 15, 16, 17, 24, 30, 32, 33, 106, 125
Tolkien, J. R. R., 189, 190, 195, 197
Tolstoy, Leo, 8, 140, 141, 205, 209
Tom Jones, 129
Tora! Tora! Tora!, 2, 96–99, 107, 213
Tornatore, Guiseppe, 213
Towering Inferno, 2, 32
Tracy, Spencer, 132, 136, 137
Trip to the Moon, A, 3, 181
Troy, 6, 44–48, 112, 116
Truman Show, The, 33
Turturro, John, 144
Twain, Mark, 10, 129, 130, 145

Underground, 160, 162, 166, 167
underground man, 158–61, 162, 165, 166, 167, 168, 169, 170, 172, 173, 174, 175, 198, 206
Union Pacific, 15

United 93, 4, 16
Ustinov, Peter, 78

Valentino, Rudolph, 12, 55–57
Varda, Agnes, 173
Verbinski, Gore, 148
Very Long Engagement, A, 206
Virgil, 7, 10, 17, 45, 77, 158
Visconti, Luchino, 207
Voltaire, 140

Wachowski brothers (Andy and Larry), 185
Walcott, Derek, 8
Wallace, William, 11
Wallenstein, 28
War and Peace, 15, 141, 203, 205, 209
Wargnier, Regis, 120
War of the Roses, The, 113
Watanabe, Ken, 107, 199
Wayne, John, 54, 59, 60–62, 84, 147, 148, 152, 198–201, 214
Weir, Peter, 67, 69
Weissmuller, Johnny, 57, 58
Welles, Orson, 172, 175, 181
Wells, H. G., 186
Whitman, Walt, 64
Who's Afraid of Virginia Woolf?, 113
Wild Bunch, The, 38
Wilder, Billy, 132, 159
Wilder, Gene, 146, 147
Winslet, Kate, 111, 125
Wizard of Oz, The, 181
Wordsworth, William, 130
Works and Days, 6
World Trade Center, 4, 16, 64
Wyler, William, 80

Young Frankenstein, 147

Zinnemann, Fred, 124, 162, 163
Zwick, Edward, 107

About the Author

Constantine Santas was born in Greece and was educated at Knox College (BA in English, 1961), University of Illinois at Urbana (MA in English), and Northwestern University (PhD in English, 1971). He taught at Milwaukee-Downer College (1962–1964) and University of Illinois at Chicago (1964–1971), and he was chair of the English Department at Flagler College from 1971 to 2002. He also served as a special lecturer in the bilingual program at the State University of Florida from 1977 to 1981. His publications include translations from Greek authors, a biography of the Greek poet Aristotelis Valaoritis (1977), several bilingual textbooks, and various articles in film and aesthetics both in English and in Greek. His first film book, *Responding to Film*, was published in 2002 (and translated into Greek in 2006), and he is currently working on *The Art of the Movie* and a translation of Homer's *The Odyssey*.